P9-DTL-618

THE TRANSFORMING
FIRE

THE TRANSFORMING
FIRE

The Rise of the
Israel-Islamist Conflict

JONATHAN SPYER

continuum

The Continuum International Publishing Group Inc
80 Maiden Lane, New York, NY 10038
The Tower Building, 11 York Road, London SE1 7NX

www.continuumbooks.com

Library of Congress Cataloging-in-Publication Data
Spyer, Jonathan.
The transforming fire : the rise of the Israel-Islamist conflict / Jonathan Spyer.
    p. cm.
  Includes bibliographical references.
  ISBN-13: 978-1-4411-6663-0 (hardcover : alk. paper)
  ISBN-10: 1-4411-6663-7 (hardcover : alk. paper)
  1. Arab-Israeli conflict—1993– 2. Islamic fundamentalism—Israel. 3. Arab-Israeli
relations—Religious aspects—Islam. I. Title.
DS119.76.S7973 2010
956.05'4—dc22   2010013568

ISBN 978-1-4411-6663-0

Typeset by Pindar NZ, Auckland, New Zealand
Printed in the United States of America by Sheridan Books, Inc

For David Spyer

Contents

Acknowledgements

I would like to thank Barry Rubin at the Global Research in International Affairs Center, IDC, Herzliya, for his support and advice during the planning and writing of this book. Also David Horovitz and Amir Mizroch, chief editor and news editor respectively at the Jerusalem Post and David B. Green, senior editor at Haaretz English edition for their enabling me to develop in shorter articles many of the ideas contained herein. Judy Heiblum of Sterling Lord is an extremely professional and committed agent without whose efforts this book could not have been written. Marie Claire Antoine, my editor at Continuum, was a consistently constructive and helpful presence as the book developed. The work and the inspiring figure of Professor Anthony D. Smith at the London School of Economics was responsible more than any other for setting me on the path of which this book is the outcome.

In addition, conversations and experiences shared with many friends and colleagues in Jerusalem and elsewhere form the bedrock from which this book has grown. In this regard, I would like to acknowledge the inspiration, friendship and influence of the following individuals: Asgeir Ueland, Lee Smith, Ezra Gabbay, Yirmy Unger, Vered Cohen, Pablo Sklarevich, Amiram Barkat, Ariel Ronen, Yitzhak Harel, Amiram Dura, Alex Grinberg, Tony Badran and Helene Lavoix.

PROLOGUE

"Not all of us will be coming back"

In the late afternoon of 9 August 2006, the unit received word that the operation into el Khiam and Marjayoun was on. We would be commencing movement at six p.m. The company was positioned on a field next to an avocado grove, on lands belonging to a border kibbutz. We had been waiting there for three days. Twice, the entry into Lebanon had been postponed. We'd spent the days checking our equipment, eating sandwiches and smoking cigarettes. Waiting. The routine of tense expectation and prolonged inactivity was one you got used to.

You can get used to a lot. You can sit next to a verdant field of avocados, and get used to the endless, sinister booming of our artillery in the morning, and the Katyusha rockets from the other side that started around 11 a.m. You can get used to scrabbling for cover in the rich dirt as the missiles fly overhead, and watching them plow up white smoke in the hills. All of that can, within 72 hours, start to feel like a normal routine. So much so that some poor, domestic animal that lies within you can even feel a little sad when it

1

hears that it's time to move on.

All the same, I was aware of the strangeness that had brought us to this point. We had come a long way from the great hopes of the 1990s. From the high-tech boom and the successes on Nasdaq and the New Middle East. All the way down through the collapse of negotiations, the ending of illusions, the return of the suicide bombers to our towns and cities, and now this, war. Who had ever believed that we would be rushing for the bus depot in confusion, like extras in some fourth-rate film about the Yom Kippur War? That we would be taking the polythene covers from the tanks that had waited patiently and motionless for precisely this moment.

The operation was into one of the areas south of the Litani river, as yet untouched by our forces. Everyone was thinking about the huge mines that had devastated a couple of the tanks heading inward at earlier stages of the war.

Nothing much you could do against the mines. I thought about them a lot. They seemed more fearsome than the other ordnance in Hizballah's armory. Mainly, I was concerned as to whether I would know what had happened. Whether there would be time to realize, with a sort of mild surprise, "We've hit a mine, so this is where it ends." Or whether the process would be too quick, and one would simply switch off. I wasn't sure which of the two possibilities seemed worse.

There were fewer jokes than usual, and no one was playing cards. We knew that we were going into the killing zone, and that it was not certain who would come out. Lebanon was the adjacent fields a few hundred yards ahead. Topographically identical, and strangely alien. The hills a little balder. No electric cables. Gray, flat roofed houses clustered on the inclines, instead of the familiar beige ones with red roofs.

With the tanks all in line against the setting sun, an elegiac mood came over us as we made the final preparations before moving off. There was time for thoughts, cigarettes, maybe surreptitious final mobile phone calls from home, or last minute adjustments.

* * *

The call had come on Friday evening. The phone rang, and after a second or so of silence on the line a recorded woman's voice was telling me to report to the agreed point from which buses would be arriving to take us north. The peaceful summer evening atmosphere abruptly changed into something cold and urgent. I had a boiling hot shower, perhaps my last for a while, it occurred to me — and dressed in the olive green uniform which I had presciently washed a few days earlier, as the scenes from the war on TV had worsened. I called my parents in London. I wrote a couple of e-mails to friends, and turned off the computer. Then I walked out of the house into the calm Jerusalem Friday evening, and began making my way to the assembly point.

Years before, I had read an interview with the Israeli journalist Amnon Abramovich, who was severely wounded in the 1973 Yom Kippur War. Abramovich had been a law student in Jerusalem when the war erupted. As I walked to the meeting point, the details of this article returned to me. I remembered his description of the transformation of his life following the severe burns he'd received when his tank was hit by Egyptian Sagger missiles.

It happened during General Avraham "Bren" Adan's failed counter-attack on 8 October 1973. Abramovich noted how one minute you're living the good life in Jerusalem, with the girls and the parties and the bars; the next you're facing surgery to rebuild your face, and burns across 70 percent of your body. The first part of Abramovich's narrative was not a bad approximation of my own life, at least on a good day. The prospect of becoming acquainted with the second was at the forefront of my mind through the weeks of the war.

The assembly point was in an Ultra-Orthodox part of town. Young, secular, and national religious Jerusalemites were gathering there when I arrived. The called-up Israel Defense Forces (IDF) fighters and the Ultra-Orthodox men mingled amiably, ongoing enmities put aside due to the strange drama of the event. After a while, I noticed an acquaintance of mine from Jerusalem, whom I hadn't seen for about ten years. We knew each other when we were students at the Hebrew University of Jerusalem in the mid-1990s and were involved in the campaign against the Rabin/Peres government's attempts to negotiate away the Golan Heights to the Syrians. In the meantime, Eli had married and had two children. We reminisced about various characters we'd known.

Some men had turned up with their girlfriends, and there were high spirits outside as people prepared to depart. For a while, something resembling the atmosphere of a café at the Hebrew University prevailed. Shouts of laughter, and friendly mockery. Mildly combative humor with the Ultra-Orthodox men, who as usual proved to be possessed of a no less nimble humor of their own.

Finally, at about 11 in the night, a convoy of buses arrived, and there was a crush as people piled aboard. I remember the Jerusalem night outside as we pulled away. The crowd of Ultra-Orthodox men watching us, now mostly in silence.

We arrived at the base in the north about three hours later, to general confusion. We collected kitbags and rifles and made our way down to the depot where the tanks were located. Maoz, my commander, was on 2A, our tank, preparing it for movement, and I shouted up a greeting to him. Kibbutznik Maoz, languid and skinny with his long black hair tied back, always quiet and soft-spoken, had a way of dealing with any situation as though it was the most natural and predictable thing imaginable. War was no exception, it seemed, and he returned my greeting with a casual wave.

The other members of our crew and the rest of the company began to arrive in ones and twos as the night went on. It was dark and the scene had an eerie quality. Piles of rifles with headlights reflecting on them. A sense of the surrounding raw nature, which made me want to stick close to the people around me. Not that there was anything out there to fear — rather that the usual layers separating the urban dweller from nature had disappeared. All the comforts and sacraments of my bourgeois existence — my right to privacy, to silence, to speaking only with those whom I wanted to speak — all had vanished. It was two in the morning, and my body was telling me that it was time to go home. But home was a long way from here. I was back in the world of my early twenties, when I served in a regular armored unit soon after moving to Israel from England. The border was up ahead, and shrouded in darkness. That was the first night of the call-up.

* * *

The enemy we were heading to engage with was quite different from the conventional Arab armies faced by Israeli forces in previous wars. It differed also from the Palestine Liberation Organization (PLO) forces that Israel had fought in Lebanon in 1982, and in the West Bank and Gaza between 2000 and 2004. The Lebanese Hizballah group had seared itself into the consciousness of a whole generation of Israelis who served in the fighting units of the IDF in the 1990s. Created by Iran, backed by Syria, it had pioneered a new form of warfare somewhere between the activities of a regular force and that of a guerrilla organization. Among other things, it was the first Islamist group to use suicide bombings as a means of war. It was comprised largely of part-time fighters, and lacked any armored capacity or heavy artillery. At the same time, it was trained by Iran, with state of the art; modern weapons systems, which it knew how to use effectively.[1]

Hizballah differed from previous enemies in other ways, too, more fundamental than military hardware and modes of organization. It was committed to a stark, uncompromising ideology in which support for the destruction of Israel formed a centerpiece. This was embedded in a Shia Islamist worldview which looked to the Iranian model of rule by clerics. Optimists had supposed that much of the movement's focus on this was a matter of mere rhetoric. They had seen Hizballah as, essentially, a Lebanese party which spoke the language of Islamism and war against Israel as a legitimating device.

This theory had been put to the test with Israel's unilateral withdrawal from southern Lebanon in May 2000. It had been proposed that this move would conclude the matter in dispute. That proved not to be the case. It turned out that Hizballah's talk of "liberating Jerusalem," as pretentious as it seemed, was a serious indicator of the movement's goals.

The issue was one of time scale. Within the context of the next five years, the idea of a Shia guerrilla organization engaging in war against Israel with the strategic goal of helping to bring about its destruction seemed detached from reality. Looking at a framework of centuries, half-centuries and decades, however, it could be seen differently. This was the framework through which Hizballah were viewing events.

The issue was one of ideology, as well. Hizballah represented a particular, Shia variant of the Islamist outlook that has proven the most effective tool of popular mobilization in the Arab world. Though at root a militia emerging from the Shia section of the Lebanese population, the movement clothed itself in the 1990s in the mantle of Arab "resistance" to Israel through its fight against the IDF in south Lebanon. In this way, it gained great kudos among circles not usually sympathetic to the aspirations of the Shia.

But Hizballah could never entirely resolve the contradiction of being an Iran-backed sectarian militia which also claimed to act on behalf of Arab and Muslim interests as a whole. In many ways, this remained the movement's Achilles heel. Hizballah would gain credit in the Arab world for activities against Israel, which it would then squander in promoting the Shia interest in Lebanon.

But this wasn't only about Hizballah, and it wasn't only about the Shia. The war in 2006 was a graphic signpost of just how much things had changed, and were going to change further, in the Middle East. Not so long before, it had seemed that the battle in the Arabic-speaking world to terminate Jewish sovereignty west of the Jordan River was beginning to "wind down." If Israel in the 1950s, 1960s and 1970s had faced the armored columns of pan-Arabism, then by the 1980s and 1990s, the only remaining foes seemed to be Palestinian demonstrators — whose own leadership, we were told, was moving toward a grudging acceptance of compromise.

The move towards peace, and therefore towards Israel's normalization in its neighborhood, might be agonizingly slow, but it seemed to be happening. The number of enemies was decreasing, the extent of the threat ever less apocalyptic. Israel had come to assume that Zionist thinker Zeev Jabotinsky's prediction: according to which the

Arab world would accept Israel as a fait accompli once it was clear that there was no other alternative, was nearly realized.[2]

The collapse of the Oslo process in 2000, and the four year low-intensity conflict that followed, put this assumption in question. But the events of 2006 — the Hamas election victory, and then the Hizballah war — all with nuclear-bound Iran lurking in the background, conclusively buried it. It was clear that the rejection of Israel had mutated again, and found a new form.

The new wave of rejectionism in the Middle East came packaged in religious garb. But in core ways, Islamism resembles the secular nationalism which it came to replace. Islamism stresses what it regards as the brittle, artificial nature of Israel. Arab nationalism had used a similar argument. The nationalist idea was that since Israel was considered to be based on a false, strange claim to nationality by a religious sect, it must surely be a feeble thing, whose destiny was to be overwhelmed by the "natural," 'indigenous' and "organic" sovereign presence in the area — the Arab nation.

The Islamists took this basic idea, replaced the Arab nation with the Islamic "Umma," and added a dose of traditional Islamic contempt for the Jews, an element of Islamic fervor for recapturing lost Jerusalem, and a certain imbibed influence from Christian anti-semitism.

The military strategy Islamism developed was also based on the view of Israel as a small and weak creature lacking the will to live, facing a vast Islamic world which would easily crush it if properly led.

The supposedly greater patience and ability to endure and sacrifice of the Muslim fighters, so it is believed [by the Islamists], will bring victory in the end — over Israel, and over the regimes of the apostates. This idea has engaged the energies of a generation in the Middle East, both among its adherents, and among those — Israelis, Arabs and Westerners — who would devote their talents to defeating it.

As for Israel — contrary to the depictions of it in the propaganda of its enemies — it has remained a far more mobilized, committed society than it superficially may appear. Seventy-nine percent of Israelis, when asked, said they would fight for their country. This contrasts with just over 60 percent of Americans, and just over 40 percent of Britons. Israel scored first in a survey of citizens of 26 democratic countries who were asked this question.[3] Israel has become more individualistic, fragmented, wealthy, and cynical. But it remains somewhere considerably above other Western democracies in its citizens' level of commitment and sense of obligation to their country.

But then again, this, while necessary, may be insufficient. No other democratic society faces quite the challenges that Israel does. Israel, and the Jews, have found themselves to be target number one in the eye of the storm of the only ideological phenomenon raising a serious challenge to the democratic West in the twenty-first century. The model for its defeat and destruction is a prolonged struggle, to be conducted tirelessly, measured in decades rather than years, by military, paramilitary, and political means. The Israel–Hizballah War of 2006 was its first major set-piece — the first high intensity engagement in the war between Israel and Islamism.

Hizballah did not expect the war of 2006. They thought that Israel's response to the kidnappings they carried out in July would be more localized, on a far smaller scale. Their intention was to free Lebanese citizens jailed for terrorism against Israel. Israel had in the past proved amenable to such exchanges, and the organization apparently miscalculated the response. But they had prepared carefully, and were able to mobilize swiftly at the start of the war.

The forces that Hizballah mobilized in the towns and villages adjacent to the border were in a certain sense comparable to us IDF reservists, in that they were not full-time fighters. Hizballah was, at the time, thought to have around 1,000 full time combatants, supplemented by about 15,000 reservists, based in the border villages and towns of its southern heartland.[4] In the sweltering days of mid-July, they, too, received phone calls or knocks on their door and, perhaps as confused and apprehensive as we were, they reported to their own places of meeting. They mobilized, and they waited, for the IDF to come in on the ground. Now, two weeks later, it looked likely that we would oblige. They were there, across the border, in el Khiam and Marjayoun, waiting for us.

* * *

We tried our best to grab a few hours' sleep on the hulls of the tanks before the morning light brought our surroundings into stark relief. By dawn, the entire company was awake. We were eating combat rations from the first day. Tuna fish and sweet corn sandwiches. One of the old comrades from the early days of the company, wiry, black-haired Alon Smoha approached me as we sat waiting for rifle practice on the firing ranges. "Look, I know you work in this field," he said, "so maybe you can explain to me what this war's all about."

I'd known Alon since 1994, and despite our very different backgrounds, in the few years prior to the 2006 War we'd established a certain friendship. Alon was from Hod Hasharon — a suburb of Tel-Aviv — of Iraqi background. He worked in a big pharmaceuticals factory, and was a fitness enthusiast. He also took a keen interest in regional politics. As for myself, I work as an analyst at a think tank focusing on Mid-East issues, and as a journalist and commentator in these areas.

Interest in Middle Eastern affairs is less widespread among Israeli Jews than might be supposed. Israelis tend to see the region as a place of dysfunction and hatred, and prefer to let their defense structures keep it at a safe distance, while they engage with other parts of the world. Alon, however, whose parents had immigrated from Baghdad in the 1950s, took a keen, sardonic, and amused view of the Arab world and political affairs in general. Every so often we used to chat and exchange opinions on these subjects.

Alon's speciality, when we were bored on company exercises, was to begin issuing long streams of orders in Arabic through the communication system. He claimed to base these monologues on Arabic wrestling commentaries that he sometimes watched on satellite TV. Sure enough, his commentaries would sometimes include sudden random Anglo-Saxon names. But that was all long before the summer of 2006.

So there, in the fading afternoon light, with the pop-popping of the rifles on the ranges behind us, Alon and I went through the reasons behind the outbreak of the conflict in which we were about to take part. We talked about Iran, about Syria, about the mess in Iraq, and the growth of a coalition that wanted to put Israel's military might to the test once again.

Alon picked at the dry earth with a stick and with a shy smile spoke about Baghdad as his father had described it to him, in the days of the Arab nationalist agitation in the early 1950s. "Power was what mattered. Not learning, or books. And Jews — less than garbage." He laughed and looked around us, and then went back to picking the ground with his stick. He went on, "They have this battle of Khaybar, you know?[5] When they beat the Jews? So they want to get back to that. They're going to keep trying." There was something about this conversation that typified army life, especially during the period of the war. Quick interactions of curious intensity. The re-affirming of links, and then something much larger coming along and separating you again.

The war had caught our company in a time of transition. We'd been formed in 1994, out of graduates of the 188th and 7th regular armored brigades. And through the tranquil years of the Oslo peace process, and then the years of the second Intifada, we'd stayed fairly homogeneous. But in the year preceding the war in Lebanon, there had been various personnel changes.

Most importantly, our old company commander, Dan, had departed for some position within the brigade staff and had been replaced by a young man in his late twenties named Yuval. Yuval wasn't living in Israel at the time of the war, as he was training as a commercial pilot in the US. So that morning he wasn't there. But we were informed that he was winging his way back to be with us.

Fortunately, we had his second in command, about whom there could be no doubt. Menash was a Sephardi Jerusalemite and one of the original officers of the company. He was short, stocky, bespectacled, and black-stubbled, possessed of endless reserves of energy, seemingly limitless supplies of goodwill, and occasional flashes of a sharp, surreal sense of humor. He was in the mold of IDF officers who grew up in the youth movements or the scouts, and for whom any problem can be solved if only a few energetic, no-nonsense and serious fellows put their minds to engaging with it.

"I don't know a great deal more than you do," Menash said that morning, as he briefed us, standing on the hull of his tank. Then he paused a bit and smiled matter of factly. "Some of you are probably thinking that you never expected we'd have to do this. I never expected it either. But that's the way it is."

We were facing the eastern sector, opposite the south Lebanese towns of el Khiam and Marjayoun. The war, since ground operations had commenced, had taken the form of sporadic raids in force by the IDF over the border, capturing towns and holding them and then retiring back to Israeli lands. The point and logic behind such activity was already being questioned at the time, and remains one of the key issues under discussion regarding Israel's tactics in the 2006 war. Ground operations had started late, in any case. Israel had erroneously believed in the first stage of the war that it could be won by air power alone. But in the eastern sector where we were, there had been little ground activity of any kind. What there was, therefore, was particularly intense Katyusha missile bombardments.

The kibbutz in which we had spent the night was largely abandoned. The little red-roofed houses were locked up and shuttered. It was strange to see the neatly tended gardens and deserted childrens' swings in the middle of a Katyusha barrage, with the missiles screaming overhead and pounding into the earth a few hundred yards away.

That night, we were awakened at three in the morning with the news that an infantry force was in trouble outside el Khiam, and we were going in to reinforce them. There was a filthy confusion in the half-light as we roused ourselves and tried to convert the tank from dormitory to fighting vehicle, to get our boots on, and get going.

We drove up to the border fence, and waited there, backed up along the road, tense, with engines running. Then, as the minutes passed, we turned off the engines and got out and sat on the hulls waiting. After a couple of hours, we got the order to stand down, and drove back to the avocado field where we were stationed. It was hard to sleep in the hot sun. We had a similar false alarm the following night.

Everyone was inwardly afraid. For the most part, however, a sort of quiet fatalism came over us. Our world had suddenly become very small. The sense of infinity and possibility that pervades the lives of young city dwellers had all gone. In its place, life was reduced to the bare essentials of hard, unpleasant work, eating and trying to keep clean. The prospect of life proving a sharply curtailed affair was waiting just across the border fence, and we knew that we'd be crossing it soon.

By the third day, when we received concrete word that there would be no further postponement, we accepted it without much fuss. There were last-minute checks to run through on the tanks. I must have checked and strengthened the tracks five times in the course of the day. Tanks have a tendency to lose tracks and become unmaneuverable in rocky-type terrain such as that we were about to enter. We had heard that the main key to surviving the Hizballah's anti-tank teams was to keep the vehicle moving, and to use the smokescreen facility liberally. Being motionless meant that you became a target, and the anti-tank teams were making good use of the system of bunkers and tunnels that Hizballah had all across the south to emerge and pick off tanks in the daylight.

In the dying afternoon light, our crew shared a last meal, sitting on the ground in the shade cast by the tank. We talked quietly and frankly about the prospect of death in the coming operation. "I'm not afraid or anything," said Maoz in his very soft and calm voice, "but I'm sad at the thought of Bar having to grow up alone." Bar was his two-year-old son.

Toward evening, as it became apparent that there really wasn't going to be another order to stand-down, preparations became frenetic, and the atmosphere charged. About ten minutes before six, which was the departure hour, I wandered into the avocado grove, alone. I went quite a way in, until I could hear the voices of the boys only in the distance. I stood there in the middle of the luscious verdant vegetation, smoking, and I said to myself: I've no claims on anyone other than myself for whatever follows. It was a curious sort of affirmation, but for some reason it helped, and I walked back through the grove to the field.

People walked from tank to tank, shaking hands with friends, wishing each other luck. I remember standing with my friend Ariel Ronen and exchanging a few brief words before we boarded. Blond Ariel, in civilian life the owner of a marketing business in Petah Tikva, was a tank driver from platoon 2. Unlike me, he had a practical, military bent to him, and was standing, watching affairs with a worried furrow to his brow. "We aren't ready for this," he said, as we shook hands. I looked at him quizzically, but he declined to elaborate, adding simply, "Not all of us will be coming back."

"We will," I reassured him, assuming the father-confessor role that I had awarded myself in the previous days. He didn't reply.

I passed by the company commander's tank. Alon Smoha was there. We didn't talk in the moments before setting off for Lebanon. Instead, as I passed by, we just shook hands. I remember his hand, lean and strong, gripping mine for a long moment, our two forearms made one, before turning toward the tanks. We had to drive up to Metullah, right on the border, which was to be the entrance point. The sun was shining, like an elegy, as we pulled out of the avocado field. The maintenance boys threw buckets of water over the tanks as we filed out, for luck. I was irritated by this, because the water left a stain on the periscope glass.

We drove on the main street, with the sound of the artillery in the distance. When we got to the ascent toward the border, in the town of Metulla, we stopped . In Metulla, there were strange scenes: the lights of the houses were turned off, as most of the residents had long since headed for the south. But by the side of the road were a group of Hassids (Ultra-Orthodox Jews) from the sect of Nahman of Breslaw, who had rigged up a makeshift sound system at the furthest point accessible to civilians.

They had recorded some songs especially for the campaign. There was one about Hassan Nasrallah which they were blaring out over and over again. The day was fading into twilight as we waited, a whole armored force on its way in, backed up, waiting for the cover of dark to enter Lebanon. There were three hundred Hizballah men in el Khiam, who were waiting, too. Meanwhile, the Bratslavers and their song about Nasrallah blared out absurdly into the night.

The media — Israeli and foreign — were there in force. The boys swapped lewd comments about the young female reporters as they shouted up to us. An Italian cameraman made a great show of delivering a speech detailing his love for Israel, which did not, of course, in any way detract from the equal love he bore for the peoples of the Arabic-speaking world. Overcome by emotion, he produced a small cigar from his top pocket. He gestured up to us. "I will give you this cigar," he said grandly, "if you will promise me you will think of me when you smoke it, later, in Israel." Itzik, our loader, who was of similarly theatrical temperament, answered him that he would certainly do so, and the cigar was duly transferred.

As the darkness came down, we received the order to move. I remember a Bratslav Hassid, standing on the roof of a car by the side of the road and blowing kisses at us as we entered Lebanon. It evoked for me a memory of the bombing of Café Hillel in Jerusalem in 2003. After the bombing, too, in the early hours of the morning, Ultra-Orthodox youths, like shadows, had flitted around the scene, amid the broken glass and the blood in the road.

We were on the dirt road toward the Good Fence. No more foreign journalists beyond this point. No more Bratslaver Hassidim. Silence except for the engine and the crackle of the internal communications. Three hundred Hizballah men in el Khiam. Mobilized civilians like us, planning our destruction. We closed the hatches and headed due north. Into the purifying fire.

Notes

1. For further details on Iranian support of Hizballah, see Kathryn Haahr, "Iran's changing relationship with Hizballah," Jamestown Foundation, *Terrorism Monitor*, Vol. 2, issue 19: October 2004.
2. See Vladimir (Ze'ev) Jabotinsky, "The Iron Wall," www.mideastweb.org. Originally published in Russian in the newspaper *Rassvyet*, November 4 1923.
3. Asher Arian, Nir Atmor, Yael Hadar, "Israel Democracy Index 2007," Israel Democracy Institute.

4. "The Challenge of Crippling Hizballah," editorial, *Washington Times*, 25 July 2006.
5. A battle fought between the followers of Mohammed and Jewish tribes living in the Arab peninsula, in 629. The battle was a victory for the Muslims, and is often cited by contemporary Islamists as the historical precedent for the expected final victory over Israel.

CHAPTER 1

History's Resurrection

Our little war in Lebanon in 2006 was the last chapter in a story of great hope, and great disappointment. The Middle East peace process was born, and could only have been born, in a moment of general optimism. It was the product of what may in retrospect have been the high point of the West's domination of the globe. The process was meant to cast the seal of this in the most troublesome of regions.

This moment seems very distant now. It has since become clear that ideas, memories, and religious loyalties are all stronger than had been imagined. At the time, however, much seemed possible. The US victory in the Cold War appeared to offer the possibility of the general rearranging of the world on the basis of a shared commitment to liberal economics and democratic government. All underwritten by US-guaranteed security arrangements. This idea held out hope for a world in which the big questions had received a final answer.

For the Middle East, long blighted by enmity and feud dressed up in ideology, the notion of the birth of such a world was of particular importance.

The new vision proposed the possibility that conflicts which had in the past been resistant to solution might now become amenable to it. After all, if politicized religion, memory, nationalism, and ethnicity were to lose their power, then it followed logically that the fire would go out, or at least weaken, in conflicts based upon them.

For an idea to reach fruition, however, a general sense of perceptions hanging in the air is not enough. What was needed, was for historical forces to take hold of the idea, and make it their own. The Middle East peace process came into being because of the meeting of a number of factors — both within the region and beyond it.

First, what was crucial was the interest of the US and the Western powers in solving the conflict. There was an awareness that the Middle East region, perhaps uniquely, was still locked into ideas and power structures hostile to the West and able to challenge them. The oil riches of the Gulf and the geo-strategic position of the region meant that the Middle East could not simply be allowed to fester in its own dysfunctionality.

This realization was presented in stark relief in the period immediately following the collapse of the communist empire in Eastern Europe. The beginning of the 1990s saw the first effort to build a challenge to the new Pax Americana in the region. This was the attempt by the Arab nationalist Saddam Hussein regime in Iraq to seize the oil wealth of Kuwait. Saddam's intention was to use his conquered riches in order to enable Iraq to emerge at the center of a regional challenge to the West and to Israel, and to unite the Arab world. Saddam, however, turned out to be the last gasp of a declining pattern, rather than the first breath of a new one.

Saddam Hussein was a sort of late caricature of the Arab nationalist leaders of the 1950s and 1960s, who had prevailed in the days of his youth. Resplendent in an unearned army uniform and beret, smoking his custom-made cigars, living in absurd opulence, he epitomized the trend of secular Arab nationalism in its dying phase. Although for a brief moment in the summer of 1990, Saddam seemed to capture the imagination of a generation of Arab intellectuals, it was not surprising that he was unable to carry through on his promise to "burn half of Israel." Instead, he succeeded in launching a number of antiquated missiles at Tel Aviv, before his forces were unceremoniously chased from Kuwait by a coalition led by the US.[1]

Following the eclipse of this early attempt to challenge American regional predominance, the Middle East peace process was born. The Americans wanted to crown their victory over Saddam, and the containing of the challenge he represented, by beginning the process of finally reconciling the Israelis and the Arabs. So they created a structure in which the sides would be brought together, and would begin talking. The process was launched at a conference in Madrid in 1991. The newly domesticated Russians were brought in as co-sponsors, together with the European Union (EU) and the United Nations (UN). The delegations arrived. The Palestinians were tacked on as part of the Jordanian team, but with an extra group of advisers appointed by the PLO.

The Israelis were led by Prime Minister Yitzhak Shamir. Speeches were made and the sides independently pledged their commitment to peace and reconciliation. Following the declarations, the idea was that serious bilateral negotiations would begin in Washington, and that agreements would rapidly follow. These would be based on a shared recognition that the age of conflicts had passed, and great prospects awaited those who realized it.

In order, however, for the structure to bear fruit, it was necessary that the various players would perform their allotted roles. For this to happen, the "lock" of objective conditions was not enough. The "key" of subjective consciousness was also essential. As it turned out, in the beginning of the 1990s, all sides — Israelis, Palestinians, and the broader Arab world — would have their reasons for taking part in the peace process. The reasons, however, were quite different, and their nature and differences contained within them are the seeds of the later failure and eclipse of the process.

For mainstream Israel, the peace process appeared to offer a chance to finally close the door on the long, exhausting struggle for the country's establishment and survival. By the early 1990s, there were latent energies in Israel, waiting to be released. The country had moved far from its austere early days as a mobilized, nationalist republic.

A highly educated, highly mobile younger generation was open to the West. The West seemed on the cusp of a golden age of open borders, information revolution, and shared prosperity. A generation of young Israelis wanted into this. The nature of their country and society had equipped them with the skills to achieve their goal.

Around the neck of this new Israel, the ongoing conflict with the Arabs hung like a millstone. There was a declining appetite for it. In the 1950s the culture of Israel had been replete with a sort of sense of wonder at the accoutrements of sovereignty — a Jewish army! A Jewish air force! A Jewish postal service! — by the 1990s, such collective self-worship was long gone, was regarded as passé and embarrassing. In Israel, where the idea of service and self sacrifice and suffering for the state was far more than theoretical for a very large number of people, the desire to move beyond it contained a sort of urgency.

This generational mood was represented in the upper reaches of Yitzhak Rabin's Labor Party, which won a narrow victory in the elections of 1992. Rabin himself was a son of the Labor Zionism of old. He was one of the great embodiments of that generation of the sons of Zionist pioneers that grew up serving the organs of the new state that their fathers and mothers had dreamed and established. But within Rabin's party were representatives of the newer generation, whose experiences and dreams were different. Among these individuals were a group gathered around the man who became Rabin's Foreign Minister, Shimon Peres.

The first, clandestine moves toward what would become the Oslo Agreements were carried out by members of this generational group, as they established contacts with members of the PLO (a crime under Israeli law at the time), and commenced a secret negotiation with them, in the Norwegian capital of Oslo.

Thus, through the conduit of the government formed by Yitzhak Rabin, a particular generational mood found expression in national policy. This generational mood went beyond politics in the normally understood sense. It saw itself as part of a natural process of normalization, of a kind which takes place following periods of upheaval, revolution, and building. The morning after had come, and it was time to look inward, and deal with the prosaic issues that are crowded out in more tumultuous times. The young guard in the Labor Party had moved beyond the old, land-based nationalism which had been as much part of their own political inheritance as it had been of their rightist opponents. They were convinced that economics and the joint desire for prosperity would trump all other considerations. This process would take place in their enemies' minds, they assumed, much as it did in their own.

In this thought, one could vaguely discern the outlines of the Marxism which was their ideological heritage. Marxism's central claim, after all, had been that the behavior of societies would ultimately be determined by economic factors and interests, which would determine the political stances taken by individuals. Those who would claim otherwise were dismissed as romantics and simpletons. The young guard in Labor, and the trends they represented were far from the socialism of their forebears. But in the economic determinism that lay at the root of their thinking, they had not entirely shed the patterns of thinking of their heritage, though they reached very different conclusions. In this sense, the peace process represented a strange and belated victory for Marx's thinking, at the very moment that the regimes who ruled in his name were crumbling.

The Labor young guard might have noted that the events of much of the twentieth century seemed to serve as a kind of warning against any easy assumption that humankind could be seen as consisting of rational economic actors. They might have remembered that on a number of noted occasions in the preceding century, the notion that politics was simply an arena in which economic interests clashed had been spectacularly disproven. But this was the time of the end of history, and they did not remember.

The route that brought Palestinian nationalism to Oslo was very different. It was not based on the fading of an apparently successful idea once it realizes itself, in a sort of natural process of birth and decline. Rather, the Palestinian national movement in the early 1990s appeared close to historic eclipse. In the first instance, this was because of a series of strategic errors which the movement had made in its alliances. The Fatah-dominated PLO, led since the late 1960s by Yasir Arafat, had been dependent on two international forces for support. The first was the communist bloc. The second was Saudi Arabia and to a lesser extent the smaller oil rich Gulf monarchies.

The Soviets had provided invaluable military, diplomatic and economic aid to the PLO. Palestinian fighters trained in the eastern bloc, and were armed with Soviet weapons. They were part of a global Soviet effort to support "national liberation" movements in the formerly colonized world (the same orientation in its embryonic form, ironically, had led to Soviet support for Zionism in the late 1940s.) But Soviet support for the Palestinians had gone beyond the merely military.

Palestinian students studied in eastern bloc universities. Soviet diplomatic support brought the PLO recognition, not only among communist countries, but also in the broader "non-aligned" movement, which again leant toward support for the eastern bloc. Beyond this, the Palestinian cause had become identified as one of the causes célèbres of the new left that emerged in the late 1960s.

In the early 1990s, this entire edifice was in eclipse. The Soviet side had been defeated in the Cold War, and, in the period 1989–1991, ceased to exist. As it went down, it took with it the various alliances it had made — like smaller boats carried down in the wreckage of a giant ship. The result was that secular Palestinian nationalism found itself without a sponsor. Of course, it had achieved the recognition first of the Arab world in 1975, and then of the EU in 1980. The Americans had initiated contact with the PLO after 1988. But all this was of only incidental importance when the main, central ally had ceased to be.

The PLO leadership then compounded its problems by offering early and highly visible support to Saddam Hussein's bid to establish himself as a regional rival to the new US hegemony. Famously, PLO leader Yasir Arafat was photographed embracing the Iraqi dictator in Baghdad shortly after the invasion of Kuwait. It was an important endorsement at the time. Saddam was trying to style himself the new

Nasir; as the symbol of the central cause célèbre of Arab nationalism, he had the power to withdraw or confer the legitimacy of that mantle. He chose to confer it.[2]

Of course, Saddam's bid was soon revealed to be form without substance. When it was over, the result for the PLO was that its former financial backers in the Gulf no longer felt inclined to support it. Saddam, after all, had made the Gulf monarchies his enemies, and had planned to make war on them for their oil wealth.

Thus, by 1991, the PLO appeared to be facing the possibility of strategic defeat. Its allies had gone. Its financial backers had gone. Israel had destroyed its military base in southern Lebanon in 1982. The Intifada in the West Bank and Gaza was petering out.

There was, therefore, a good reason for the organization to buy into the chance offered by the opening of the peace process. It promised to save the PLO from the threat of irrelevance. The PLO had been debating the issue of how to deal with the surprising longevity of Israel since the early 1970s, and had been moving slowly toward the notion of accepting the creation of a Palestinian state in Gaza, the West Bank and east Jerusalem — as a way station, or as a final settlement, depending on who was asked. In 1988, in Algiers, they appeared to endorse the original UN resolution for the partition of the country (Resolution 181), making the peace process of the 1990s a possibility.[3]

The PLO reflected the state of the larger Arab nationalist culture of which it formed a part. In the 1990s, this outlook was fading. Not as a result of weariness born from success — as was the case with Israel and Zionism — but as a result of weariness born of failure. Arab nationalism had erected a great edifice of furious rhetoric over the previous half century. Palestinian nationalism was its emblem. But there was nothing much to show for all the words. By the 1990s, Arab nationalist rhetoric had turned into a faded fig leaf for a number of police states in the region. Near-defeat brought the PLO to the peace process.

This fact marked the nature of the process from its very beginning. It meant that, while the PLO had a clear interest in entering the talks which offered it a lifeline, the talks themselves were not based on similar or even particularly comparable processes taking place among Israeli Jews and Palestinian Arabs.

The documents which the process produced may perhaps best be understood as attempts to disguise or postpone realization of this reality. The Oslo Agreements, or more officially the "Israeli-Palestinian Interim Agreement on the West Bank and Gaza Strip" differ significantly from the usual type of document that brings a conflict to resolution.[4] The usual order is that a conflict is resolved when the two parties have found a formula for its resolution to which they can both agree. But the 1990s peace process was not like that.

The Oslo agreements lay down an incremental process which was intended after a period of building trust to produce a final status agreement between Israelis and Palestinians. The accords are a perfect artifact from the age of the end of history. The idea was that since it was known that the natural state of conflicts is that they are amenable to solution, what was needed was for the two sides to get to know one another over a set period of time. In the course of this, ways of settling issues of deep dispute would emerge. Then, after a five year period, the sides would re-convene, and conclude the deal.

In this way, issues of sharp division remaining between the two sides were concealed. Thus, on the future of Jerusalem, or of the refugees of 1948, the two sides remained in essence irreconcilable. But these specific differences were indicators of a greater flaw.

The flaw was that the two sides had come to the peace process with quite different assumptions and goals. The Israeli side wanted to wrap up the final arrangements of what they regarded as a confirmation of their historic victory in creating and defending Jewish statehood. The PLO was based on a whole regional political culture that to its very core rejected this verdict. It had come to the table because it had nowhere else to go.

There were undoubtedly individuals within the organization who had made their peace with what looked like the historical realities of the situation. But the PLO leader Yasir Arafat seemed able to hold within himself entirely contradictory impulses simultaneously. This, at least, was what was indicated by his statements and actions through the years of the peace process.

So, Israel came to the negotiating table as a result of a decline in nationalist fervor and commitment in the country, of a kind typical of successful movements half a century after their moment of success. But no comparable process of examining of core assumptions was noticeable in Palestinian thought. On the contrary, the assumption of the absolute justice of the Palestinian cause, and the absolute immorality of that of Zionism/Jewish nationalism remained entirely unassailed. This core assumption was then made to fit uneasily with the fact of the negotiating process, which was taking place as a result of dire political necessity.

On this basis, a set of fragile political arrangements were put in place, from early 1994 onwards. These allowed for the creation of a Palestinian Authority in the Gaza Strip and part of the West Bank. The uneasy relations between this entity and Israel, and their eventual collapse into open conflict in late 2000 defined the decade of the 1990s in Israel.

This was not, however, the way it felt during the period. Large parts of the country set about in the 1990s creating a sort of post-conflict culture, even in the absence of an actual end to the conflict. The point of the process for Israelis was not particularly to reconcile with and get to know the neighbors. Rather, the idea was to make a deal precisely so that they could forget about the neighbors and open out to the world.

Life in Israel is possessed of a fabled intensity. Israelis can apply a kind of fervor to pleasure seeking, consumption and enrichment of which more staid parts of the world could not conceive. The 1990s were a non-stop party in the center of the country. The Nasdaq was booming. The country was awash with venture capital. Investment in start-up ventures dreamed up by young entrepreneurs was at a premium. There was a real estate bubble along the coastal plain, as the physical infrastructure emerged to service this new world — malls, glittering towers, restaurants. It was all as though the promise had been fulfilled.

International concerns such as Intel located their research and development facilities in Israel — a recognition of the Israeli ability in fast and creative thinking.

The political culture rapidly adapted to accommodate this change. Discussions took place along the lines of "for 100 years, the conflict has acted as a kind of glue, binding us together. What will remain to unite us now the conflict is over?"

The problem with all this was that it was not mirrored by concrete progress in the political and diplomatic sphere. While large sections of the Israeli public gratefully turned their backs on the tedious squalor of the conflict, in fact the conflict was not over. The Oslo process had not succeeded in building the bridge between the two sides that it appeared momentarily to presage. Instead, the two societies continued to exist in their parallel realities. The one hooked into an emerging global reality, the other into part of a region that was being left behind by that reality.

The result was that every so often, the frenetic activity of the coastal plain would be brought to a halt by an explosion. Terror attacks at Beit Lid in 1995, in the Apropos Café and the Mahaneh Yehuda Market and so on. The periodic bombings would come as stark reminders of a quite unresolved situation a few miles to the east. But they failed to impact on the more general mood.

Elements of the religious public loyal to the religious nationalist fervor that swept the country in the late 1960s and early 1970s were of course furious at the turn of events. A young representative of the most extreme circles within this public assassinated Rabin in 1995. But neither this act, nor the subsequent election of a government overtly skeptical to the thinking behind the peace process, was enough to throw it off track.

The right wing government of Benjamin Netanyahu which took power in 1996 did not depart from the framework of Oslo. Rather, Netanyahu continued negotiations — and in the city of Hebron, territorial concessions. Netanyahu in any case lost power to a government of the left in 1999.

The talks trundled on, and the perception grew in Israel that somehow the peace process was an inherent aspect of reality. It was assumed that there would be ups and downs, but the "process" had become a familiar part of life.

Reality, however, if forbidden entry, will tend at a certain stage to force its way in. The Oslo process was limited in time. It was made possible because it agreed to postpone discussion of core issues of the conflict, such as borders, the future of Jerusalem, and the issue of the refugees of 1948 and their descendants. But it agreed to put off the discussion for five years, not indefinitely. At a certain point, the end game had to begin. So, in 2000, the government of Ehud Barak took the first moves in initiating a process intended to begin the final act. With the reluctant agreement of the Clinton Administration, the sides gathered to try to wrap up the process in talks at Camp David, in the summer of that year.[5]

The summer of 2000 was a curious, febrile time in Jerusalem. Anyone who kept their ear close to the ground could feel that something bad was brewing. The disconnection between perceptions on both sides had reached an extreme point. Israelis partied on through the economic boom, and the TV talked about the crystallizing "agreement" with the Palestinian Authority. On the Palestinian side, things looked rather different. There was widespread disillusionment, and new movements and directions were emerging to feed off it.

Palestinian discontent derived from a number of factors. On the one hand, the PLO bureaucracy, who had arrived from Tunis at the start of the process, had proved prone to corruption and dismissive of the rights and interests of the local Palestinians. As a result, there had emerged in the territories a very visible class of bureaucrats who had grown rich and fat from the peace process and the opportunities it had offered.

There was also a very pervasive sense that the peace process represented in fact a surrender to Zionism, and the acknowledgment of its victory. It would include, after all, the final recognition of the partition of the country, against which Palestinian nationalism had come into being in order to fight. Presumably, it would also include something less than the fulfillment of the "right of return" of refugees and their descendants that formed a central motif in Palestinian national identity.

So, there was resentment, anger, and far from the conference rooms of the peace process, there was also a growing sense of an alternative.

First of all, on the ground in the Palestinian territories since 1987, the Hamas movement offered a totally separate set of strategies and symbols. Hamas had emerged from the Muslim Brotherhood in Gaza in the late 1980s, at the time of the outbreak of the First Intifada. The movement was the response of the Brotherhood to a smaller Islamist current, Islamic Jihad, which itself had been formed by Palestinians inspired by the Islamic revolution in Iran.

Hamas had carried out an implacable opposition to the peace process since the 1990s. Its bombings and killings were the punctuation that came to Israeli towns and cities, reminding the forgetful that the conflict had not ended.

But there was another example, from a little further afield, which offered a particular inspiration to those convinced that historic compromise with Zionism was neither desirable nor necessary. In May, 2000, against the background of a determined public campaign, Ehud Barak ordered the unilateral withdrawal of Israeli forces from the 10 km wide "security zone" in southern Lebanon. In doing so, Barak handed victory to the Iranian backed Shia militia Hizballah, which had been fighting the IDF in southern Lebanon since the mid-1980s. The model offered by Hizballah was one of implacable resistance to Israel's existence, separated from any possibility of a political process or hope of reconciliation.

This example, this possibility was in the background, as the parties met at Camp David to try to bring the 1990s to a successful conclusion. A close observer of the situation might have noticed signs of the underlying mood. The university campuses of Israel were rocked by demonstrations and counter demonstrations in the course of the summer.

Arab-Israeli students and their leftist Israeli-Jewish allies faced off against rightist Israeli counter-demonstrations in a series of angry encounters. For the first time, Hizballah flags were seen among the Arab-Israeli demonstrators at Haifa University.

I remember one such demonstration outside the Frank Sinatra Cafeteria at the Mount Scopus campus of the Hebrew University of Jerusalem.

I had been working in the university library when an acquaintance rushed in and told me there was something going on outside the cafeteria. We went down to take a look. A crowd of leftist and Arab students were facing off against a similarly sized group of right wing Israeli and Jewish counter-demonstrators.

Beefy, amused university security types kept the two crowds separate. I remember the growing, visceral rage of the chanting as the minutes wound by. There was a sort of strange communication in it, as chant answered chant. At one point, in a basic re-statement of the point under contention, the two crowds began simply to yell at one another the rival names for the area of land under dispute. The Jewish demonstrators began with a raucous calling of "Eretz Yisrael, Eretz Yisrael" (the Land of Israel in Hebrew — which has connotations of something much older and deeper than the UN Partition Plan of 1947).

The Palestinians and their supporters picked this up after half a minute or so, and responded with a rhythmic chanting of their own of the word "Filastin" (Palestine) over and over. Something slightly comical about it, and something disturbing.

The second notable aspect was the utter indifference displayed towards the two warring groups of demonstrators by the vast majority of students. Crowds wandered by, perhaps glancing at the scene with a little smile of indulgence. This was still Oslo-time. Who could understand this curious attempt to raise the old atavistic spirits?

Thus it went on, the chanting echoing off the walls of the Frank Sinatra building away into the dry desert air, a gorgeous blue sky up above. Through the glass walls of the cafeteria, some young students looking out — but mostly not looking out; mostly engaged in other things. The same cafeteria that would be destroyed by a Hamas bombing a little year later, when the matter had been very much decided. The last days before the fall.

Similar demonstrations took place in Haifa and Tel Aviv. At that time, people thought they were the last gasp of the past — though of course they were actually harbingers of the future. The fact that the students demonstrating with Hizballah flags were Palestinian citizens of Israel might have offered an additional clue to give pause to those who were convinced of the triumph of economics over politics. These young people, after all, were by any measure beneficiaries both of Israel's modern economy, and of the chances represented by the peace process. Yet they — and their numbers in the summer of 2000 were growing and visible — evidently found the "resistance doctrine" of Hizballah and Hamas to be a more attractive proposition.

The demonstrations were not the only clue available. There were those who had been predicting an explosion in the Palestinian territories for some time, because of the absence of economic development as a result of the peace process. This was in spite of the fact that the Palestinians had become the largest beneficiaries per capita of aid in the world.

The endemic corruption and incompetence of the PLO ruling stratum in the territories, not helped by the closures imposed by Israel following violence, had led to large scale unemployment and frustration with the process. In many ways, the regime created by the PLO in this period resembled those of the other military-nationalist regimes in the Arab world that had emerged at the same time as the movement. One difference was that Arafat and the PLO did not possess the tools of repression available to similar regimes in Syria and Egypt.

The Camp David negotiations of course did not produce the desired final status agreement. Rather, it was discovered at Camp David in the summer of 2000 that issues that had appeared intractable in the early 1990s had not been made more amenable to solution through the process of acquaintance and joint effort of the 1990s.

On the core matters of Jerusalem, borders and refugees, differences soon emerged in the course of the negotiations. The deliberations continued for 13 days. In the course of them, a proposal for Israel to concede 92 percent of the West Bank and the entirety of Gaza to a new Palestinian state was made. The proposal was rejected by the Palestinian delegation, with no alternative offered.[6]

The hastily prepared summit then turned into a Sisyphean experience for the US mediators. President Clinton at one point accused Arafat of having "been here for 14 days and said no to everything." In the final Israeli offer, the Palestinians were to be given sovereignty over the Christian and Muslim neighborhoods of Jerusalem, and over seven of the nine Arab neighborhoods of east Jerusalem. The Palestinian Authority would also receive custodial responsibility over the Temple Mount/Haram al-Sharif, though it was to remain under Israeli sovereignty.

On refugees, US mediation was unable to come up with a formula acceptable to both sides. Palestinian negotiators made clear that any formula that seemed to remove their peoples' hope of returning to what was now Israel would be unacceptable. The result was that no coherent proposal of any kind was reached on this issue. In any case, since the Palestinian delegation turned down the arrangements on borders and Jerusalem, the summit did not reach the point of also arriving at disagreement over refugees. Rather, it broke up in acrimony after two weeks.

The failure at Camp David did not immediately presage the end of the Oslo process. On the contrary, the believers went on believing, throughout the remaining months of summer. However, something had shifted. At Camp David, the carpet was pulled from underneath two core assumptions of the 1990s peace process. The first was the belief that the incremental web of connections built up by Oslo would prove sufficiently strong to hold the weight of the core issues of the conflict. This had proven not to be so.

The second, more fundamental issue put to the test at Camp David was the notion that the conflict was in essence a matter of differing claims over a piece of real estate. This idea received a severe blow as a result of events at the summit. The issues that caused the summit to fail were not related to practical, substantive, solvable matters, but rather to ideological and symbolic ones.

Yasir Arafat, in the course of the two weeks, dismissed Israeli claims of attachment to Jerusalem's Old City. The PLO leader claimed that the Jewish Temple had not been located in Jerusalem at all, but rather in Nablus.[7] It proved impossible to induce Arafat even to offer an alternative proposal to that made by Barak at the summit. Rather, the Palestinian position was that their compromise was in accepting the existence of Israel in the remainder of the land outside of the West Bank, Gaza and east Jerusalem, and that it was therefore unfair to expect them to make further concessions.

Saudi Prince Bandar concluded later that Arafat was incapable of making the transition from revolutionary to statesman.[8] But the PLO leader's position was indicative not only of Arafat's personal psychology and character. Rather, it was deeply rooted in the political culture from which he had emerged, which he had helped shape, and of which he was a chief symbol. Arafat had entered the peace process not because of any transformation in attitude. He and his colleagues had never been part of the change in mood that had underlain the Israeli journey to Oslo. The Israeli change of mood, of course, did not derive from any outbreak of altruism. Rather, it was rooted in a sense that the world was changing, values changing, new possibilities and forms of success becoming feasible.

None of this in any way affected the outlook of the PLO leader or his colleagues. He had entered into the process because he had few alternatives, and to see where it would lead him. The fact that Arafat and the PLO leadership were not part of the more messianic transformation of attitudes of which the pioneers of Oslo sometimes spoke was not lost on the Israelis.

Rabin, at the start of Oslo, had spoken of a "great revolution," which he depicted as spreading "in Moscow, and in Berlin, in Kiev and in Johannesburg, in Bucharest and in Tirana." This revolution, he said was now "reaching Jerusalem, Tel Aviv, Beersheva, and Tiberias. We are undergoing the revolution of peace."[9]

These phrases were undoubtedly the work of a speechwriter. Rabin did not sound like that when he was choosing his own words. But anyway, no one would have suspected that the Palestinian leadership in any way shared this perspective. What was, however, assumed, was that this leadership had the same bottom-line perception of interests and time as did their Israeli and Western counterparts. This, it was assumed, would be the meeting point.

At Camp David, this was precisely what did not happen. US Middle East Envoy, Dennis Ross, in his memoirs, pointed out that a considerable gap existed between Arafat's stance and that taken by more junior members of his delegation. He also notes, however, that when he spoke with them about this, they pointed out to him that only Arafat could "deliver" on an agreement.[10] This was because Arafat was the "keeper" of the symbolic level of politics, wherein legitimacy was situated. But this symbolic level contained within it real impulses and directions and strategies. It was not simply a colorful and folksy cover to be put over the gray rationality of shared interest.

Arafat could speak of struggle and humiliation and revenge and Islam and pride in past victories. This was what gave him legitimacy. But precisely because he also genuinely thought in these terms, he was quite incapable of reaching the kind of agreement envisaged by the architects of Oslo. The change they had foreseen was largely illusory, the forces represented by Arafat stronger than expected. It was these forces, in a new guise, which would go on to define the next chapter in the conflict, not those of the peace process.

The parties returned empty-handed from Camp David at the end of August. Although a half-hearted statement emerged from the summit to the effect that negotiations would continue, it was obvious that something had been broken. A theory had been tested, over a period of seven years, and had been found wanting.

The strange atmosphere grew in Jerusalem in the remaining months of summer. Something would soon come to fill the void. In the meantime, the brief Middle Eastern autumn, which is followed rapidly by winter, was beginning.

The fall came on 28 September. The spark which began it was the decision by Likud leader Ariel Sharon to visit the Temple Mount/ Haram al-Sharif in Jerusalem. This decision was met by massive

Palestinian protests, which turned into running battles with the police and Border Guard in the Old City of Jerusalem. It started on a weekend which also marked the Jewish New Year — Rosh Hashanah. I was at home in Jerusalem that weekend, and I decided to take a walk to the Old City, to see how much had changed.

Over the period of the peace process, Jerusalem's Old City had become a bustling tourist venue. It was popular with Israelis from west Jerusalem and beyond, who would fill the Hummus restaurants on Saturdays. On the Saturday of Rosh Hashanah 2000, all was transformed.

There was white smoke rising as I entered the Old City via the Jaffa Gate. The narrow alleyways, which should have been full of tourists and visitors on a Saturday afternoon, were almost deserted. There were stones strewn around from the recent clashes, and teams of Border Guards in riot gear moving through the area.

One of the tourist shops, which offered a range of t-shirts to supporters of either of the sides in the conflict, was open. The ones saying "don't worry America, Israel is behind you," were still hanging next to the ones reading "Free Palestine." This, I had always thought, testified to the triumph of free market economics over both nationalisms. But now the rival shirts were hanging there mute and absurd, with no one coming to buy them. And martial Arab songs were blaring out of the speakers at the entrance to the shop. The stones strewn in the alley were the only audience.

Abu Shukri, where I liked to go for lunch on a Saturday, was deserted. Usually it was impossible to find a chair at 2 o'clock on a Saturday afternoon. Israelis and Palestinians, mutually gorging themselves, would fill the place up. Now, there was nothing but chairs. One of the waiters who I knew, nervously glanced at me and addressed me in English, instead of Hebrew. All was changed.

Abu Shukri had always occupied a rather strange balancing point. A number of the waiters wore the beards of devout Muslims, and there were Muslim Brotherhood stickers and posters on various of the walls. These were in Arabic only, however, and hence it had been common to see affluent young families from Tel Aviv eating hummus and kebabs under a poster proclaiming that Islam was the solution. It had worked. For a while. Not any more.

In the alleyways, a small group of Germans who looked like young political activists were making their way towards the Damascus Gate, led by a thin woman in her early 30s. She was speaking to them in low, urgent German tones. They passed a Border Guard team heading the other way. The Oslo process, of course, had seen its days of unrest before. There had been terror attacks, demonstrations. This was different.

In the days that followed, rioting and gun-battles spread throughout the country: through the West Bank, and in areas of heavy Arab population within pre-1967 Israel. The killing of 12-year-old Mohammed al-Durrah in Gaza on 31 September brought things to a new level of intensity. Later, there would be claim and counter claim regarding who was responsible for this incident. But at the time, it had the effect of galvanizing opinion in the Arab world.

For a brief moment, in the balmy days of late September, it looked as though a general ethnic war between Jews and Arabs in the area of former Mandatory Palestine was about to break out. The 1949 ceasefire lines, the possession of Israeli citizenship, negotiations, peace processes, all for a moment seemed about to be shrugged off like useless detritus. With the basic issue — of ownership and sovereignty — to be contested by blood once again, as in 1948.

The unrest spread to Israel's Arab population. In Wadi Ara, mobs blocked the roads, stoning cars, attacking motorists and Jewish civilians. An elderly Jewish man, Jan Bechor of Rishon LeZion, was stoned to death by the mob in the area of Jisr a-Zarka. The police responded in force. Thirteen Arab rioters, citizens of Israel, were killed in the first days of October 2000.

What characterized the actions of the security forces in these early months was chaos and improvisation. No one had included the prospect of the sky falling in as a scenario for consideration. Stretched thin, facing scenes without precedent, they responded to the violence of the mob with heavy force.

By the end of the first week, 60 Palestinians and five Israelis were dead. American attempts to broker an early ceasefire were unsuccessful. On 4 October, Arafat rejected a US call for an end to the violence. The PLO leader was not involved in the planning and execution of the violence itself. But his was the guiding strategic hand.

In early October, two IDF reservists took a wrong turning on their way to reserve duty at a detention facility north of Jerusalem. As a result, they ended up in Ramallah, and were arrested by the PA police. A mob descended on the police station and the two men were lynched. Their battered bodies were abused by the crowd. This action led to the first major Israeli incursions into the PA controlled cities of Ramallah, Gaza, Jericho, Nablus and Hebron.

The framework of Oslo was coming apart at the seams. As it did so, the ideas upon which it had rested were also shaking on their foundation. Frantic attempts to save the enterprise took place in the autumn of 2000, to no avail. Various new diplomatic initiatives were tried. Clinton came up with a new set of proposals, which included greater concessions to the Palestinian side.[11] There was a last ditch meeting between the sides at the Bolling Air Base in Virginia. But something stronger was working against it.

It has since become clear that the violence that erupted that autumn was not entirely spontaneous. Rather, the Sharon visit to the Temple Mount was used as the spark by elements among the Palestinians to launch an uprising. The initiative seems to have come from elements in the Fatah command.

Tanzim militia leader Marwan Barghouti was the man who directly took the decision to use Sharon's visit to the Temple Mount in order to foment violence. But as the Fatah leader in the West Bank, it is unlikely that he would have acted without the knowledge of his superiors.

Barghouti had emerged as a young leader of Fatah during the First Intifada. He had been seen as one of the main proponents of a compromise peace with Israel. However, he also headed his own militia faction within the larger movement. After the events, he revealed that "I knew that the end of September was the last period (of time) before the explosion, but when Sharon reached the al-Aqsa

Mosque, this was the most appropriate moment for the outbreak of the Intifada."[12] On the evening of 27 September, Barghouti appeared on a local TV station, and called on the public to go to the al-Aqsa Mosque the next day, to confront Sharon. In the first clashes, four Palestinians were killed.

The example that inspired those responsible for the launch of the Second Intifada was that of Hizballah in southern Lebanon. It was not the Shia Islamist philosophy of Hizballah that was relevant here, but rather Hizballah's successful use of paramilitary activity in order to achieve a political result. This was the aspect which the Palestinian strategists sought to emulate.[13]

Baghouti had set about building a force within Fatah to carry out armed struggle, and pioneering the unfamiliar cooperation between Palestinian nationalist and Islamist forces that would characterize the second "Al-Aqsa" Intifada. This force, alongside the Palestinian Islamists of Hamas, would now be launched at Israel.

Years of fire and smoke had begun. In Jerusalem, new and strange sights. We watched in wonder as the tanks headed for Gilo on the southern edge of the city. How strange to see them deployed for action, in a suburb of the capital. The siege was drawing in. Just across the valley, in Beit Jala, the gunmen of the Fatah-Tanzim would come up from Bethlehem in the night. There would be wild firing across the valley. In the months to come, the sound of guns from the south would be a normal nightly occurrence, and later a matter for gallows humor. Not at first, though.

The city filled up with journalists on expense accounts, and various varieties of political partisan. The foreigners who had come to share in normality and hope were departing. Others who had come to partake of chaos and suffering were arriving. I remember one evening in a bar in the Finegold Courtyard, saying goodbye to a group of German medical students who were cutting short their trip. "My parents, you know," said blonde Lucinda, smiling a little shamefacedly at this admission of not quite maturity.

The Arabs from the east side of the city who used to come to eat and drink in the bars were already starting to stay away. Reservists stationed in Gilo came up to sample west Jerusalem's offerings of night life. Sophisticates from the coastal plain, they feigned scorn and condescension, in their olive green fatigues and boots.

Young European leftists come to support the Palestinian cause clustered in their hostels and sometimes would deign to move among us. They would wander the city, secure in their limitless rightness and an accompanying ignorance of sometimes epic proportions. There were pro-Israel partisans too. Often Americans, often Christians, who would tell us of their love for the people of Israel.

This love was a curious thing because of its sincerity and often transparent guilelessness. It could be comforting because in the years to come, often the only foreigners who wanted to brave west Jerusalem of the suicide bombings were these Christian types from Oklahoma and Tennessee and other American states very far from the Jewish experience.

It was now obvious that the 1990s were over. It was now obvious that the hope that sanity was about to begin its long reign was come to nothing.

We also knew that the punctuation of bombings that had marked the quiet years was likely to become a flood. The first of the explosions in Jerusalem of the Second Intifada came on 2 November, in the Mahaneh Yehuda market area. It happened on Shomron Street, a little turning off the main road. They left a car bomb there, and it exploded at just after three in the afternoon on 2 November, on a clear, pale Jerusalem afternoon. There were two killed. A man called Hanan Levy, and a woman called Ayelet ha shahar Levy, who was in the process of moving into a new house. Islamic Jihad claimed responsibility.

Reserve call up notices began to arrive for young men across the city. For me, too, and I headed down to Gush Etzion in the rain and mud of the last days of the year. "Goodnight hope and hello despair" went a sad song of that time, "Who is the next in line and who is in the next queue?" The song was by Yehuda Poliker, a son of Holocaust survivors from Salonika and one of Israel's best-loved singers.

For what it was worth, the "end of history" moment had given Israelis a fair ride in the 1990s. For a few years, an illusion of normality had prevailed. All this was to be swept aside in the autumn of 2000. In those early stages, it was not yet possible to grasp the deeper significance of what was taking place. But what was clear was that the great hope of the triumph of economics over politics had been revealed as a chimera. Human motivation remained an altogether more complex affair.

Rational self-interest, it appeared, could be interpreted variously. The lives of nations could be imagined in infinite ways, which cut across any easy power of prediction. Armed sets of symbols. But the blood and the suffering would be real enough. And the change that they wrought would clear away the detritus of one generation of leaders and call forth another. And would cast the region into another dark time. Those who had set the wheels in motion would not be the ones to navigate the journey. History, too soon eulogized, had risen again in Jerusalem.

Notes

1. For the best description and analysis of the Saddam Hussein regime in Iraq, see Kanan Makiya, *Republic of Fear*, University of California Press, 1998.
2. See Barry Rubin and Judith Colp Rubin, *Yasir Arafat: a Political Biography*, London, New York: Continuum, 2003: 122.
3. Ibid: 112–16.
4. *Israeli-Palestinian Interim Agreement on the West Bank and the Gaza Strip*, 28 September 1995. Ministry of Foreign Affairs, Jerusalem.
5. See Dennis Ross, *The Missing Peace: the inside story of the fight for Middle East peace*, New York: Farrar, Strauss and Giroux, 2004: 650–712 for the most authoritative account of the Camp David summit.
6. Ibid.
7. Efraim Karsh, "Arafat's Grand Strategy," *Middle East Quarterly*, Volume XI, No. 2, Spring 2004.
8. William Simpson, *The Prince: the secret story of the world's most intriguing royal, Prine Bandar Bin Sultan*, Regan Books: 2006: 263.
9. "Address by Prime Minister Yitzhak Rabin to the General Assembly of the Council of Jewish Federations," 18 November 1993. Source: Israel Ministry of Foreign Affairs. http://www.mfa.gov.il/MFA/Foreign+

Relations/Israels+Foreign+Relations+since+1947/19921994/138+ Address+by+Prime+Minister+Rabin+to+the+General.htm?Display Mode=print Accessed: 1/9/09.

10. Ross: 768.

11. "The Clinton Parameters," as published in *Haaretz* (English edition), 1 January 2001.

12. "Marwan Barghouti, Fatah-Tanzim and the Escalation of the Intifada," Jerusalem Center for Public Affairs, Volume I, no. 16, January 2002. The quote is taken from an interview given by Barghouti to the London-based Arabic daily newspaper *al-Hayat* on 29 September 2001.

13. See for example, the comment made by senior Fatah official Farouk Kaddoumi: "We are optimistic — Hizballah's resistance can be used as an example for other Arabs seeking to regain their rights," Hussein Dakroub, Associated Press, 26 March 2002. For further detail on PA planning for the Second Intifada, see David Samuels, "In a ruined Country," *Atlantic Monthly*, September 2005.

CHAPTER 2

Muqawama: Islamism's Rise

In the winter of 2000/2001, I served as a reserve soldier, patrolling the roads and the hills of the Gush Etzion area, south of Jerusalem. It was freezing, icy rain and winds. My memory of the time is mainly one of ice-cold hands, which I was not sure could work the rifle. It was a time before the IDF had fully internalized the nature of the struggle that was being waged against it. So there was confusion. Oslo still existed. This meant there were areas into which Israel did not have the right of pursuit. It also meant that the informational structures that had once covered the West Bank like a web were no longer there.

The Palestinian organizations, with Hamas chief among them, were waging a war against Israeli civilians in the area. They had calibrated that this was the way to affect Israeli policy. The army was, for them, mainly a nuisance. The "war" thus took the form of efforts by the Palestinian organizations to kill drivers on the roads from Gush Etzion to Jerusalem, and then to escape back to the Palestinian autonomous areas before the army jeep patrols had time to apprehend them.

It wasn't a particularly hard task for them. The car with the

41

gunmen would wait at the exit to a village. Others would radio the location of the two patrols on the road. The gunmen would then pull out. A few days before we headed for Gush Etzion, they killed Dr. Shmuel Gillis, a well known hematologist from the Hadassah hospital, this way as he drove home to Carmei Tsur in the evening.[1]

It was frustrating, Sisyphean work in the Gush that winter. We couldn't see the enemy. We also knew quite well that he was watching us. On one night, shots were fired at one of our patrols from a house in the village of El Aroub. The patrol organized a ridiculous, puffing chase after nothing through an adjoining field by way of a response. Another time, we had reports of armed men in an olive grove, and I took part in a fruitless dash at 2 in the morning through the fields. After ghosts. With the sound of a wedding party taking place incongruously somewhere in the distance.

Ours wasn't the real war. The army was just holding the line at that time on the roads of Gush Etzion. The real war was a shadowy one taking place usually out of our range of vision. It was being fought between the General Security Service (Israel's internal security agency) and the Palestinian organizations. It was a war for information. The General Security Services (GSS) were in the process of trying to re-build their knowledge of the activities of the organizations, so that we, or rather those that came after us, would be able to work in a slightly less blind way.

Every so often, we stumbled across them. One night, a colleague of mine and I, seconded to the police for 24 hours, were sent to grab some rest in a room next door to where a suspect was being interrogated. The Druze policeman with us snored peacefully as the man screamed and begged in the next room. I lay there in the bed next to the wall. The Druze snoring on one side and the screaming just the other side of the wall — sometimes interrupted by a low voice, too quiet to make out the words. It was a long night.

A few nights later, Tsahi Sasson, a civilian from the Gush, was shot dead outside of the village of Tsriff. One of our unit's patrols found him dead in his car. No sign of the gunmen. In retaliation, the army created a new guard outpost at the entrance to the village, where soldiers would be placed on guard like sitting ducks in case the gunmen in Tsriff felt bored with killing only civilians.

I stood outside there myself on a few occasions. Luckily, the gunmen weren't interested. It seemed no way to fight a war — and we weren't. We were just holding the line, as bullets from unseen gunmen came down like rain every night from El Khader, on the road to Jerusalem. The GSS and police methods, and the army as iron fist and stone wall, would deliver change further down the road. But that was all a long way off. When I got back to Jerusalem from the Gush it was raining and I slept for a long time.

The low-intensity war that broke out between Israelis and Palestinians in the autumn of 2000 was fought by the Israeli security forces against an alliance of Palestinian militias and organizations. The key components were the Hamas movement and the al-Aqsa Martyrs' Brigades, which emerged from within the shell of Fatah. The smaller Islamic Jihad movement was an additional, junior partner. The traditional dividing line in Arab politics was between secular nationalists and religious conservatives. For many years, the secular nationalist element among the Palestinians had appeared the more revolutionary.

In the 1980s, before the First Intifada, the Muslim Brotherhood was treated as a slightly embarrassing family joke by young Palestinian nationalists. Like a country cousin. But a complex series of processes was to transform this, leading up to the situation from 2000 on whereby the Islamists would set the tone, with the younger generation of nationalists largely adopting their model.

Muqawama — the term means, in Arabic, "resistance" — is the preferred designation for the Islamist and nationalist forces currently engaged in war with Israel. It is, literally, Hamas's middle name. "Hamas" stands for "Harakat al Muqawama al Islamiyya" or Islamic Resistance movement. Hizballah, meanwhile, refers to itself as the "Muqawama al Islamiya fi Lubnan," or "Islamic resistance in Lebanon."[2] These forces adhere to a shared doctrine of attrition and "death by a thousand cuts" which they wish to inflict upon Israel. The application of this doctrine has underlain the fighting between Israel and the Islamist enemies on its borders since the 1990s and in intensified form following the collapse of the Oslo peace process in 2000.

Radical Islam among the Palestinians has a history. The Muslim Brotherhood had long maintained an active branch west of the Jordan River. One of its former members was PLO leader and Fatah founder Yasir Arafat. Fatah itself commonly made use of Islamic imagery. The very term "Fatah," in addition to being a reverse acronym for the Arabic letters for Palestine Liberation Organization, also denotes an Arabic word which means "to open," but which is also used to mean conquering a country on behalf of Islam.

The Palestinian national movement in its earliest incarnation was led by a cleric — Amin Husseini, Grand Mufti of Jerusalem. Among its early heroes was the Muslim preacher Izz a Din al Qassam, killed by the British in the West Bank village of Yabed in the 1930s. Some of the most famous theorists of radical Islam have emerged from among the Palestinians — including Abdullah Azzam, generally seen as the ideologue of al-Qaida, and Taqiuddin al-Nabhani, founder of Hizb ut Tahrir. The post-1968, Fatah-dominated PLO avoided overt statements of secularism. Thus, the famous goal of the "democratic, secular" state has no equivalent in Arabic, where the parallel expression removes the term "secular."[3]

But it was the foundation of Palestinian Islamic Jihad from a disparate group of smaller Islamist groupings in 1979–1980 that set the scene for the modern renaissance of Palestinian Islamism. The physician Fathi Shqaqi and Abd al Aziz Awda, both with backgrounds in the Muslim Brotherhood, were the founders of this small movement. Their inspiration was revolutionary Iran, and they adopted a number of aspects of Teheran's Shia revolutionary creed — including the concept of rule by clerics quite alien to the Sunni Palestinian tradition.[4]

This 'ecumenical' aspect of Islamic Jihad served to keep the organization a small and somewhat esoteric project among the Palestinians. It eschewed political activity, favoring an exclusively military orientation. Islamic Jihad saw itself as a vanguard, elitist organization, and it scorned the prospect of patiently building up support among the Palestinians. Rather, the movement engaged from the outset in violent acts of terror against Israeli targets.

Islamic Jihad was the first group to combine Islamist ideology with a Palestine-centered military strategy. The movement had its roots in the Muslim Brotherhood, but split from it. It lacked the deep roots in Palestinian society that the Brotherhood possessed by virtue of its history and its welfare structures. Hamas, however, did not constitute a split from the Palestinian branch of the Muslim Brotherhood. Rather, the movement was a result of the wholesale turn of that branch toward a focus on paramilitary and political activities.[5]

Unlike Islamic Jihad, Hamas thus had a real base in Palestinian society. The "Dawa" (Islamic relief work) structures of the Muslim Brotherhood in the Gaza Strip and West Bank were extensive. They included an education system, day care centers, health facilities, soup kitchens, a sports league and orphanages. Since the early 1970s, the Muslim Brotherhood had been developing this infrastructure, far from the headlines in either Israel, the West or the Arab world. It had gained them a reputation for clean hands, and the respect of a large part of the Palestinian public. This was not the part of the Palestinian public that tended to speak English and mix with foreign correspondents, so the development went largely unrecorded.

It was noticed, however, by the Israeli authorities, and plausible rumors have circulated ever since that Israel was particularly tolerant of the activities of the Islamists because it saw them as building a politically quietist counterweight to the nationalists of the PLO. It is hard to imagine now, but there was a time when greater religious observance and attendance at the Mosque were thought to have an adverse affect on the likelihood of political activism. Hamas's forerunner organization, the Mujama never engaged in military activity and was never declared illegal by the authorities.

So when the Muslim Brotherhood decided to move into the realm of paramilitary activity, it could draw on a large, existing structure on which to base itself. Hamas was formed in the Gaza Strip in 1987 following the outbreak of the First Intifada in December of that year. The movement's military wing, the Izz al-Din al-Qassam Brigades, emerged a little later, in 1992.

Qassam began to compete with Islamic Jihad and the secular

Palestinian organizations in violence against Israelis from the moment of its foundation. But Hamas really impacted on the consciousness of Israelis with the wave of suicide bombings that disturbed the semi-calm of the Oslo years in early 1996.

It was at this time that the bus bombings, Shahids (martyrs) and the rest of the soon to be familiar paraphernalia of Islamist terror against Israeli civilians came into being in the conflict. The wave of attacks in 1996 followed Israel's killing of Yehya Ayash, a Hamas master bomb-maker. They led to the only serious attempt by the Palestinian Authority to crack down on Hamas activity in the course of the Oslo years.

The attempt was half-hearted and of no long-term impact. And so by the time that the peace process collapsed in 2000, Hamas, and to a much lesser extent Islamic Jihad, were established as the new and rising force in Palestinian politics.

Hamas's strength was based on a combination of factors: it had established a reputation for clean hands, in stark contast to the deeply corrupt Fatah nomenklatura installed by Arafat in the PA in the Oslo period. Through its inheritance of the Dawa networks of the Muslim Brotherhood, this lack of corruption was widely known and respected among the public. Hamas was new, untried, untainted by the perceived failure of the peace process and by the inherently humiliating involvement in it — since the process was always seen as a grudging acceptance of unavoidable reality.

Hamas possessed the immense legitimating power of religion in a traditional society. Finally, Hamas could present itself as something new, perhaps the wave of the future. This was important because it would enable the movement to re-capture the badge of legitimacy still possessed by those who engaged in political violence with the enemy, for the maximum goal.

The latter aspect would prove crucial in the period of conflict that opened up in the autumn of 2000. Hamas and Islamic Jihad were no longer seen as only, or primarily, groups representing a religious political outlook. Rather they, and in particular the former, were seen by many as bearers of a doctrine and a means of resistance that might well prove the answer to the lies and disappointments of the diplomatic process.

For this reason, their outlook and ideology were able to some degree to "vault" over the divide — hermetic elsewhere in the Arab world — between secular nationalists and Islamists. And in 2000, in the divided, chaotic structure of the Fatah movement, there emerged militia groups led by and consisting of men whose outlook was in many ways similar to that of the Islamists. Many of the fighters of the al-Aqsa Martyrs Brigade, for example, were no less religiously observant and no less militant in outlook than were their compatriots in Hamas. Some of them were in Fatah for family and clan reasons rather than a particular ideological decision.

So at the outset of the fighting in 2000, Hamas and the al-Aqsa Martyrs' Brigade of the Fatah movement were poised to test the shared theory according to which the Zionists had ceased to be the fearsome foe of yesteryear, and would now be forced to yield in a war of attrition.

The tactical assumption they shared was that attrition could be used to force Israel to retreat. Strategically, Hamas was committed to the destruction of Israel, and to the remaking of the area between the Jordan River and the Mediterranean Sea as an Islamic Waqf (endowment).[6] This was in contrast to Fatah, which officially accepted an outcome of a small Palestinian state in the West Bank and Gaza alongside Israel.

In practice, however, the strategic goals of the two movements did not stop them from cooperating, because their view of the immediate future was similar. They shared a view of how to turn the apparent weakness of the Palestinians into strength, and the apparent strength of Israel into a vulnerability.

Israel's technological superiority would be bypassed and its citizens, who wanted above all to be left alone to pursue their private, atomized lives, would be assaulted. This would happen time and again. The process could take years. But there was time, because the Palestinian Arabs, in the estimation of their leaders, were not one of the peoples made transient and atomized by post-modernity and globalization. On the contrary, their poverty and lack of development set them on a different trajectory.

This was the doctrine which led the low-intensity conflict that began in 2000 and petered out in 2004. It was supposed to signal the end of the age of defeats.

The Palestinian organizations had an initial advantage, because the structures laid in place by Oslo meant that they could operate against Israeli targets and then escape back into the areas of Palestinian autonomy. The Palestinian Authority now existed in a sort of legal no mans land — simultaneously engaged in de facto conflict with Israel while at the same time remaining formally in a peace process with it. This state of affairs was responsible for the winter we spent in Gush Etzion chasing murderous shadows.

The factor that hurried the decline of the Oslo framework was the Hamas bombing campaign, which began in earnest in 2001. Like most brilliant military ideas, the Hamas suicide bombings were deceptively simple. All that was needed was a young man, or in a few cases young woman, who was willing to die, a requisite amount of explosives, and a gathering of Israeli civilians and the picture was complete. There was no shortage of volunteers for the muqawama.

The suicide bombings took a heavy toll of Israeli life in the course of 2001. Places of entertainment were a particular favorite among the bombers. The Dolphinarium disco in Tel Aviv was bombed in June 2001, the first of the really large scale acts of terror of the period. Twenty-one people were killed, most of them young female Russian immigrants to Israel. In August, the bombing of the Sbarro Pizza restaurant on King George Street, Jerusalem, resulted in 15 people killed and another 130 injured. Another bombing, on the tourist pedestrian walkway of Ben-Yehuda Street, claimed 11 lives, leaving 188 wounded.[7]

The bombings transformed life in Israel, and especially in Jerusalem. After they took place, the city center would empty for a period. Only a few reckless souls felt confident enough to go back to the area where death had just visited. This meant that the entertainment centers of west Jerusalem became like a weird and empty movie set.

Sandy-colored plaques listing the names of the dead appeared, and the debris was rapidly cleared away. If you felt brave, you could walk around in the middle of the evening. No one else would be there. Just you and the memorial plaques. After a few days people would begin to return to the city center, and within a week or so things would be as they had been before.

One of the noticeable aspects of the period of the suicide bombings in Jerusalem was that the interim period in which people stayed in their homes after a bombing grew shorter as time went on. Explosions, the sound of helicopters overhead, the scream of ambulances became part of normality.

People even began to develop their own little rules for ascertaining if the sounds you could hear were actually evidence that another attack had taken place. One version was to count ambulances. According to the rule, if you heard two ambulances that was fine or at least explainable. If it was three, that was evidence that something was up.

The rules had an obvious function of offsetting the human dislike of uncertainty. They created the feeling that despite it all, you had control over your own destiny. They didn't always work. For example, another rule was that places of entertainment that were close to official buildings and facilities were held by some to be safer. This was because the presence of large numbers of security personnel in these areas was thought to make it more likely that a terrorist might be apprehended on his way to his mission. As a result, it was expected that the organizations would choose places where this factor would not apply. But this assumption proved erroneous.

I was sitting in the Mike's Place bar one evening, chatting with the young barman, who was also an immigrant from London. It was a Saturday, in the early spring of 2002. He got a call from a friend of his who was a reporter on Israel's Channel 1 news program. I sat at the bar and watched him listening, nodding, silent. Then he hung up and turned back to me and said, "Gur says that Moment's been bombed. It hasn't hit the news yet."

Moment was situated almost next door to the Prime Minister's official residence on the corner of Balfour and Gaza Streets. As such, it was in one of the most heavily guarded and policed areas of the city. This had not been of assistance. On that night of 9 March 2002, a Hamas suicide bomber had entered the crowded café and detonated his charge. Eleven people were killed.

I wanted to get home as quick as I could. The quickest route back to my apartment on the German Colony was straight down King George Street, which would take me past Moment. So I set off from Mike's Place in the direction of home.

By the time I passed the cafe, the security forces had placed fences along the road, and the media had arrived. There was a scene of utter chaos and desolation in the building itself. It had been an elegant little place, and I had been there several times — on dates and other meetings.

From the road, I could see that the whole of the interior was blown out, with mess and debris everywhere, and the floors stained with blood. Lines of TV cameras were filming. The black skullcap wearing members of Zaka (an Ultra-Orthodox volunteer group) were inside the building — their job was to make sure that all body parts were taken for burial. The police and Border Guards were stopping anyone from getting too close to the scene.

By a bus stop a little apart from the scene, quietly, a line of black filled plastic bags were laid out. Each had a number on it. For a moment, it wasn't clear to me what these were. Then I realized. Zaka were nearing the end of their evening's work. In my innocence, I had long wondered why it was that many victims of terror attacks were buried in coffins, rather than as is more usual in Israel, sheeted and wrapped in a prayer shawl. Now I understood why. These were the bodies of the dead, or what remained of them. Set back a little in the center of a terrible silence. The corpse of the place itself and the corpses of the victims.

I saw an Israeli government spokesman giving an interview to one of the cable news channels. He was holding some tiny shards of blue and metal in his hand. These, he was saying, were what remained of a woman's jewellery, which he had picked up from the floor of the café.

The corpses of jewellery. It was the closest that the bombing had come to me up to that point. Perhaps ten minutes from my home. There was a small crowd gathered there, but no one said very much.

After a few minutes, I asked a middle-aged man standing next to me where he thought all this would lead. He made a gesture with his hand as if to dismiss the inadequacy of my question and curse the enemy with a single movement. "To war," he said, and turned away with a look of disgust.

I left the area a few minutes later. The news channels all had continuous coverage for the best part of the night, as was usual. The debris was quickly cleared away and the building boarded up. This was a notable aspect of the response to suicide bombings — the immense haste with which all evidence of the bombing was repaired and removed. The hunger to re-impose the illusion of normal life.

And then, once the clearing up was done, in the weeks that followed, another of the little sand-colored stone plaques with names on it appeared at the site. There were stories in the media in the days that followed that two of the eleven people killed were a couple close to the date of their marriage. They were buried together. It reminded me of a poem by Abba Kovner, the Hebrew poet and partisan of Vilna who eulogized his dead sister and her never-to-be wedding. "We will set the table without you, my sister. The marriage contract will be written in stone."[8]

The bombings grew in intensity, and reached their height in mid-2002. On 31 July of that year, Hamas placed a bomb in the Frank Sinatra Cafeteria at the Hebrew University of Jerusalem. The bomb was in a bag, placed under an Israeli newspaper. Seven people, students and university employees, were killed in the explosion. It took place in the cafeteria next to the square where the rival demonstrations had taken place in the summer of 2000, in the last days of the peace process.

Among the dead were a number of Americans, including Ben Blutstein from Harrisburg, Pennsylvania and Marla Bennett from California. Both were students at a religious studies college in town. Ben Blutstein was also a DJ who performed once a week in a bar downtown. I had seen him around; a very young, heavily built man with a beard and a big knitted kippa. He had cut an incongruous figure in the Diwan bar, owned by Farid, a former social worker from Nazareth, where leftist Israelis and Palestinian young professionals had mixed in the high days of the 1990s. Hamas, it appeared, specialized in the removal of all such incongruities.

In the tradition of such things, a small photograph of him appeared on the bar wall a few weeks later.

The bombing at the Frank Sinatra Cafeteria was aimed at the community of immigrants, university types and bohemians of which I suppose I was a part. As a result, it echoed closer. Ben Blutstein and his hefty presence behind the turntables in Diwan. But also Levina Shapira, another of the dead from that day, whose sister, Daniella Lehrer, was a friend of mine who owns a bar and restaurant in the Feingold Courtyard, in central west Jerusalem. And also David Gritz, son of Norman and Novenka Gritz, friends of friends whom I later visited in their home in Paris.

Norman Gritz was a professor of languages in Paris, an American by birth. His son had won a scholarship to study Jewish thought, and had arrived in the country a week earlier. The family weren't Zionists, nor were they particularly interested in Israel, though Norman was Jewish. But the Hamas bombing of the Frank Sinatra Cafeteria, like the other bombings, had in it an element of coercion, not only of the people whose lives were extinguished. The families and the survivors were henceforth made to be part of something which to many of them was incomprehensible.

Norman Gritz came from the courteous world of Paris and the École Nationale for language studies, and his son, with his interest in Jewish thought, also wanted to pursue activities on this high and subtle level. The intention of Hamas bombings was to prevent the possibility of pursuing such activities in Israel without reference to the national and political struggle going on there. From this point of view, targeting the innocent had a positive advantage.

I met Norman Gritz for the second and last time in Paris, in the Gritz's family apartment. Norman had a certain kind of warm, twinkly smile which I associate with Eastern European Jews. We sat facing each other in the late afternoon, talking not about the bombing but about Israel and about Jewish history. Novenka, who was Croatian born and spoke little English, came in to bring us coffee and smiled shyly.

Norman Gritz was broken by a sadness that was beyond words and gestures. Hence, he smiled quite a bit. Outside — a European city and the sound of its traffic. David had been their only child. They had been, he said, worried at his decision to travel to Jerusalem of the suicide bombings but they had kept their fears largely to themselves.

At that time — it was a year after the bombing when I traveled to Paris — France itself was being seen as a center for renewed anti-Jewish activity and street-level agitation. I was there to attend a conference, but also to interview a young man from a Zionist youth movement involved, supposedly, in organizing a response to attacks on Jews by young Muslim immigrants.

A general sense of the return of a dark, gloomy, un-natural and oppressive reality suffused everything. Norman was immensely kind and courteous, and I think slightly surprised that I had looked him up again, after the first time we met in the house of our mutual friends in Jerusalem.

He did the things that I think he thought were expected of him, talking a little about David and his interests and hopes and ambitions. They showed me his room in the small and elegant Paris apartment. There was a sense of some sort of light that had been extinguished. In spite of their welcome, I felt like an intruder; someone who wished to inquire as to facile political logic in the bottomless tragedy they had experienced. They did nothing to give me this feeling, but I felt it anyway. We said goodbye as the evening shadows were growing longer, and off I went. I left Paris three days later and I never saw Norman Gritz again. He died of cancer a few years later, in 2006.

The bombing at the Frank Sinatra Cafeteria felt like only the latest episode in an endless wave of tragedy descending on the country at that time. In retrospect, however, it took place at the moment when the attacks began to decline, and something approaching normal life began to become possible again. Operation Defensive Shield which preceded it set the basis for a process of rebuilding the rules of engagement, intelligence networks and defensive measures which by 2004 would reduce Palestinian terror attacks on Israeli civilians to close to zero.

There was a sense at the time in Israel of a war for national survival. On the one hand, this seemed absurd. Israel's conventional abilities vastly exceeded those of its enemies. On the other hand, the enemy was adapting its approaches in order to try to nullify this advantage. The intention was to turn this back into a straight fight between two roughly equal populations. From this point of view, the notion of Israeli Jews fighting for their survival did not seem so very ridiculous. And the increasingly hazardous nature of daily life in Jerusalem between 2000 and 2004 offered confirmation. The nature of the war was changing.

In Operation Defensive Shield, Israel delivered its answer to the attacks of the preceding months. Thousands of prisoners were taken, and new facilities were established for guarding them. One of these was Machaneh Ofer (Camp Ofer), a converted military base north of Jerusalem, outside Ramallah. In August 2002, a month after the bombing at Frank Sinatra, and three months after Defensive Shield, my unit was mobilized once more for reserve duty. Most of the unit went off to the Nablus area. However, a small detail was sent to guard at Mahaneh Ofer. We received a briefing from our platoon commander before heading off.

He said a number of perpetrators of the worst terror attacks of the last year were currently being held there. He mentioned, for example, the "Silwan cell," which had carried out the Moment bombing and the bombing at Frank Sinatra Cafeteria. The cell consisted of four residents of the east Jerusalem village of Silwan, which was a half hour walk from my own home in the German Colony. The names of the four were Mohammed Odeh, Wissam Abassi, Aladin Abassi and Wa'el Kassam. All were men in their late twenties or early thirties. All were members of Hamas. Their pictures had been in the paper.

This meant that for the next two or three weeks, I was going to be guarding, among others, the men who had killed Norman Gritz's son David, Daniella's sister Levina, and Blutstein the DJ from the bars. It meant that the people who had created the black, numbered body bags by the bus stop outside of the shell of the Moment café would now be under my care — the care of myself and my friends from the 188 Armored Brigade.

Mahaneh Ofer was distinguished by a distinct smell of rotten eggs that clung to every corner of the place. It looked and felt like a prisoner of war camp, not like a prison. Later it became a regular jail, they built a perimeter wall, and the prison service took over from the army. At that time, however, it was a chaotic arrangement of barbed wire and tents, and a cookhouse and old, rusty guard towers. The freshly minted Palestinian prisoners lived in two rows of barbed wire compounds. Then there was a wall of large plastic barriers, behind which the IDF soldiers lived in identical tents and identical conditions to those of their wards.

It was a flyblown, squalid place. The military police who were detailed to guard it were lazy and disorganized. They spent their time on duty flirting via the radio with the girls who ran the switchboard, and watching as the inmates transferred messages to each other by throwing them wrapped in socks from compound to compound. A different military culture to the one that I knew — the Armored Corps, with its mixture of gung-ho attitude and anal attention to detail. This crowd seemed like a Tel Aviv beach party in uniform. The army had sent us here to create a different impression, we were told. I suspected this was only a pep talk, and really we were just making up the numbers.

The prisoners lived in compounds separated according to political affiliation. There were compounds affiliated with Fatah and Hamas, and one area within the Fatah domain for the Popular Front for the Liberation of Palestine (PFLP).

The system was designed so that there would be minimum contacts between the army and the inmates. Each wired compound had a representative, a senior member of the organization to which the prisoners were affiliated. The representative was known as the "shawish." We would escort the military police officers around the area of the jail for which we were responsible in the mornings as they discussed matters with the shawish.

The three shawishes from the three different organizations in our part of the jail were a study in contrasts. The PFLP was represented by an older, balding, jeans wearing type, clearly influenced by the 1960s generation. His name was Shaqer and he sometimes wore a Che Guevara t-shirt. He enjoyed engaging the soldiers in political discussion, and explaining that they were acting as pawns of the United States. Shaqer, however, bore no apparent malice against them for this. He was a friendly soul, always beaming, affable. There weren't enough of his men to have a whole compound to themselves, so they were in with the Fatah contingent.

The Fatah representative was a small, thin man with a moustache, called Khaled. His relations with the Military Police and the soldiers seemed most straightforward. There was sufficient similarity that there was no wondrous sense of opposites meeting and pondering one another. Rather, he and the other Fatah representatives engaged in fairly natural, unaffected relations — in Hebrew — with the staff of the jail.

Unlike Hamas, Fatah was engaged in a relationship of formal cooperation with the authorities in Mahaneh Ofer. This meant that every so often, the various Fatah shawishes would be collected out of the compounds and taken for a private meeting with a civilian employee of the IDF, called Moshe. This Moshe's job was mainly to deal with the coordination of provision of food and other service to the compounds, and to pass any particular issues, complaints or requests from the inmates on to the appropriate authorities. This was not sufficiently grand for him, however, and he liked to pretend that his job also consisted of obtaining information through subterfuge from the prisoners, in the manner of an intrepid intelligence agent who moves among the enemy.

Since he spoke no Arabic, and was known by the inmates as a representative of the authorities, this was a somewhat ludicrous pretension. Nevertheless, Moshe liked to indulge in it. "Ya Fawzi," he would call out to one of the prisoners, "you're no longer just one of the Shabab of the Fatah. You should be showing more responsibility." Statements of this kind would delight the inmates, who would ask Moshe what the matter was and advise him to take a rest.

In the chaotic and confused atmosphere of Mahaneh Ofer, Moshe was something of a liability. He liked to engage in elaborate displays of hospitality with his Fatah shawishes, and would march them off to a hut he maintained for this purpose somewhere within the jail. A soldier would be detailed to accompany them. The hut was located near the outer wire, and it would have been relatively easy for the five hefty Fatah men to have jumped on the soldier and Moshe. Perhaps one of them might have been shot, but they could have managed it if they'd been prepared for that.

I took part in these meetings on a couple of occasions. They were strange. Moshe arranged plastic bottles of coke and orangeade, and Noblesse cigarettes and sunflower seeds on a white table. He and the Fatah shawishes would sit there, and discuss mundane matters of food provision and bed shortages, sometimes laughing and engaging in eastern displays of theatrical affection and status. The soldier escorting them (myself, on the occasions that I witnessed these meetings) would be entirely ignored and would feel inferior and left out. He, however, was engaged in a different line of activity in the prison, which would involve shooting any of the shawishes dead if they tried to make a run for the road below, a mere 50 yards or so away. None of them did, luckily, on the occasions when I was escorting them.

The third shawish represented the Hamas movement. His name was Salah, and he was a thin-faced, black-bearded, very dark-skinned and always impeccably dressed little man. Hamas officially had no contact with the authorities, so Salah did not take part in the meetings with Moshe.

Each day, Salah would dress in gray patent leather shoes, gray trousers, a white shirt and a gray tie. Thus suitably differentiated from his surroundings, he would set about his mundane but important work of trying to make sure that the inmates in his compound lacked for nothing when compared with their Fatah rivals.

He had no official channels with which to achieve this, and so needed to be a subtle diplomat. Salah would stand by the fence of the compound, with his brow furrowed and his thin hands gripping the fence, and he would wait for the military police officer to pass by on his rounds, accompanied by the two soldiers detailed him.

The military police officers were all 21-year-old boys, but the nature of their work imbued them with a different style from regular army officers. They would affect the worldliness and slightly contemptuous sense of superior knowledge that is a condition of policemen everywhere. Interaction in military settings always carries with it an excess of testosterone and groping for status. The military police officers took this to new levels. Their training seemed to encourage them to see themselves both as fellow soldiers and as police — attempting to exert authority over other members of the IDF as well as over the prisoners.

Salah, the Hamas shawish, therefore, was set the task of how to appear cooperative without being supplicatory, of how to be a Hamas man in an Israeli jail in 2002 and at the same time, unofficially, ensure that his own men received blankets in the winter, food parcels and visits to the medical staff and the rest of it. He would engage the passing lieutenant in good Hebrew (we poor ordinary soldiers would, once again, be treated as extras).

Salah would begin with a discussion of the politics of the day; he particularly liked drawing the officer in to share his amused contempt at the Fatah-led PA leadership. He had a special dislike of PA Foreign Minister Ahmed Qureia (Abu Ala), and liked to share his views of Qureia's latest actions, which he regarded as both contemptible and amusing. He would relate some anecdote to the lieutenant, and then stare off into the distance, as if considering the transient nature of things with his sharp brown face screwed up. Then he would casually drop in a remark about a boy in the compound who had stomach pain and needed to see the doctor, and the lieutenant would nod and say he'd deal with it. Salah would smile and nod and gracefully withdraw. There was something absurd about his natty gray outfit against the backdrop of the squalor and mess of the camp. Also something oddly impressive.

In general, the jail ran smoothly enough. The days passed in mundane routine. Behind Salah, among the Hamas prisoners in the tents with their beds pushed closely together, were the four men who blew up Moment and the Frank Sinatra Cafeteria. I tried to remember their faces from the newspaper and would look from one to another of the Hamas prisoners as we passed by, trying to discern something which might offer some giveaway sign. Nothing, of course. Which of the men hosing the compound floor, endlessly all day, wasting the prison's water as though it was Zionist too, preparing delicious-smelling falafel in their tents, taking part in lessons during the day and fervent sing-songs at night, building wooden models of the al-Aqsa mosque, smiling at us as we went by, which of the shawish Salah's men were the ones with the blood of my friends on their hands?

It was a war of unwanted intimacy. Four faces among the Hamas prisoners belonging to the same men who had produced all that: Norman Gritz in his apartment in Paris in the lengthening shadows; the broken jewellery on the floor of the Moment café; the many lives shattered in the explosion at the cafeteria.

The enormity of the losses might lead one to think that surely the bombing had been perpetrated by some huge and monstrous force, some giant, terrible creature. But here were the people who had done it, lazily sunning themselves in the slow afternoon, somewhere among their colleagues — receiving consignments of fresh vegetables once a week from the Israeli authorities, which also treated them if they had stomach pains. Here was their representative, an artful little man in gray patent leather shoes and a matching tie. Hard to make it fit.

War among the people, they call it in schools of strategic studies. On the weekends, on leave from Mahaneh Ofer, I'd head back to Jerusalem. I liked to go to Diwan, where Ben Blutstein had DJ'ed. Now it had become the haunt of left wing foreign students who supported the Palestinians, mainly continental Europeans. I would sit there quietly and think about Salah and Shaqer and Moshe, and Ben Blutstein and Norman and Novenka and David Gritz. The immense certainty of the International Solidarity Movement volunteers next to me would ring out in three different languages.[9]

I remembered Salah four years later, when I was in Ramallah to cover the Palestinian election campaign. I remembered the way in which he had sought to differentiate himself from his surroundings, and the slightly comic but impressive sense this had created.

Unlike the Fatah types, Salah and his friends did not deal in posturing. They were not interested in proving to us that they were in the right. Rather, in their eyes, they were part of a process of setting the universe back in order. And we temporarily dominant Jews could make as much noise as we liked in the process, but it was about as significant as the clucking of hens on their way to the slaughterhouse. On this basis, Salah was even friendly, in a cool, half-ironic sort of way.

Open racism against Arabs is rare in educated Israeli circles. But a sense of cultural superiority is quite deeply ingrained. This led to a tendency not to watch carefully and take seriously what people like Salah were saying — which was to prove a mistake.

In Ramallah, on 25 January 2006, it was a day of politics — the day of the Palestinian parliamentary elections. Ramallah was known as a secular and pro-Fatah town, but the Hamas-led list "Change and Reform" also maintained a considerable presence on the ground. The conventional wisdom was that Fatah would win, though Hamas, who were new to the political game, might make some gains.

Observation of the campaigns on the ground, though, might have offered clues as to the contrary. I spent the day wandering the town with a Norwegian journalist colleague. The Fatah presence on the ground consisted largely of young men, some of them armed. There were sound systems set up near Manara Square at the center of the city. Young Fatah members in black and white keffiyehs, waving Palestinian flags, were dancing around to their movement's songs. Vehicles transporting well-groomed, armed young men, with huge Fatah and Palestinian flags held from the windows, were cruising through the town.

We spoke to some of the armed men, and they were keen to show off their gleaming M-16s on election day — announcing themselves as members of the "Fatah Tanzim–Marwan Barghouti." There were representatives of various smaller lists. But Hamas activists were also in the town. They presented a rather contrasting impression.

First of all, what was interesting was the much larger number of young women activists among the Hamas cohort. The men among them were much quieter than the Fatah members, and seemed more square, somehow. The Fatah boys had a certain theatrical swagger which the Hamas activists seemed deliberately to avoid. The women were all in hijab, and many of them wore a green ribbon around their heads to show their Hamas affiliation. Some of them were students and spoke English.

Hamas's move towards politics had come partly out of necessity. By 2004, the real sense of crisis of the 2000–2002 period had passed. The Israeli military and intelligence structures had adapted rapidly to the changed situation following Oslo. After 2002 and Defensive Shield, Israel had gone onto the offensive and in 2004–2005, this had resulted in a series of assassinations of Hamas leaders. The movement had found it increasingly difficult to successfully launch operations. The acceptance of a ceasefire (the "Hudna") and a move toward politics enabled Hamas to turn back towards the social welfare structures it had maintained throughout. In 2006, it sought to translate its combination of clean hands, religiosity and extreme militancy into political power.

The signs should have been obvious. Elsewhere in the region, where free elections had taken place, Islamists had won (in Algeria, for example, and in Turkey.) This hadn't happened with the Palestinians because Yasir Arafat had owned the key legitimating symbols of religion and militancy against Israel. But, by 2006, Arafat was gone, and his successors were ruling over a rickety kleptocracy in those areas of the West Bank that remained to the PA after Operation Defensive Shield.

On the ground, Fatah could pull out these crowds of raucous young men, many or most of them probably on the movement's payroll. Hamas fielded quiet, studious looking young men and women, who were probably not on its payroll. Corruption would come later, but at that time the general and largely correct sense was that these young people were clean.

There were material aspects too. Whereas the PA educational and welfare systems were in a mess, starved of funds because of corruption and Israeli sanctions after 2002, Hamas maintained its parallel systems very effectively. There were always ways to bring in money from Saudi Arabia or Qatar or Iran, and the system kept on working.

This applied in all areas. The Tanzim men might enjoy riding around Ramallah in their big white cars. But if they found another use for their brand new weapons outside of posing, their movement would take poor care of them. It was generally held that Fatah did not look after its prisoners in Israeli jails and their families properly. Everything depended on a person's standing in the pyramids of power and patronage of which the "movement" consisted. Such considerations did not apply to Hamas, who had many quiet, modest and committed mid-level activists like Salah to call on.

Given all this, we should really have been suspicious when the exit polls that evening predicted a clear victory for Fatah. And the assembled community of journalists, pundits and analysts should not have been all that surprised to wake up in the morning, turn the radio on and find out that the exit polls had got it wrong and Hamas had just won the Palestinian Legislative Council (PLC) elections.

Twenty–twenty hindsight is easy, of course. And one tends to arrange the past so as to make sense in light of subsequent events. Yet the contrasting groups of activists in Ramallah should have made it clear. A combination of the easy to comprehend and the less easy. The young men dancing themselves to a frenzy with their Fatah songs in the main square. And by contrast, the industrious, thin men and their hijabed young women, smiling a lot, but shyly, talking softly; a sort of happiness about them.

It does no good to remind oneself that their ideology is a creed of hatred and destruction that seeks the total negation of the rights of the other side. It is of no use to remind oneself that the Hamas movement's founding charter is a litany of historic accusations against the Jews, which manages to combine elements of the European anti-Semitic tradition with traditional Islamic contempt and suspicion. It won't really help to recall again Norman Gritz in his apartment in Paris, and the silent dead outside the Moment café. None of it is excused or forgiven by realizing and acknowledging that Hamas on the streets of the West Bank in January 2006 was a revolutionary movement, that felt the wind of history at its back.

It is hard to quantify or identify the presence of revolutionary élan. But it can be present in movements committed to dark and backward ideologies just as much as in those committed to furthering the totality of human freedom. That is the deeper meaning of what could be sensed in all of the encounters described here. Hamas's project was not merely to lead the Palestinian movement. It intended to transform it into something new, a branch of a region-wide, Islamist movement committed to total victory over the enemy.

Hamas was able to capture the latent energies of rejectionism that have been present in Palestinian thinking throughout. At the heart of this is the absolutely rock solid conviction that Israel is a transient, artificial phenomenon. This belief took nationalist form for a period, but has now been comfortably embedded in an Islamist world view.

It appears to be completely impervious to empirical refutation. It does not matter how many times one reiterates the lines about Israeli material development, and the strong sense of nationhood felt by the Jews, and their history, and their suffering. Hamas among the Palestinians is now articulating the deep sense of strategic optimism that has always characterized the Palestinian and broader Arab and Muslim view vis à vis Israel. According to this view, the existence of Israel is in opposition to the natural state of affairs in the region, and to the usual laws of human development. Since this is the case, what is required is to keep the struggle going, never to give in, until the final victory.

The introduction of a religious and even eschatological element into this core outlook was the key innovation made by Hamas.

In late 2008, I traveled again to Ramallah to interview a Hamas member of the PLC. The movement at that time was existing in a sort of semi-legal twilight — its members subject to arrest by Israel and to harassment on the part of the Palestinian Authority security forces. It was holding power in Gaza, and undoubtedly its base was still strong in the West Bank. In Gaza in July 2007, the noisy young men of Fatah with their shiny new weapons had the chance to go up against the quietly fanatical men of Hamas, and Fatah was defeated hands down. The result was that a furious Fatah for the first time made real efforts at cracking down on Hamas in the West Bank.

My interview with the Hamas PLC member (who I'll call Nizar) took place in English, in an anonymous office block in the city. Nizar did not look like an Islamist. With his moustache and close cropped black hair, he rather resembled a smart junior officer of an Arab police force. He delivered a series of talking points designed to show that peace with Israel was impossible because Israel did not want it, and understood only force. At the same time, he denied that Hamas was a religious movement, claiming that there were Christians in its ranks, and that he himself was not a particularly religious man. He had moved from Fatah to Hamas, he said, because of the latter's policy of resistance. It was a practiced performance, given no doubt to many foreign visitors, and it was no more enlightening than a prepared speech by any other professional politician.

At the end of the conversation, however, as he relaxed, he began to expound on the nature of the Israeli enemy. In precise terms, in clipped and fluent English, Nizar explained the basis for Hamas's strategic optimism.

The Israelis, he said, nowadays just wanted to be left alone. Gone were the days when they sought to expand and conquer. The Zionist project, he said, had begun with the desire to create a Jewish state between the Nile and the Euphrates rivers. Then because of Arab resistance, this ambition had shrunk to a desire to expand Jewish control to the entire area between the Jordan River and the Mediterranean Sea. Determined Arab and Muslim resistance had now shrunk Zionist ambitions even further. Now, all the Israelis wanted was to be allowed to keep what they had. But this, too, was only a stage.

Nizar spoke without emotion, in a polite but neither warm nor friendly way which I had learned was the characteristic Islamist style. It conveyed gravity and a sort of understated hint of menace. A young, very thin, ginger-bearded Hamas man brought in two glasses of tea on a brass tray and put them on the table, leaving without a word. Nizar continued his exposition.

The Jews, he said, came to the land for two reasons — to make business and because of the land's holy status in their religion. As they realized, however, that their attempt to build a religious sovereignty was impossible, and that there was no way to make business there, so they would leave. The fact that the Jews, in his view, now wanted only to be left with the current situation, was proof that the way of resistance was correct, and was in the process of delivering the victory. In his view, an ultimate military victory against Israel was unlikely to be necessary. Rather, the constant maintenance of pressure at a certain level would suffice to bring out the contradictions of Israel and its un-natural essence, such that eventually it would simply wither away.

Israel's aversion to military casualties, he continued, was a further indication of its growing feebleness. It meant that Israel would prove unable to win decisive military victories over its enemies any longer, because it lacked a citizenry willing in sufficient numbers to pay the ultimate price for its continued existence.

Here was a genuinely held ideological position. Nizar, unable to leave Ramallah because of fear of arrest at the hands of the IDF, harried by Mahmoud Abbas's security forces, was calmly confident of the utter inevitability of the victory of the Muslims in the slow, long war of attrition of which he was a part.

In a room in a quiet office, in a corner of Ramallah, I found the explanation at the heart of the force whose murderous shadows we had chased in Gush Etzion in 2000, who had brought the fire and smoke to the Moment café, the Frank Sinatra Cafeteria, the Dolphinarium and all the other places, that had cast the heavy pall in the apartment of Norman and Novenka Gritz in Paris, that had watched us in irony and silence at Mahaneh Ofer, and that had swept Fatah aside in 2006 and 2007.

The contours of the kind of society envisaged by Hamas were meanwhile emerging into reality in the movement's enclave in Gaza after 2007. Here could be seen the blueprint for what Nizar, Salah,

Mohammed Odeh, Wissam Abassi, Aladin Abassi and Wa'el Kassam were trying to create.

Hamas's rule was brutal and brooked no opposition. Their control was complete. The Gaza public space rapidly became very noticeably Islamic. Few women were to be seen without the hijab. New security forces and organizations were created to enforce Islamic norms in public. The "Propagation of Virtue and Prevention of Vice Security Force," a police force operating directly under the Ministry of the Waqf (Islamic Endowment), was tasked with patrolling public areas to ensure that rules of modesty and other Islamic norms were observed.

These rules were applied stringently, and were draconian. Mixed bathing was prohibited on Gaza's beaches. Women were no longer allowed to smile and laugh when bathing, and men were prohibited from bathing shirtless. From the summer of 2009, compulsory wearing of the hijab was introduced in girls' schools.

The Gaza judicial system also became Islamized, and Islamic social controls increased. When, in 2007, Hamas tried to ban a book of Palestinian folk-tales — "Speak, bird, speak again" — there was a large public outcry. By 2009 in Gaza books and certain styles of dancing and singing were routinely prohibited with little or no public comment.[10]

The process of the establishment of a mini Islamic republic of Gaza was not powered only from above. Rather, the grassroots proliferation of extreme Sunni Islamic sects, and of similar sentiments among Hamas activists drove it along.

There had once been a clear dividing line between the extreme, Salafi (al-Qaida style) viewpoint and the Muslim Brotherhood ideology of the first leaders of Hamas. This dividing line faded in Islamist Gaza. The process of radicalization did not stop with Hamas. And disappointment with Hamas did not mean a return to secular nationalist politics.

Salafi Islamist groups proliferated after the Hamas takeover. These groups operated both within Hamas itself, and in the wider society. In the movement, their influence was particularly strong in the armed wing, the Izz a din al-Qassam Brigades.

A myriad of such organizations proliferated, helping to shape the tone of the society. The Jund Ansar Allah, Jaish al Umma and Jaish al Islam were three of the largest. These groups and others like them were responsible for a wave of honor killings, attacks on Gaza's small Christian population and attacks on internet cafes and other facilities deemed "un-Islamic" which characterized Gaza in the post 2007 period.

These more extreme groups had no chance of seizing power from Hamas. But they were the products and the fruits of the society the movement was creating — a society whose only measure of legitimacy is Islam, and whose only policy is the pursuit of war until victory over Israel.

The emergence and rise of the muqawama wasn't a matter of ideology and theorizing for its own sake. The Islamist movements were developing a praxis for struggle based on turning the nature of Arab and Muslim societies from an advantage for their enemies into their own advantage. They were unshakably convinced of their eventual victory. It meant that the prospect was for a long, long conflict to come. They hoped by the end of it to have dried out and exhausted and depleted their opponent. State borders, treaties, international law — all would be not confronted but bypassed.

It was a strategy intended to blend pre-modernity with ultra-modernity. It was intended to create a campaign against which Israel's air force and armored divisions and secret weapons would be rendered useless. The internal integrity of this view and its adherents was undoubted.

What I saw in Gush Etzion, Jerusalem, Ramallah, and Mahaneh Ofer, and what underlay Hamas rule in Gaza, was an ideology in the upwards stage of its historical trajectory. It was filled with integrity and determination. In the manner of adolescents, it dismissed its enemy and the obstacles before it as of little consequence.

Notes

1. For a short summary of the work and career of Dr. Shmuel Gillis, see the website of the Hadassah Medical Organization: http://www.hadassah-med.com/English/Eng_SubNavBar/TheDoctors/Gillis Shmuel.htm Accessed: 12.10.09.
2. See Hizballah's official English-language website "Islamic Resistance in Lebanon" — http://english.moqawama.org/index.php Accessed: 12.12.09.
3. Alain Gresh, *The PLO: The Struggle Within*, Zed Books Limited. London and New Jersey, 1988: 49.
4. See Holly Fletcher "Palestinian Islamic Jihad," Council of Foreign Relations, April, 2008. http://www.cfr.org/publication/15984 for a background introduction to Islamic Jihad. Accessed: 17.5.10
5. Matthew Levitt, *Hamas: Politics, Charity and Terrorism in the Service of Jihad*, New Haven and London, Yale University Press, 2006: 8.
6. See Hamas Charter, 1988. http://www.mideastweb.org/hamas.htm Accessed: 15.5.10.
7. All figures from Israel Ministry of Foreign Affairs website. http://www.mfa.gov.il/MFA/MFAArchive/2000_2009/2001/12/Suicide%20 bombing%20at%20the%20Ben-Yehuda%20pedestrian%20mall Accessed: 17.5.10.
8. Abba Kovner, "My Sister," in the *Penguin Book of Hebrew Verse*, London: Penguin Books: 563. (Translated by Ted Carmi.).
9. The International Solidarity Movement — a pro-Palestinian movement founded in 2001 that organized foreign volunteers to visit the West Bank and Gaza and undertake a variety of activities designed to aid the Palestinians in their struggle with Israel.
10. See, by the author, "The Islamic Republic of Gaza," *Jerusalem Post*, 29 September, 2009.

CHAPTER 3

A New Jerusalem

So, was the enemy facing the jihadis truly of such little consequence? They had correctly identified some unmistakable trends in Israeli society, but had drawn the wrong conclusions from them. They had noted superficial weakness, but not the strength that lay within it. Israeli society itself was in a state of change and flux, as it adjusted back into conflict mode.

Every year, a large commemoration event takes place at the site where Israeli Prime Minister Yitzhak Rabin was murdered in 1995. Supporters of the Oslo peace process and the path of Israel's moderate left come to listen to the leaders of Israel's center and left parties as they eulogize their fallen leader and lament the faltering of his path.

It might have been expected that a murdered prime minister would become a generally unifying national symbol. This is not what has become of Rabin's memory in Israel — perhaps because of the deeply controversial legacy of the Oslo process he initiated. So the November gathering at Rabin Square (formerly Kings of Israel Square) in Tel Aviv is a place where one can take the temperature of one of Israel's political camps.

But it is more than that. The Israeli Zionist left is not simply

69

another of the political camps in the country. Rather, it is the element that more than any other was responsible for the establishment of the State of Israel, and for the construction of the key institutions of the state. So, in a way perhaps hard for outsiders to grasp, the gathering at Rabin Square is a gathering of mainstream Israel, of the traditional upper bourgeoisie, of what was once presented as the Israeli norm — secular, largely of East European origin, self-consciously pragmatic in outlook, disliking nationalist displays of emotion, secure in its self-image as the most deeply "Israeli," as well as the most deeply sane, of Israel's various political tribes.

2006 was no ordinary year. The annual November gathering took place three months after the bloody and inconclusive Second Lebanon War. The war made a deep imprint on the Israeli consciousness. It seared home to the country the awareness that a larger enemy, with real abilities and with patience, had made Israel's disappearance its strategic goal. The commemoration for Rabin took place in the atmosphere of confusion and gloom that followed this realization.

The keynote speaker at the commemoration that year was David Grossman, one of Israel's most prominent novelists. Grossman's son, Uri, a tank commander in the 401 Armored Brigade, had been killed three months earlier, in one of the final engagements of the Second Lebanon War. The 401, together with infantrymen of the Nahal Brigade, had been kept waiting, amassing on the border, for two days prior to being sent in. The ceasefire agreement that would end the war was already in an advanced state of negotiation. They had walked into a Hizballah ambush in a place called Wadi Saluki.

In the eastern sector, we had heard the firing from further west on that Saturday night, and had known that an attack was taking place. The tanks of the 401 had been backed up in the valley, and the Kornet missiles had reaped a terrible harvest of men and machines.

The air was, therefore, thick with poignancy as David Grossman made his speech that evening. His calm and dignity only added to this sense. Grossman took the opportunity to launch a measured but uncompromising attack on Israel's political leadership. He depicted them as "hollow" men, lurching between opinion polls and legal investigations.

It is for these passages, and Grossman's subsequent refusal to shake the hand of Prime Minister Ehud Olmert, that the speech is most often remembered. However, there is an earlier passage which is yet more significant, I think.

In it, Grossman depicts what sounds like an unbearable historical dilemma for Israelis. He eulogizes the path taken by Yitzhak Rabin, and explains it in the following terms:

"Yitzhak Rabin took the road of peace with the Palestinians, not because he possessed great affection for them or their leaders. Even then, as you recall, common belief was that we had no partner and we had nothing to discuss with them. Rabin decided to act, because he discerned very wisely that Israeli society would not be able to sustain itself endlessly in a state of an unresolved conflict. He realized long before many others that life in a climate of violence, occupation, terror, anxiety and hopelessness, extracts a price before which Israel will be unable to stand."[1]

In this way Grossman explains the reason for Yitzhak Rabin's turn, after a lifetime of military activity in the Palmach organization and then in the IDF, and suspicious, zero sum politics, toward a policy of seeking a compromise peace with the PLO in the early 1990s.

This statement has implications of enormous importance. Grossman locates the reasons for the turn toward accommodation with Palestinian nationalism not in hope, but rather in something close to fear. Peace, this statement seems to suggest, became essential because Rabin saw that Israeli society was no longer able to sustain war. What were the reasons? What were the factors that led Rabin to draw this conclusion? Grossman does not go into detail in this regard. But the near despair inherent in its merely being asked, and the enormous vulnerability that it engenders, are very apparent.

After all, if it is indeed the case that the infliction of violence and terror on Israel will exact from it a price that it will be unable to pay, and if, as we have already seen, there are forces in existence in the politics of the region that regard the creation and continued existence of Israel as an affront against both man and God, then there is an obvious logical inference to be drawn from this. Namely, that those forces committed to Israel's demise would be well advised to apply the maximum pressure on Israel in precisely these areas, for the maximum period of time, since victory, though it may not be immediately within reach, is achievable and perhaps inevitable.

Grossman was enmeshed in personal tragedy at the time that he gave this speech. His very presence gave off a sense of enormous dignity and profound pain. Yet his speech was not simply a cry of anguish. Rather, he had identified a central strategic question facing his country.

Israeli society has undergone great change in the last three decades. This change has to some degree mirrored — at perhaps a more accelerated rate — a transformation in the larger Western world. The Jewish state in its first years was a place of uncommon ideological coherence. It was democratic in the sense that the possibility of a change of power through elections existed. But it was a mobilized, republican, ideological democracy — created by idealists, peopled largely by refugees.

With the decline in secular ideologies in the Western world in general, and with the growing distance from the days of the founders, this cohesion began to fade. Zionism raised formidable structures for the defense of the Jewish people. The structures survive. But the spirit that animated them has faded. The old secular Jewish nationalism embodied by the founding generation was on the way out by the end of the 1960s. The sons — of whom Yitzhak Rabin was a classic representative — were a generation of the "end of ideology."

The expectation at that time was that the great fires of the days of foundation would subside, and life would become a great deal calmer. Boredom and alienation might be an issue, but that would be all. The sons of Labor Zionism met their enemies, the secular Arab nationalists, on the field of battle, and vanquished them in bloody, high-speed warfare, in 1967 and 1973. There, it was hoped, the tales of blood and sacrifice could end.

This morning-after flavor is present in embryonic form already in much of the Israeli literature of the 1960s. It may be felt in the first stories of Amos Oz and A. B. Yehoshua. There is a turning inward. We have won, their work seems to say, and now we must have the really important conversations about who we are, and who we want to be. Arab nationalism's challenge intervened — but it was defeated.

But it was in the subsequent decade that these changes really got under way. They may partly be explained simply by the passing of time. In the early 1970s, the last of the generation of the founders were departing the stage. Those dreamers and builders for whom Jewish rights in the Land of Israel, the dangers of anti-Semitism everywhere else and hence for whom the justice and urgency of the Zionist project were a given, would no longer be around. The generation that rose to prominence in the 1970s and 1980s was skeptical of collective endeavors, tired of exhortations to struggle and sacrifice, searching above all for normality.

All this was fine and natural, and resembled similar processes in other states founded upon the ruins of European colonialism in other parts of the world. Elsewhere too, the secular ideologies of nationalism and socialism had performed their work and were declining. The "end of ideology" in Israel in no way meant the socio-economic failure of the country. On the contrary, the new individualism was to prove the motor for entrepreneurial success. Still, the passing from nation-building and military affairs to commerce made sense only on the assumption that the enemy too was passing through an analogous process.

For a considerable period of time, this was exactly what appeared to be happening. Arab military-nationalism was the force that had emerged to "carry" Arab rejection of the creation of Israel, after the monarchical and civilian regimes failed to snuff the country out at its birth in 1948. And Arab nationalism met its Waterloo in 1967, never recovering its élan after that point. So, if Israel in the 1970s grew tired of its version of collectivism and nationalism, then some among its most significant enemies in the Arab world also grew tired of theirs.

The watershed moment of the peace negotiations with Egypt was a direct result of this process — and everything appeared to be going according to plan. External defeat and internal failure had caused Egypt to abandon its pan-Arab ambitions and to turn toward the West. A pragmatic rapprochement with Israel was an essential part of such a process.

So the Israeli version of tiredness and post-ideological maturity dovetailed with the Egyptian version. Egypt was the factor that gave the Arab side a conventional military option. The Egyptian military had performed well against Israel in the first days of the 1973 war. So its removal from the strategic equation was of paramount significance. Syria to the north remained locked into a timewarp of Arab nationalist rhetoric. But Syria was too weak to pose a serious conventional threat. All this meant that by the 1980s and 1990s, the only serious piece of remaining business, in order to complete the consolidation of Israel's victory and survival, was to close a deal with the Palestinian Arabs — Israel's first, nearest and perhaps last remaining foe. This, at least, was how it looked.

Were all this to have proven itself in reality, then the fatigue noted by Rabin and expressed so eloquently by Grossman, would not have mattered. It might have offended the sensibilities of the right wing of Israeli politics, and conservative intellectuals might have warned against the dangerous decline in national cohesion. But ultimately this would have been of little consequence. The peace process of the 1990s was meant to be the final act in this. Once the tired, disillusioned Palestinian nationalists signed their agreement with the post-ideological leaders of Israel, all could then move on. The naïve illusions and their terrible cost could be jointly wondered over by future generations, and would no doubt soon seem as distant and arcane as the dispute between Roundheads and Cavaliers or Romans and Carthaginians.

The problem, as we have seen, was that the deeply felt Arab rejection of Israel's presence did not vanish with the fading of its Arab nationalist carrier. Rather, it was inherited by the enemy and successor of Arab nationalism within regional politics — the movements of radical Islam.

This meant that Israel by the end of the 1990s was faced with an uncomfortable situation. Israeli society had reached a level of urbanity, sophistication, and detachment that made it increasingly difficult to sustain the citizen-soldier ethos that had formed the basis of its success. Achievement in Israeli society was no longer defined by a military career, or involvement in politics or the state bureaucracy. The ethos of the Israeli elites had moved beyond such things.

Statistics showed that the sections of the population that had once constituted the serving elite of the society were now, increasingly, going through a stage of self-privatization. This was an ongoing process, of course, neither started nor completed in a short period. The elite in question was precisely the section of society who would have constituted David Grossman's audience on that night in Rabin Square in the early winter of 2006. This section of society, the secular, largely Ashkenazi, middle and upper middle class, had been the bearers of the version of Israeliness best known to the world.

This public had also traditionally been one prepared to make great sacrifices for Israel. There had been a sense, ultimately, that Israel was "their" project. Theirs was the "beautiful" Israel of kibbutz, secularism, and European-style culture. This Israel lost electoral power in 1977 to Menachem Begin's Likud, which represented an alliance of outsiders — all the various factors in Israeli society not invited to the "beautiful Israel" party. Jews of North African and Asian origin, the religiously observant, the Ultra-Orthodox, former fighters of the Irgun and Lehi undergrounds.[2]

But although this elite version of Israeliness lost political power in 1977, and never regained its hegemony, it remained dominant in many areas of life. In the universities, the media, upper ranks of the military, free professions, upper ranks of the civil service, and of course in cultural production.

Israel today no longer possesses a single, authoritative cultural identity. Rather, a multiplicity of political tribes and interest groups compete for dominance. The elite version of Israeliness, meanwhile, no longer seems so sure of the justice of Zionism and Israel's cause. The intellectual mood has long been one of iconoclasm. There are few sacred cows remaining. The history of Zionist settlement and colonization, the political system, and now also the military and the security forces have all been thoroughly de-mythologized in elite opinion.

The nation as construct and fiction, Zionism as a movement of settler-colonialism, the framing of Arab and Muslim opposition to Israel in the language of anti-colonialism and civil rights — all these have combined to bore away at the moral and ideological foundations of Israeli sovereignty, also in the eyes of those sections of society who were once its main standard bearers.

This process is no longer merely a latent, or potential one. It is being reflected in concrete ways in terms of which sections of society are most involved in Israeli public life, and as a consequence, which ideas come increasingly to hold sway. The pattern emerging is one of a change in elites. At its most banal level, this may be seen in the cliché of the political quietism and political non-engagement of the secular, upper-middle class elite of Tel Aviv.

There is a Hebrew term — 'bu'a (bubble) — used to describe this phenomenon. It describes the widespread decision of economically successful citizens to withdraw from public engagement and to focus on their careers, friends and private lives. It is hardly a phenomenon unique to the Tel Aviv conurbation or to Israel. But it contrasts with the almost abnormally high levels of engagement of Israelis in the public life of their country in the past.

The crucial point to note is that this process of growing ennui and disengagement is society-wide in Israel, but is affecting the various sectors of society with different levels of intensity. It has of course been widely noted by Israel's enemies, and is cause for great rejoicing in their circles. Hizballah leader, Hassan Nasrallah made the focus on and exaggeration of this aspect of the Israeli reality into one of his movement's trademarks.

After the unilateral Israeli withdrawal from Lebanon in 2000, and still more following the inconclusive Lebanon war of 2006, the propaganda of Hizballah and its allies sought to portray Israel as a sad, lost and fearful place. Hizballah websites are particularly fond of detailed studies of the enemy. Israeli society is referred to as the "Spider's Web" — the term used by Nasrallah in his victory speech in Bint Jubail in May 2000. The term is meant to indicate the perceived flimsiness and weakness of Israel.

A closer look at social processes in Israel, however, indicates that the disengagement, fatigue and disillusion which Nasrallah is fond of pointing out is distributed unevenly across Israeli society. The secular, left of center culture that gathered at Rabin Square, and that still holds the commanding level in many of the idea-generating centers of Israeli society does not speak with unquestioned authority to that society. Rather, quite different ideas and allegiances exist, and produce quite different conclusions and patterns of behavior. Away from the cultural centers of the elite, a different set of loyalties pertain.

One measure of this process is military service. Service in frontline units of the IDF was once a badge of status for members of the Israeli elite. Since the First Intifada of the 1980s, and with gathering pace in recent years, this is ceasing to be the case. Rather, the sons and daughters of Israel's secular elites prefer increasingly to avoid the rigors of service in combat units. Service in the military no longer offers the status that it once did. This has become so because of the decline in the republican patriotism of Israel's early years.

What is happening as a result, however, is not the general decline into fractiousness and ennui which the ideologues on the other side would like to see. Rather, as the old elite steps back into self-privatization, its place is being taken by new forces, formerly marginal or hardly heard from in Israeli society. The Israeli military was once the great Zionist melting pot, with the secular Ashkenazi Israelis at the top defining the tone and the behavior patterns. The melting pot aspect to a degree remains, but what has been coming into being in the Israeli military over the last decades is an army increasingly dominated by formerly peripheral groups in Israeli society.

Most important and most visible of these groups is the national religious community. Religious Zionists, with their distinctive knitted skull-caps, are emerging as the dominant group in the fighting units of the IDF. Their rise has been visible on every level. Overall, around 30 percent of all junior officers and non-commissioned officers (NCOs) in IDF combat units now belong to this community.[3] However, if one takes a closer look at the figures, the issue becomes more striking. The national religious community is gradually rising in the military hierarchy. Other population groups, meanwhile, increasingly over-represented in front line units of the IDF, are new immigrants from the former Soviet Union and Ethiopia, members of Israel's Druze community, and lower class Israelis of North African and Asian origin.[4]

Involvement in combat and elite units of the military, of course, is only one gauge of public commitment. But in a society entering a long period of protracted struggle against an enemy committed to its destruction, it is a fair measure of which population groups remain most committed to the society's professed goals. What is taking place in the Israeli military is that the long-established elite of secular Israelis of European origin is giving way to something new. A new elite, more Jewishly observant, perhaps more narrowly nationalist, less European in origin and in outlook.

I remember a particular incident in the wake of the 2006 Lebanon War that brought home this change of elites in a peculiarly affecting way. It took place at a memorial gathering for a comrade of mine who was killed in an operation in the Lebanese eastern sector in the last days of the war. Alon Smoha died a few meters from me, in a cornfield in a valley below the town of el Khiam. We carried his body back on an armored vehicle across the border.

Alon's family had a memorial event at their house to mark a year since his death. In the year since the war, the unit acquired a new brigade commander. His name was Aryeh, and he was very much in the mold of the national religious style of IDF officer. He was a thickset, bearded, black haired man in his late 40s. American-born, living in a settlement just east of the Green Line, Aryeh had served as a deputy battalion commander in our battalion when they had put it together in 1994. His commitment to the reserve army had led him to take battalion commander and brigade commanders' courses. I remember him standing there in the back garden of the Smoha family's house that afternoon, somehow entirely at home and yet a little alien all the same.

One of Alon Smoha's favorite songs was a very famous Israeli folk melody from the period of the 1948 war. We had sung it at his funeral when the 2006 war was still on, and we always sang it at memorial events too. The song is one of the anthems of consensual Israeliness. It is called "Shir Hare'ut" (song of friendship) and it was written by Chaim Guri during the war of 1948, to commemorate his dead comrades from the Palmach.

It has a sweet and wistful feel to it, in the style common to Israeli songs of the time. There is military pride in it, but no triumphalism. "We will remember all of them," goes the chorus, "the beautiful of forelock and of countenance, because friendship like this will never allow our hearts to forget." And in the next line — "Love sanctified in blood, you will return to flower among us."

The memorial event to mark a year since Alon Smoha's death also marked the consecration of a Torah scroll in his name. In the course of the evening, various people were invited to come to help roll the paper on which the Torah was written around the wooden holders, or write in one of the final few words to the Torah. The five books of Moses, of course, are one of the foundation stones of the Judeo-Christian West. But they are also the founding national story of the Jewish people. It was in this sense that they came into focus that evening on the Sharon plain. Aryeh the brigade commander performed the writing and the rolling of the scroll with great aplomb, smiling behind his thick black beard.

Then at a certain point, we all rose and sang Shir Hare'ut, this anthem of the old Israel. I wondered if Aryeh would join in with the song. I remember even at the time attaching a peculiar importance to this question, without quite knowing why. I watched as everyone began to sing. Aryeh did not join in. I wondered if he would at least sing the chorus. He did not. Rather, he stood stiffly and very politely as we sang Chaim Guri's song, like a diplomat attending a celebration of a community for whom he has great respect, but only limited acquaintance.

Chaim Guri's song is an emblem of the old Israeli consensus. But Aryeh's language for self-sacrifice and commitment was a different one — one more concerned with Jewish tradition and texts. This is an extreme example, to be sure. I have no doubt the brigade commander knew the song. But he chose not to sing it. It signified something. An important shift.

In the early days of Zionism, people used to talk about the "rustle of history's wings." The Jewish presence in the country, as is well-known, was re-established step by hard-earned step. So, an official speaking at a ceremony to mark the establishment of a new community, or a new school, or the opening of a new cowshed at a collective settlement might mention that he hears the "rustle of history's wings" about the opening of the facility. The same feeling seems to me to attach to the brigade commander Aryeh and Chaim Guri's song.

The changes in the army were mirrored by broader patterns of social engagement. The passion for politics that was once one of the most characteristic elements of Israel began to fade in the 1990s. There was a growing and largely justified cynicism toward the professional political class. Israeli elections up until the early 1990s were raucous, engaged affairs. One would see crowds of people gathered together, wearing the colors of different parties, arguing and shouting. By the first decade of the new century, such a scene would have been anachronistic. Voting levels at election time were falling.

But again, where political passions were in display, it was largely among populations who had been far from the center. The outward-looking, educated, secular Israel of the urban conurbations was indeed tired of nationalism, and skeptical of the old collective ideals, which were largely fading. But what was happening was not that the old statist Zionism was taking the country down with it. Israel was not, as leftist ideologues and Arab nationalists had long predicted, separating off into warring tribes.

Rather, the European style Zionist ideologies which had shaped the country and battled each other were being replaced by something new, more amorphous, less recognizable, which was emerging from below, and from outside of the recognizable ideological divisions of the country. This new, Israeli nationalism was at once more ethnic, more provincial, less European, less clearly defined, less open than the country had previously seemed. It was neither recognizably Ashkenazi, nor recognizably Sephardi, neither rigorously secular nor strictly observant. The mass of Israelis could find themselves somewhere within its broad and loosely defined borders.

Hizballah and its allies like to pride themselves on their deep knowledge of Israeli society. But the point they and their allies have missed — because of the fury and hatred of Israel which is the root of their thinking — is the emergence of this new, Israeli Jewish national identity and nationalism. This new Israeliness is steeped in a comfortable, not particularly rigorous attachment to the symbols of Jewish tradition. The political party that knows how to read its code best is the Likud, and this underlines the status of "natural party of government" which this party has enjoyed in Israel for the best part of the last 30 years.

It is noteworthy that Israeli politics at the time of writing are currently dominated by the Likud, and two parties which in essence emerged from it — Kadima and Yisrael Beiteinu. In the Eighteenth Knesset, these parties between them controlled 71 seats out of a total of 120 in the parliament. Each of these parties emphasized a slightly different aspect of the consensual Israeliness whose support they sought. Yisrael Beiteinu, which depends largely on the votes of Russian immigrants, focused on an ethnic appeal of the most direct kind, in response to the growth of nationalism and Islamism among Arab citizens of Israel. Likud sought to combine a hard-edged Jewish nationalism with a more sophisticated regional and geo-strategic focus. Kadima promoted a slightly softer edged version of the same orientation.

The new Israeliness bears little resemblance to any of the Diaspora Jewish communities from which Israeli Jews hailed. It does not resemble significantly the blueprint for the new nation that Zionist ideologues assembled. It also does not fit with the hopes of those far-leftists who would like to imagine the growth of a new national identity that could replace Zionism and form the basis for a US or EU-style state of all its citizens on the shores of the Mediterranean.

This is because the version of Israeli national identity that holds the Israeli center is entirely inseparable from Jewishness — even among its secular adherents. Jewish Israel does not see itself as a new country. It is a self-consciously new-old one. The Temple Mount, the Hebrew language, the Jewish festivals, and the sense of being a revived and ingathered nation are all basic aspects of the self-perception of this public, which today constitutes a critical mass of Jewish Israelis.

These loyalties are worn without the visceral intensity of a nation seeking sovereignty, of course. They are the markers of loyalty of a nation already two generations from the fight for sovereignty. A nation which has grown accustomed to success. All the same, they are the elements that hold the Israeli Jewish public together.

This identity has emerged in a state of constant conflict with the Arab and Islamic worlds. It is a version of national identity designed to survive in hostile climates and as such, paradoxically very much at home in the Middle East. In its nationalism, its sentimental attachment to historic symbols, in its defiant tone of self-righteousness, the mainstream discourse of Israel has produced a form of Jewishness with deeply local coloration.

I think of Alon Smoha and his family and all this is clear to me. And I am aware that this Jewish nationhood is not a matter of play-acting and discussions of identity, but rather is part of a century of on-off warfare, which shows no signs of being close to its end.

The Smoha family of Hod Hasharon are a good example of the kind of unforced, non-ideological Jewish and Israeli patriotism which now forms the bedrock of the State of Israel's existence. Smoha is instantly recognizable to Israeli ears as an Iraqi Jewish name, and the Smohas came to Israel with the mass of that ancient Jewish community in the 1950s.

They came during a period of Arab nationalist agitation against British colonialism and then against Zionism. They were witnesses to the effective demise of Iraqi Jewry, which had existed since the destruction of the First Temple and the exile of the Jews to Babylon in antiquity.

The Smoha family house is in the town of Hod Hasharon in the heart of the Sharon plain in central Israel. The family has lived there since their arrival from Baghdad in 1950. Hod Hasharon is host to one of the central concentrations of Iraqi Jews in Israel.

Shimon and Shoshana Smoha had three sons. Alon, the eldest, was my comrade in the reserve army for 12 years, from 1994–2006. I knew Alon well in the context of our frequent turns of reserve duty. I first met his family only after his death, when they would often invite members of the unit back to their house after memorial events at the Hod Hasharon cemetery, where their son is buried.

The Smoha family clearly existed politically somewhere in the area right of center and left of the radical right. But the specific political stance is not what is important or characteristic. What makes the Smoha family for me emblematic of the underlying ethos of the Israel in the process of being born is the seamless link in their lives and in their outlook between attachment to Jewish tradition and Israeli patriotism.

This is captured in a number of aspects. I remember Shimon Smoha describing to us the circumstances of how his son had received the call that informed him of our mobilization in 2006. The family gathered around the Shabbat table, making the blessing over the wine, over a pure white tablecloth. The phone ringing, and all of them knowing what it was and what it meant.

Alon, of course, had cleaned and packed his uniform days earlier, as the news from the north had worsened. So his bag was waiting for him quietly in his bedroom. He came back to the table and they finished the Shabbat family meal. Then he left for the north.

Afterwards, Alon's friend Eitan picked up the bag from where it had been left, with all the others, next to a tent in a field in Kfar Giladi, when we had headed into south Lebanon and the night.

Shimon Smoha is a quiet, soft-spoken and very dignified man who bears an astonishing resemblance to his eldest son. When he was in mourning, I saw how his beard grew, describing the same shape on his face as had his son's during the war, when there had been little time for shaving.

At the events to mark a year since his son's death, he described to us how his son was with him from morning until evening. How when he rose up early for the morning prayers, he felt Alon's presence, which did not leave his side. He wept only once, when he reminded us that Alon, though 35 at the time of his death, had not yet found a wife, nor "built a home in Israel," nor raised a family.

The contention of the forces currently engaged against Israel is that the country is, as they often describe it, an "artificial entity." What they mean by this is that Israel, in their view, is based not on a natural, organic nationhood, but on a strange attempt to re-imagine a "religious" identity as a national one. This is an old, Arab nationalist claim, and the nationalists themselves inherited it from the Soviet communists, who believed they could come up with a neat set of criteria by which the category "nations" could be judged. Undeserving attempts could then be rejected.

With the Islamists, the definitions are less rigorous, and the lack of rigor might lead one to suspect that there is an element of disingenuousness going on. Sometimes, if one listens to the speeches of Hamas and Hizballah leaders in Arabic, it is apparent that there is no real sense being conveyed of this bogusness of Jewish and Israeli identity.

Rather, the Jews are presented as a genuinely ancient and historic presence — and one that has been a baleful and cunning enemy of the Muslims since the emergence of Islam. The "Bani Israil," Jewish tribes (or tribes of Judaized Beduin) in the Hijaz, were among the earliest opponents of Mohammed's mission. The traditional Muslim attitude of mistrust mixed with contempt rather than hatred is informed by the stories of the venality of these tribes and Mohammed's eventual defeat of them.

It is considered by Israel's enemies that the smallness of the country in terms of population, size and resources when compared with its enemies, coupled with this inherent contradiction, must bring its defeat in the long term.

But whether or not the argument about the flimsiness and shallowness of Jewish identity is sincerely expressed, or expressed merely to make common cause with opponents of Israel in the West, it is sustainable only on the basis of the denial of a profound reality. For me, at least, this reality is best seen and grasped through the example of families like the Smohas.

Two years after the war in Lebanon, I traveled back to Hod

Hasharon to speak to Shimon Smoha and Dekel, one of Alon's brothers. Hod Hasharon is one of the many towns in Israel rarely visited by foreign correspondents, which is a pity. It is a place where not everyone speaks English, and not everyone is looking to get their message through to the outside world. But the real Israel lives in such towns.

I wanted to ask the Smoha family about their assessment of Israel's state of health. I felt like I was searching for something hidden in the country, which they could help me to find. The events of the summer of 2006 were fresher in my mind two years on than I had expected them to be. Not a day went by when I didn't replay and re-live what happened in the morning of August 10 outside the town of Marjayoun, in the events that ended in the death of Alon Smoha. These events had not left.

Sometimes I would wake up suddenly in the night with my heart banging on the inside of my chest with a speed and strength I would not have believed possible. I didn't know what had happened in my sleep to cause this. Only the room in the dark and the pounding at locomotive strength in my chest. I knew that meeting and spending time with the Smohas would raise all that up again, but also that I needed to do this to get to the essence of what I was seeking to understand regarding Israel, and its likely response to the long war that had been declared upon it.

So, Shimon, Dekel and I sat in the front room of their house on a quiet evening just before Pesach, 2009, and discussed the matter of Israel's national strength, Jewish history, the wars that had been, and those still likely to come. I noted that there were those who claimed that our nation had grown tired, and that we would no longer be able to sustain the sacrifices necessary.

Shimon's response was curt and brief: "If we're tired, then we won't exist. It's forbidden to tire. If we're tired, then we'll have to accept any script that they want to write for us. But we're not tired." Shimon's words were delivered slowly and evenly, after consideration, all in a strong, musical Iraqi accent. But his son Dekel was full of rage and energy, the words spilling out of him for his lost brother, and for his contempt at those who had lost faith. He counted off Jewish history on his fingers:"This nation has passed through the exodus from Egypt, countless wars in conquering the land, the destruction of two Temples, the Holocaust, and this nation is alive and living and breathing. While empires rise up and live and fall, this nation goes on living."

And I knew, as with Nizar the Hamas man in Ramallah, that my instincts had been right and that here was the essence of the thing I'd sought. Our conversation veered from the personal to the national and back again; over the officers of the unit, and Alon's friends, and how much they cared, and how much they stayed in touch. And over the details of the call-up. How Shimon had finished saying the blessing over the bread, and then the phone had begun to ring. He didn't answer the phone on Shabbat, but one of his sons had picked it up, and had turned to Alon and said "Alon, you've got a recorded message." I remembered receiving the same recorded message, I suppose at the same moment, in my apartment preparing for a night's drinking with an American journalist friend. How Alon had left the table to fetch the bag he had prepared, had returned and finished the Shabbat dinner, and then had left his home for the last time. And how if we're tired, we won't exist, but we're a small nation that knows how to unite in times of crisis, in all its simplicity and strength.

They showed me a film that our comrade Arik had taken of Alon standing on the hull of the Merkava 3, in the field next to the avocado grove at Kfar Giladi. They were discussing the prospects for Betar Jerusalem in the coming season. "Israeli players don't want to work hard," Alon was saying with cheerful disdain, "I believe in hard work. But they'd rather just piss around." And then, as Arik tried to say something else, "Never mind, that's all nonsense. The main thing is that we should all get out of this and come home safely." And then he had thrown his head back and raised his hands, beseeching the almighty and recited the first words of the Shema, the most holy prayer in Judaism: "Hear, o Israel, the lord our God, the lord is one." A day before Marjayoun.

"It's enough that the enemy killed my son," Shimon continued, when I asked him how the loss had affected his family, "I won't let them destroy my family as well." And then, by way of conclusion: "We need to make the memory of all those who fell eternal. To remember them. And to be strong."

I am only able to give excerpts from this discussion, which continued for an hour and a half. I hope I am able to convey its flavor, and the eeriness of seeing this film for the first time, and hearing the voice of the dead man, again, for the first time in over two years, just as though he was standing in the room. There was something stark and immensely strong in it all. A sort of harsh male energy, wedded with a very great hidden tenderness.

Before I left, as we shook hands, Shimon summed up for me what he wanted me to take from the meeting. It was the only time in the course of the meeting that the matter of fact tone in which he spoke cracked slightly, to reveal the sadness for his lost eldest son. I felt a very great weariness in his voice, though it wasn't the weariness that the muqawama thinks it sees in the Jews. Only the private, deep fatigue that war and bereavement plant in peoples' bones: "The Shema Yisrael that he said — you saw it. He believed in the justice of the way. We know that we're the few against the many, that we have no other country, that we need to guard it, and sometimes — that we also give our lives for it."

That was all. That and the tales that Shimon's own father told him of the "Farhoud" in Baghdad in 1941, when their Arab neighbors had taken part in the anti-Jewish riots that formed part of Rashid Ali al-Ghaylani's pro-German coup — and the message they had taken with them from this experience, of utter self-reliance.

This stark Jewish self-reliance is half of what Israeli Jewish identity is built upon. The other part is built on the premise of the return to life of the dried bones of Jewish sovereignty which were carried about by the Jews through the years of Diaspora. And both of these were there, in the air, and in the words of the dead man's brother, and the father whose son came to life in his face when he smiled.

Jewish tradition contains within it as a central motif the idea of a remembered, fallen sovereignty, which will one day be revived and remade. Rabbinic Judaism also developed a tradition of political quietism, and the notion that this would take place as part of a divine process. This has much to do with the fact that Rabbinic Judaism as we recognize it today emerged in the context of a series of political catastrophes that befell the Jews as a result of ill-judged attempts at rebellion against Rome in the province of Judea. But the important point is that the notion of Jews as a people who once possessed sovereignty is hard-wired into Jewish tradition.

The idea of Zionist nationalism and of the creation of Israel was in essence an attempt to build a renewed nationhood on the basis of this fossilized memory of sovereignty and peoplehood that Jews imbibed in their tradition. Jewish identity for most of subsequent history prior to the Enlightenment was a primary matter for Jews, not a matter of a hyphenated sub-allegiance. All the same, the prospect of sovereignty still seemed straight out of the world of fantasy for many contemporaries of Zionism's emergence. As unreal as Ezekiel's vision of the bones in the valley, taking on flesh and walking again.

Zionism was not invented out of thin air. A slow move of Jews back to Ottoman Syria began even prior to the movement's emergence, made possible by administrative reforms in the Empire. It took the tragedy of European anti-Semitism, and then the expulsion of hundreds of thousands of Jews from the Arab world in the wake of the creation of the state in 1948, to turn Israel into a living reality.

But the point is that the fundamental idea has worked. Through the medium of the creation of the society, and above all the development of the modern Hebrew language, the ghostly memory of sovereignty contained in Jewish tradition has been re-established in the place where it originated. This sovereignty, like all real sovereignty, is a fleshy, gross, bloody thing, which owes as much or more to the sword as to the book. Yet, its opponents miss the strength of its grounding, of its underpinnings.

There is Shimon Smoha, weeping for his dead son who never "built a house in Israel." What does this Hebrew phrase mean? There is an obvious, prosaic meaning. But there is another meaning too. To "build a house in Israel," in Jewish tradition, means also to create a Jewish home, the repository from which tradition can be handed on.

The brigade commander rolling the text of the Torah scroll, the Smoha family and their white Shabbat table on the evening of their son's departure. These elements are utterly alien both from the Judaism of the Diaspora, and from the secular, austere, East European Zionism that dominated Israel's first years. But these images reflect an old new reality which has come into being. They reflect an identity which people will live and die for. "Renew our days — as of old" goes the Jewish blessing.

This Israeli-Jewishness is the complex of belief and identity upon which Islamism and its allies have declared war to the death. It is possible that the professed contempt, which I have found repeated again and again, has within it an element of propaganda or psychological warfare. If it does not, then it represents a profound misreading and underestimation of the nature of the enemy, which it seems to me will have a telling influence on the outcome of events.

* * *

I should make clear that I am neither an advocate, nor really an inhabitant of the new Israeli-Jewish identity which I have been trying to describe and encapsulate here.

I have lived in Israel for 20 years, arriving from London in my early twenties. The Israel with which I grew up, and to which I felt a profound attachment from my earliest childhood, was not the country of the Smoha family and Aryeh the brigade commander. It wasn't the long-lost secular, socialist "beautiful Israel" of the Rabin Square demonstrators either.

It was an imagined and largely imaginary place that existed in our minds as a fertile, strong, proud, and beautiful answer to the sufferings of the Jews in Europe, and to the long humiliations of exile. I grew up in the 1970s, so it was the Israel of Yoni Netanyahu, who led the commandos in the Entebbe Raid. It was the country of Soviet Jewish immigration, which waited to welcome the oppressed Russian Jews at the end of their long journey. It was the land that I learned about, spoken of in tones of a sort of staunch love by relatives of my grandparents' generation. A rightness in it beyond reproach. It was the land of Menachem Begin and the Irgun Tzvai Leumi, whose exploits I can remember being debated by my loyally British-Jewish father and one of my uncles, around our kitchen table 30 years after the fact.

Most of all, for us, for me, Israel was the answer to something. Centuries of oppression of the Jews, of powerlessness, of bent backs and un-physicality, culminating in the incomprehensible wiping out of the greater part of Europe's Jewish population in the 1940s. Here was the mechanism by which none of this could ever happen again. At the core of it — a Jewish state with nuclear weapons. And around the core, values — of courage, of defiance, of dignity.

I received this inheritance in different ways from both sides of my family. On my father's side, in the image of my grandfather, who was one of the people who helped to create the Jewish Legion, the Jewish infantry brigade that marched with Jabotinsky under General Edmund Allenby, and took part in the bloody campaign that Allenby fought to wrest the land from the Turks in 1917–1918.

The Legion was the first regular Jewish fighting force since the Bar-Kochba revolt in the second century. My grandfather, Samuel Spyer, was a diminutive Jewish tailor from the East End of London. He served for two years with a British infantry unit in France before volunteering for the Legion. As its regimental sergeant major (at the age of 21), he played a key role in organizing and training it. He died when I was two years old, so I have no memory of him. Yet the sense of him, the little moustachioed sergeant major of the Jewish Legion, was a constant presence, along with the stories of Orde Wingate, and a certain cult of toughness, hard knocks, and muscularity that I learned at home.

On my mother's side, there were the remnants of her family from Lithuania and from Ukraine, who arrived on the shores of Israel in 1949. Her cousin Moshe, a partisan from the Polish forest, who slept in a box on Haifa port, and then raised his family in a little two roomed house provided by the Jewish Agency in a neighborhood of

Holocaust survivors called Kiryat Bialystok, in the nondescript town of Yehud outside Tel Aviv.

It was these stories and experiences, of history and pride and defiance in the face of adversity, which enthralled me as a young man and which made me want to join my own fate to that of Israel. The idea of our submerged people, long accustomed to outrage, long grown used to swallowed insults and swallowed pride — finally rising again into sovereignty. The idea of the birth of a kind of heroic Jewish pragmatism and realism — forged in the fires of historical necessity. This seemed to me something worth defending and it was this that led me after graduating from the London School of Economics to volunteering for the 188 Armored Brigade, and to service in Gaza and in the West Bank, and on the Lebanese border in 1992–1993.

After the army, I worked in public service for a number of years, in the Prime Minister's Office and the Ministry of National Infrastructures. Then I went into the world of think tanks and journalism. For a while, the sense of living history in Israel remained central to me. But as one builds a life in a place, any living place, so ambiguity and difficulty and complications crowd in. Thankfully. The Spartan, heroic country that I had imagined in my youth would be an unbearable place to live. It would be good only for songs, sung at a safe distance. No one would have wished to make their life in it.

But the important point is that the things I dreamed had only a tangential relationship to the complex, fractious Israel of Rabin Square and Hod Hasharon. And it is fairly hard, with the best will in the world, to find much of a connection between the pristine, simple, pure images of self-sacrifice that gripped me as a young man, and the immensely difficult working-through of tradition in the context of democracy that is a key issue of modern Israeli reality.

This, it seems to me, is evidence of life. The Israeli-Jewish society that has emerged, partly because of the heroic ideas and ideologues, and partly in spite of them, is not a symbol of anything else. It is not a response to a historic experience in another place. It is what it is — a real, breathing, living country that gets up in the morning and works and argues and reconciles and makes its loyalties, in its own language and in its own interests.

The Jewish cultural trappings that were revived in the hot-house atmosphere of early Zionism have now become natural. And as the twentieth century ideological fervor has subsided, a real and living society has emerged. This society is indeed less overtly "mobilized" than the country at the moment of its birth. The key question that is currently being put to it is whether the critical mass: demographically, culturally, linguistically, diplomatically, economically, and militarily, which the Jews in Israel have built up over the last century, will be sufficient to carry it through the latest version of the rejection of its presence by the Arab and Muslim cultural milieu that surrounds it.

Old ideas are declining. New versions are emerging. Israel is in the process of a change of elites. The country and the society will not conform to the desires of Western Diaspora Jews. It will not be a new Europe, or a new US, for that matter.

Yet none of this presages decline for Jewish Israel itself. Broken-hearted David Grossman, after all, was eulogizing a son who gave his life to protect the residents of Israel's north. For all the issues he raised, this fact remains salient. And broken-hearted Shimon Smoha, whose son died in the same cause and in the same cursed war, was able, in Hebrew words that no news organization carried around the world, to articulate his regret in terms that offer clues as to the true cultural sources which have been at work in the establishment of Israeli society.

The Zionist project has been achieved and transcended. The European nationalist outlook that formed modern Zionism is fading. But beneath and around it is growing something else that is being formed through the fusion of Jewish sovereignty, Jewish tradition, and Middle Eastern reality.

It is this immensely powerful complex of images and ideas that currently forms the bedrock of Jewish Israel. Of course, the presence of this process is no guarantee of success or the long-term viability of the country. Perhaps the forces arrayed against it and for its destruction will eventually prove the stronger. But understanding its presence is crucial for understanding the nature of the conflict currently opening up in the Middle East. Jewish nationality is not a matter of ideological debate. It is a real and living thing; a thing that sometimes people give their lives for. Some of its best sons are buried in the red soil of the Sharon plain, and others in Mount Herzl in Jerusalem.

Notes

1. Excerpt from speech given by David Grossman at the Rabin Memorial, November 2006.
2. The Irgun (National Military Organization) and Lehi (Fighters for the Freedom of Israel) militias emerged in opposition to the military policy of the official Zionist leadership in the pre-1948 period, and were neither acknowledged nor commemorated by the State of Israel in its first 30 years.
3. Stuart Cohen, *Israel and its army: from cohesion to confusion*, Routledge, London and New York, 2008: 127.
4. See Cohen *op. cit.* for a wider discussion of this issue: 107–36.

CHAPTER 4

The Middle East Cold War

The nature of the transformed conflict is such that it cannot be understood purely from within the limited space of Israel and its immediate surroundings. Behind the Islamist organizations fighting Israel, stands a regional alliance and a complex regional reality. In order to understand the meaning of the events outlined here, it is necessary to take a focused look at some of the larger political processes currently at work in the Middle East region.

The broad contours of the conflict between Israel and Islamism, which is what is under discussion here, are made possible by the intersection of three related projects and processes. The first is the emergence of Iran as the main strategic enemy of Israel, and the decision by a dominant radical elite group within the Iranian regime to make the destruction of Israel a central goal. The second process is the rise of various versions of radical Islam as the most important political trend in the Arabic-speaking Middle East.

The third, less central, element is the information revolution, which has profoundly transformed the way that political community and identity are built, reducing the ability of states to control access to alternative versions of events and, no less importantly, the process whereby information is produced and consumed.

The result is the emergence of a new cold war in the region. This pits an alliance largely consisting of various Islamist forces, led by Iran, against a loose, unstated coalition of pro-Western states, of widely differing ideological loyalties.

Iran is the home of the first Islamist revolution. That epoch-making event took place in 1979. And Iran is currently going through the convulsions of something resembling a second revolution, but within the regime, not against it.

This is a process familiar to history. A few years, or a few decades on, and the fighters of the revolution look around themselves and see only decay. Little to show for the years of sacrifice. Revolutions always deliver less than they promise. The Islamic revolution in Iran, which promised a new era of purity and which has created a deeply corrupt, deeply unpopular regime, is an extreme example of this historical truism.

The elite of the young activists who made the Iranian revolution are older now, and advancing towards the centers of power in the regime they helped to create. They are aware of the gap between their hopes and the reality of Iran. Their hope is for a revival of the original flame of the revolution. If the economy is failing, and corruption and indifference are everywhere, if the regime is unpopular at home, and isolated internationally, there are those within the ruling oligarchy who believe that a return to the pure, hard, Islamist ideology of 1979 can reverse all this.

President Mahmoud Ahmedinejad is the most well-known of the group of men planning the return to what they regard as the purity of the revolution's first days. Ahmedinejad emerged and rose due to his association with the radical conservative circles associated with this goal. The "Principalists," as these circles are known, are organized within a series of interlocking conservative political organizations. Ahmedinejad was a member of the Abadegarane Iran e-Islamic group, under whose auspices he won the Teheran Mayoral elections of 2003. This group is in turn part of a larger conservative umbrella group called the Osulgarayan, which brings together a variety of civil society groups.[1]

Ahmedinejad's election to the presidency of Iran in 2005 offered clear evidence that the Principalists were on the rise. Their subsequent victory in elections to the Majlis (parliament) in 2008 confirmed this.[2] There have been ups and downs, but the Principalists are a rising force within the regime. They are dominant within the regime's Praetorian force — the Revolutionary Guards Corps. Supreme Leader Ali Khamenei is considered to be sympathetic to their cause, as was evidenced by his staunch backing for Ahmedinejad during and after the disputed presidential elections of 2009.

The issue of Israel, and the broader question of Iranian regional policy are of interest to the Iranian radical conservatives for two reasons; one of them is ideological, and the other pragmatic. Ideologically, the spread of the Islamic revolution is a central goal of the regime. The 1979 revolution, after all, was never considered to be an event limited by national borders. Rather, the fall of the Shah was intended by those who brought it about to usher in a general process of similar Islamic revolutions across the Middle East. As with other ideological revolutions, early optimism in this regard proved misplaced.

The desire of revolutions to export their model overseas, and the failure to achieve this, is an additional factor which the Iranian experience shares with other countries and other ideologies. Thirty years after the revolution, the crop of successes on the Teheran model is meager indeed. Still, for the radical conservatives and their allies, the belief in "Muslim" identity as their basic political loyalty, and the desire to create a bloc of genuinely Islamic states, with Iran at their head, remains an article of faith.

This is not, however, merely a matter of selfless idealism. The Iranian regime is unpopular at home, and lacks legitimacy. It has signally failed to cure corruption, usher in the rule of the just, or even to effectively administer Iran's own economy. Rather, it has managed to turn the country, with its vast resources, into an inefficient, bloated and sluggish place. An area in which the regime may, however, be able to buy the loyalty of the populace is that of foreign affairs.

Assertion beyond Iran's borders is the point at which the Islamist ideology of the regime and the traditional patriotism and imperial memories of Iranians are able to meet. So projecting Iranian power and influence across the Middle East, and leveraging these into major regional power status for Teheran has an instrumental value as well as an ideological one for the rulers of Iran. It is currency which they hope to convert back in order to buy domestic legitimacy.

The current leaders of the Islamic regime in Teheran are not immune to nationalist feelings, any more than previous representatives of supposedly supra-national ideological regimes in other places and times have been. And Iran, like the Arab world, is a place with a shining and glorious past, of which its peoples are justly proud.

As an Iranian colleague once put it to me, "Iran is a civilization which belongs in the league of China and India, not that of Iraq and Jordan." If the Islamic regime can manage to build the place of Iran on the world stage — thus the radical conservatives believe — this will play an important part in legitimizing the regime in the eyes of broad swathes of the people obliged to live under its rule.

But Iran, as it attempts to build its influence in the Arabic-speaking Middle East, has an additional pair of problems. It is not Arab. And it is not Sunni Muslim — the religion of the great majority of the inhabitants of the region. In fact, Iran is a historical enemy of the Arabs. So, there is a certain very acute in-built tension in the Iranian desire to style itself as the natural leader of the region, on the basis of a shared Islamic identity.

It is here that the issue of Israel becomes relevant. Commitment to the destruction of Israel is an integral part of the Islamist ideology that currently rules Iran. Organizational links have existed between the Iranian revolutionaries and the Fatah organization since the 1970s. So the fervor expressed by Ahmedinejad, and the non-stop drum beat of anti-Israel propaganda that emanates from Iran is undoubtedly heartfelt.

The Iranian regime remembers the close links between Israel and the Shah's regime in Iran. The regime sees the establishment of Israel through the prism of supposedly anti-imperialist arguments. An eminent British analyst of Iran once described to me a private conversation with an Iranian official, in which Israel was described as the "droppings left behind in the region by the goat of the imperialists."

This description lacks the smoothness of the pronunciations of some of the regime's representatives and apologists. It is, however, an accurate expression of Teheran's position. The regime has adopted the Arab nationalist view of Israel as an "artificial" entity. The by now familiar contrast is made between nations and nationalisms which are seen as "authentic" to the region, and Israel, which is deemed a construct, not based on any real and organic nationhood.

But notwithstanding the sincerity of this position, it also plays an instrumental role for the Iranians. They are strangers in the Arab Middle East. But there is one issue that may be able to "trump" their outsider status. This is the issue of the Arab-Israeli conflict. The Palestinian problem, and the broader question of Israel's establishment and survival, remain the most emotive issues within the politics of the Arabic-speaking world. Arab countries may have made their pragmatic arrangements with the Jewish state, but anti-Israel passions remain the defining issue of Arab politics. As such, Iran has an obvious interest in laying claim to the Palestinian issue — and in seeking to demonstrate that it is capable of more effective action on behalf of the Palestinians than are the Arabs themselves.

It is for this reason, as well as for any genuinely held ideological views, that Iran has been engaged in the process of attempting a sort of hostile takeover bid of the Palestinian national movement over the last decade. The mechanics of how this bid is playing itself out are crucial to understanding the developing strategic situation in the Middle East.

All of this, of course, is taking place under the shadow of the Iranian nuclear program, and is part of Iran's motivation for pursuing the nuclear option. An Iranian nuclear capability would facilitate and accelerate the Iranian drive for regional power, and the regime's drive for greater legitimacy at home. There is consensus support in Iran for the regime's nuclear ambitions, on the basis of nationalist feelings. Regionally, meanwhile, a nuclear capacity would vastly increase Iran's freedom of maneuver in supporting organizations engaged in violence against Israel, and in threatening and subverting Arab countries opposed to its advance.

Before going on to look in detail at the system of alliances that Iran has created to advance its bid for regional hegemony, it's important to consider the nature of the wave of ideological ferment on which Teheran wishes to ride to dominance in the Middle East.

A profoundly important process is currently transforming the major countries of the Middle East. This process is the Islamization of regional politics. In all major countries of the region, the most popular political forces are those identified with one or another form of political Islam. Islamist movements — the Muslim Brothers in Egypt and Syria, Hizballah in Lebanon, Hamas among the Palestinians, the Islamic Action Front in Jordan, today possess, more than the adherents of any other stream, that vital ingredient necessary for political success in the Middle East — large numbers of young men willing to kill and die in the service of the idea.

In Egypt, Jordan and Syria, and probably also among the Palestinians, if elections were held tomorrow, they would almost certainly be won by Islamist political forces. This is apparent from observation of the various occasions in which Islamists have been permitted to stand in free elections. Among the Palestinians, of course, Hamas won parliamentary elections in 2006. In Turkey and Iraq, Islamist parties have come to power via the ballot box. In Egypt, in late 2005, the Muslim Brotherhood won 88 of 444 seats in the parliament, despite being permitted to stand for only one third of the total number of seats.[3]

But it is not only the quantitative popularity of Islamism which is important. It is also the quality of its support. After all, in Iran itself, after thirty years of Islamist misrule, the mullahs would be swept from power if free elections were held — yet the regime is in no danger of falling. This is because free elections — that is, elections in which candidates other than pro-regime Shia Islamists are permitted to compete — are not going to be held, and the people that oppose the regime lack the organization and are probably unwilling to pay the price that would be required in order to seize power by force. The unrest that followed the presidential elections of June 2009 has not fundamentally altered this situation. The protestors are undoubtedly sincere and determined. But the radical conservatives rising within the regime are no less so.

In the Arabic-speaking countries of the Levant, and in Iran, that element of the population most committed to political ideology and to political action favors the Islamists. In some countries, such as Syria, the regime has found its own way to the Iran-led regional bloc. Elsewhere, such as in Jordan, the existing institutions of the state appear strong enough to resist the efforts of the Islamists to bring them down. But throughout, it is the Islamists who are the possessors of a clear and vivid ideology, of resistance, self proclaimed cultural authenticity and furious anger at the West. They also have the confidence that comes from the feeling that their idea is in the ascendant.

Islamism has no serious competitor at the present time in the battle for the hearts of the broad masses of the populations in these countries. The small trend of pro-Western secular liberalism lacks organizational ability. The regimes themselves are in most Arab countries strong enough at the moment to fend off Islamist attempts to topple them. But the Islamists are the ones who have captured the sense of shame, humiliation, and desire for retribution which remains the most powerful political currency in the Arabic-speaking world.

This language — of outraged dignity, of desire for self-sacrifice and glorious revenge — is the salient factor of Arab political culture. It applies, of course, only to privations placed by the enemies of the Arabs on their dignity — not to instances of the reverse. It is for this reason that the Arab League can band together to defend the mass-murdering President Omar al-Bashir of Sudan, while at the same time issue cries of apparently sincere moral outrage at Israel's actions in Gaza.

But contradictions aside, this latent presence offers the key to political legitimacy in the Arab world to whoever can successfully lay claim to it. Islamist movements currently possess it — inherited from the now largely discredited movements of secular Arab nationalism.

And it is these forces that Iran wishes to aid, in order to use them as a passport to bypass Iran's foreignness to the Arabs, and to build the Islamic Republic's regional presence.

The third element that must be borne in mind in considering the transformation currently under way in the politics of the region is the information revolution. Modern communications have served to make possible a real and deeply felt sense of political community across state borders. The project of the Islamic revolution of 1979 and of Islamism more generally is the creation of an overarching "Muslim" identity, replacing narrower national, state, and ethnic allegiances. This project is utopian and probably bound in the end to be frustrated by the strength of other identities held by Muslims alongside their allegiance to Islam. However, the sense of belonging to a shared Muslim "Umma" has been increased among educated Muslims by the ability of modern media to create a shared conversation.

Preachers such as the Doha-based Egyptian Yusuf al-Qaradawi, and media channels such as al-Jazeera and the Hizballah-controlled al-Manar, transmit an easily assimilated message of cultural and religious self-assertion. Once, pan-Arabism promised to bring down what it regarded as the artificial borders dividing the Arabic-speaking world. This project long ago foundered on the rocks of political reality. Since the decline of pan-Arabism, the divisions in the Arab world have grown yet stronger, and state borders are in no danger of falling — even among the small emirates of the Arab Gulf, where little resembling a modern national consciousness existed to support loyalty to the state. Yet modern communications have made possible the sense of a shared political and cultural space which in a more modest but significant way has transcended state borders.

This creation of a shared "conversation" across the region — with the issue of Israel and the Palestinians as a central subject — has increased the potential "soft power" impact of Iran's attempt to depict itself as the champion of the region's "dignity." This is because popular sentiment across the region is in tune with the stances of defiance and resistance (muqawama) that are the key ingredients of the ideology that Iran wants to promote.

Iran has not been slow to move to take advantage of the opportunities thus offered.

Teheran has invested in satellite television stations and radio networks in several languages, more than 100 newspapers and magazines, a dozen publishing houses and countless web pages and blogs administered by the Iranian Revolutionary Guards Corps, as part of the country's public diplomacy program.

Iranian financed charities and mosques have proliferated across the region. Within this vast network, operatives of the Revolutionary Guards overseas wing, the Qods force, and Hizballah have operated openly or on a clandestine basis.[4] This non-benign version of outreach has succeeded in creating a vast number of supporters and sympathizers of the Iranian project. These people see Iran as a rising, unstoppable power, engaged in a long struggle to replace the tired and ailing United States and its allies in the region.

Thus, a number of elements are coinciding. A radical Islamist leadership that wishes to build Iranian regional power — for both ideological and instrumental reasons — is emerging. This leadership hopes to take "ownership" of the Israeli-Palestinian conflict — the most emotive issue for the region. Islamist movements are rising to prominence throughout the Arabic-speaking world, and the revolution in communications is facilitating the strengthening of shared political and cultural ties and perceptions across state borders.

All these elements are together serving to revolutionize the nature of the conflict between Israel and its enemies. Both new enmities — and, paradoxically, new alliances — are being formed in the wake of these processes. A cold war is emerging in the Middle East, with the Islamist and Iranian challenge to Israel's existence one of its central fronts.

The rival alliances each consist of a series of interlocking strands. To understand the nature of the emerging conflict, it is necessary to take a closer look at both of them.

The Iranian regional alliance contains three sovereign states as firm members — Iran itself, Sudan and Syria. It includes a number of Islamist paramilitary movements, most importantly the Lebanese

Hizballah and the movement of Muqtada al-Sadr in Iraq, but also Palestinian Islamic Jihad. Hamas is also increasingly being drawn into the alliance. In addition, the Gulf emirate of Qatar has in recent years moved closer to Iran.

The alliance led by Iran is not simply a matter of ideological commonality. It brings together elements that superficially differ in this regard in quite significant ways.

Syria, the other central sovereign member of this alignment, is ostensibly a secular state. In reality, it is a family dictatorship. The Assad family has held power since 1970 and has managed the impressive feat of handing power from father to son under a supposedly republican system of government. Officially, power is wielded in the name of the secular, socialist Ba'ath Party. This has led some observers to conclude that Syria's involvement with the Islamists in Teheran must be merely a marriage of convenience.

Supporters of such a view consider that since the ideology of the secular, socialist Ba'ath is in opposition to that of the Mullahs in Teheran, any alliance between them must surely be shallow and based purely on immediate self-interest. Syria has thus been portrayed as the weak link in the alliance, and it has been suggested that Damascus might easily be tempted away from the Iranian-led bloc.

This, however, represents a misunderstanding — both of Syria and of the nature of the Iranian-led alliance. The Syrian alliance with Iran is not a new development. It dates back to the early 1980s, and to the first days of the Islamic Republic of Iran. On a superficial level, the alliance emerged from a common interest in opposing Iraq. The ostensibly common ideological roots of the Assad and Saddam regimes in Syria and Iraq did not stop them from becoming bitter rivals.

But there was always more to it. Syria's main asset in its dealings with the region has been characterized by the eminent Middle East scholar Fuad Ajami as its "capacity for mischief."[5] The country is small, weak, and lacking in natural resources. It is led by a regime focusing on a single family and more broadly on the minority ethno-religious group that this family belongs to (the Alawis).

But this regime presents itself as the bastion of Arab defiance, the "beating heart of Arabism," as the usual phrase has it. The claim is not merely a verbal one. Syria has backed it up by offering support and shelter to many organizations engaged in fighting Israel and the West in the region. These have included Hamas and Islamic Jihad, as well as the Kurdish Partiya Karkeren Kurdistan (PKK), the Palestinian PFLP, and other groups. Support for these organizations, and Syria's nationalistic stance, have enabled the country to punch above its weight in the region, and have earned the regime greater legitimacy at home — among the Sunni Muslim majority population of Syria. There is also every reason to assume that Syria's stance accurately reflects the genuine world-view of the senior elite of the country and its leadership. It is this stance, of Arab nationalist radicalism, based on the firm foundations of both regime interest and genuine commitment, which has underpinned the two-and-a-half decades long Syrian-Iranian alliance.

The ideological position being promoted by the Iranians is not based solely on Islamism. Rather, the notion of "resistance" is the larger, vaguer, and more generic stance upon which Iran is staking its claim to regional leadership. The roots of this notion run deep. A trend in the Iranian elite towards borrowing ideas from the fashionable "third worldist" ideologies of the day preceded the Iranian revolution. Such thinkers as Ali Shariati and Mahmoud Taleqani pioneered a trend that supporters of the Shah called "Islamic Marxism." This was used as a term of abuse, rather than an accurate description of this trend.

But the fact was that these thinkers, most importantly Shariati, sought to combine the traditional martyrology of Shia Islam with the fervent sense of victimhood and desire for violent redress that characterized the movements of the radical left. Such an approach constituted an important trend in the 1979 revolution. Following the revolution, of course, the Islamists turned on their erstwhile leftist partners and destroyed them.

But this has not prevented the current rising elite in Iran from seeking to present Teheran as the center of resistance to inequity and injustice in the region, and the focus for the assertion of the dignity of the peoples of the Middle East. This message is far more "ecumenical" and inclusive than a narrow, sectarian call would be. It is a message with which Syria can easily identify and which it can echo. Both Iran and Syria are brutal, authoritarian regimes which use the language of "resistance" and "dignity" as their brand name. So both in terms of self-interest and in terms of ideology, the Iranian-Syrian alliance is strong and deep.

Regarding the non-state elements in the Iranian-led alliance, the most important are the Lebanese Hizballah organization and the Palestinian Hamas.

Hizballah is a creation of the Iranian Revolutionary Guards Corps. It is important to clarify this statement. First, the Shia of Lebanon have played a key role in the development of Shia Islamism over the last half century. It was in Lebanon that the Iranian cleric Musa Sadr developed much of the distinctive modus operandi which has characterized this trend. Many of Hizballah's first cadres were drawn from the Amal movement that Sadr created before his disappearance in 1978. Secondly, the sense of historic exclusion of the Lebanese Shia which Hizballah has come to represent is genuine and deeply historically rooted. Still, the precise organizational roots of Hizballah can be traced to the period immediately following the Islamic Revolution in Iran, and Israel's invasion of Lebanon in 1982.

The crucial event leading to the foundation of Hizballah was the dispatch of 1,500 members of the Iranian Revolutionary Guards Corps (IRGC) to the Bika'a valley, in East Lebanon, in 1982.[6] Their mission was part of the early attempt by Iran to spread its revolution across the region. In 1978, during Israel's first major incursion into southern Lebanon, the Shia population of the south had been largely quiescent. Some were even supportive of Israel because of the difficult situation they had faced living under the de facto control of the PLO throughout the 1970s. In 1982, the situation would prove very different. The Iranian drive to export the 1979 revolution was the crucial factor of change. Having first attempted to propagate their message in Amal, the IRGC men then set about creating a framework for a separate, pro-Iranian, Shia "resistance" movement in Lebanon.

A subsequent split in Amal brought a number of seasoned officials of that movement over to their side. Five hundred Iranian Revolutionary Guardsmen established themselves in the town of Baalbeck, after the bulk of the original force returned to Iran.[7] It was in Baalbeck that Hizballah was founded as an umbrella group bringing together various Shia elements that supported the Iranian revolution, and accepted the key principles of governance of the revolution.

It is worth noting that the current contours of the Iranian-Syrian alliance were already apparent at this stage. Syria was interested in the establishment of a force to challenge Israel and the US in Lebanon, and so Syria chose to open the Bika'a area to the Iranian Revolutionary Guards personnel, allowing them access to the area via Syria's border with Lebanon.

So, from the outset, Hizballah as an organization was a product of the Iranian Revolution. The movement was and remains committed to the key principle of the revolution — "vilayet a faqih" or rule of the jurisprudent. This innovative principle is the basis for the clerical regime established by Ayatollah Khomeini in Iran. Hizballah leader Hassan Nasrallah describes himself as the representative in Lebanon of the current Iranian Supreme Leader, Ali Khamenei.

Hizballah's status as an Iranian creation and client organization is visually very apparent in southern Lebanon. Portraits of Khomeini and Khamenei are to be seen alongside the movement's leaders. Hizballah has grown in visibility, of course, because of its successful guerrilla campaign against Israel in southern Lebanon in the period 1982–2000, and its subsequent war with Israel in 2006.

Over time, and with large scale financial and practical aid from Iran, Hizballah has emerged as a powerful political force in Lebanon. Simultaneously, the movement has built up parallel military and security structures in the country, which have enabled it to conduct its own foreign policy. Hizballah decides when the country goes to war, without consulting other political forces. Hizballah's intelligence structures stretch across Lebanon — controlling security at the Rafik Hariri international airport. The movement maintains a sophisticated, Iran-supplied internal communications network. It has built up a formidable arsenal courtesy of Teheran and Damascus north of the Litani River since the 2006 war. There is every reason to believe that an infrastructure closer to the border has been re-built, into which this arsenal could be moved in the event of war with Israel.

In 2009, Hizballah appeared on the verge of becoming the key political force in Lebanon. The movement's activities are not limited solely to the Lebanese arena, however. Rather, in cooperation with its sponsors in the al-Qods (Jerusalem) force of the Revolutionary Guards, evidence has emerged that Hizballah is engaged in activities on behalf of Iran and its Islamic revolution across the region.

Thus, Hizballah men have been implicated in arms smuggling from Sudan to Gaza, in preparing a cell to act against the Egyptian regime, in facilitating terror attacks by Palestinian groups against Israel — notably the Islamic Jihad movement and elements within the al-Aksa Brigades of Fatah.[8] There are also indications that Hizballah men have played a role in training Shia insurgent groups in Iraq.[9] The movement maintains a department, known as unit 1800, whose job is facilitating aid to other movements and coordinating activities in cooperation with the al-Qods force of the Revolutionary Guards, which has a similar function within the IRGC.

Iran's relations with its Palestinian partners are more complex. Its deepest and most long term connection is to the Palestinian Islamic Jihad movement, which arose largely in response to the Iranian revolution of 1979. Islamic Jihad, according to many accounts, has become a fully fledged subsidiary of Iran, operating largely under the direction of the Iranians and Hizballah. Islamic Jihad, however, is a small group of declining political significance among the Palestinians.

Iran also maintains relations with Hamas and with elements of Fatah. With regard to Fatah, Iranian support is directed through Unit 1800 of Hizballah and was much in evidence in the years of the Second Intifada. It took the form largely of financial inducements to cells of the armed wing of Fatah, in order to aid them in carrying out terror attacks on Israelis.[10] Because of its divided and shambolic nature, Fatah proved vulnerable to penetration of this kind. Many younger Fatah military activists are themselves religiously observant.

This, coupled with the very disunited nature of Fatah, has rendered it vulnerable to the penetration of Iranian interests and money.

Regarding Hamas — unlike Islamic Jihad, as noted earlier, this movement has genuine and deep roots in the Palestinian polity. It also adheres to a conservative Sunni Islam which has little in common with the ideology of the Iranian revolution. Nevertheless, since the 1990s Hamas has been engaged in a process of drawing closer to Teheran. This process reputedly received a boost in 1992, when over 400 Hamas activists were exiled to southern Lebanon by the government of Israel. In the course of the 1990s, Hamas founder Sheikh Ahmed Yassin visited Iran, and the levels of financial and other aid offered by Teheran to Hamas increased throughout the decade and the one that followed it.

Estimates of the precise numbers regarding Iranian assistance to Hamas differ. Most researchers agree that the Iranian tendency is to pay for results, so support for Hamas has increased at times of unrest, when the organization has been engaged in attacks against Israelis. Thus, by 1995–1996, Iran was reputed to have transferred around $50 million to Hamas, according to testimony in a US court.[11] The year 1996 saw the highest number of Hamas terror attacks until that date, and was the year of the first suicide bombings on buses — a technique which was later to become particularly associated with the movement. By the end of the decade, however, Israeli figures suggest that Hamas was receiving around $3 million annually from Iran. Contributions picked up again as Hamas spearheaded the low intensity war usually known as the "al Aqsa Intifada" in the first years of the new century.

Support from the Gulf to Hamas dried up because of US pressure on the Saudis to crack down on backing for terrorism following September 11, 2001. Hamas had been reluctant to come to rely too much on Iranian support, for fear of losing its freedom of action. There are also real ideological differences at stake. Hamas emerged from the Palestinian branch of the Muslim Brotherhood movement. The trend within it is currently toward even more stringent and intolerant versions of Sunni observance. Within Hamas's military wing, there is a growing tendency toward Salafism — an extreme, anti-Shia interpretation of Sunni Islam. There is a natural tension between this tendency and the increasing ties between the movement and Iran.

Nevertheless, necessity is forcing Hamas further and further into the Iranian-led alliance. The movement's victory in 2006 elections, and its subsequent seizure and holding of the Gaza Strip in June 2007, have brought its activities and its needs to a new level of seriousness. As Hamas approaches the possibility of making a serious bid for control of the Palestinian national movement, so its links with the pro-Iranian alliance become more crucial. The achievement of this goal is only imaginable on the basis of the alliance with Iran. No other ally can provide the weaponry, training, and funds that will maintain the semi-sovereign, besieged Gaza enclave, and enable Hamas to pose a real challenge to its Western-backed Fatah opponents.[12]

In early 2009, revelations emerged of the extent to which Iran and Hizballah were engaged in arming and training Hamas forces in Gaza, and in smuggling weaponry into the Strip. The weaponry arrived by way of another adjunct and veteran member of the alliance — the Islamist regime of Omar al-Bashir in Sudan.

The revelations indicated the extent to which Iran and its allies were able to operate in close collusion with one another — with state sovereign members of the alliance, along with Hizballah, uniting to defend the alliance's franchise among the Palestinians and its foothold on the Mediterranean, the besieged Hamas enclave in Gaza. Iranian aid is not only financial and material. Rather, Hamas cadres have undergone training in Iranian training camps, with the intention of building Hamas's military capabilities to levels similar to those developed by Hizballah under Iranian tutelage.

Economically and militarily, Hamas's Gaza entity depends increasingly on Iranian aid. The Gaza enclave is in the process of metamorphosing into a fully fledged Islamist mini-state. Since the coup of July 2007, Hamas has constituted the sole ruling force within the Gaza Strip. Under its jurisdiction, an ever more stringent Islamic regime is under construction in the Strip. Events in Gaza demonstrate the dynamic of the meeting point between the Iranian interest from above, and popular Islamist agitation from below.

The Hamas enclave in Gaza is defined by the interaction of these two forces. The superior commitment of Hamas fighters when compared to the forces of Fatah enabled them to drive Fatah from the Strip in 2007. Iranian aid and training has underwritten the subsequent survival and development of the enclave. Hamas forces performed poorly against the IDF, however, in Operation Cast Lead, and the rulers of Gaza are determined to improve their military abilities. Their role-model is Hizballah, and they want to create a military force with abilities parallel to that of the Lebanese Shia group. Iranian aid is the key element in achieving this. So Hamas is drawing closer to its Iranian allies. This is not to the liking of all in the movement, but it is probably unavoidable.

Islamist fervor, however, is not simply a mechanism directed from above. It also has its own logic. In Gaza, as discussed earlier, the momentum from below is forcing Hamas in the direction of a greater Islamization of society.

All these elements — the increasing Islamization of society, the proliferation of small Islamist sects, and the growth of increasingly radical positions within Hamas itself — are direct by-products of the construction of a jihadi enclave in Gaza, from which all more moderate Palestinian streams have been expelled or else suppressed. What is emerging in Gaza, as in Hizballah-controlled southern Lebanon, is a Levantine blueprint for the kind of societies the rising elite in Iran hope to see emerge throughout the region: steeped in religious observance, repressive, and geared above all to the successful prosecution of war.

So the main components of the pro-Iranian regional alliance are Iran itself, Syria, and Hizballah. The logic of Hamas's position is drawing the movement closer to Teheran. The Sunni Islamist Sudanese regime is a client of the Iranians, and has based itself on the Iranian model.

In addition to this core, Iran has a number of other regional allies. Qatar is playing a strange and ambiguous role in the regional cold war that is currently developing in the Middle East. The Gulf emirate has close relations with the US, which maintains one of its largest regional air bases in Qatar. But Qatar is seeking to ride the wave of opportunity presented in the region by the rise of Iran, the popularity of Islamist radicalism, and the communications revolution. By drawing closer to Iran, and championing radical positions on its enormously popular satellite channel, al-Jazeera, Qatar has managed to increase its presence in regional diplomacy, seeking to make itself a natural point of mediation between the two camps.

As relations between the Iran-led camp and its opponents have worsened, so Qatar has found this role harder to sustain. Increasingly, as was illustrated by the two rival Arab summits that took place during Israel's Operation Cast Lead in Gaza in early 2009, Arab states are being forced to choose with which camp they wish to be identified. Egyptian President Hosni Mubarak's failure to attend an Arab League summit in Doha following the Gaza operation was evidence of Cairo's anger at Qatar, and the growing rifts in the Arabic-speaking world.[13]

In addition to the adjunct membership of Qatar, the pro-Iranian alliance supports a variety of Islamist insurgent movements throughout the region. The Sadrists in Iraq, Shia oppositionists in Kuwait, Bahrain and Saudi Arabia, Jihadists in Egypt, and other manifestations of Islamism across the region all benefit from the assistance of Iran and its proxy Hizballah.

A major question regarding the new cold war in the Middle East is the position of Turkey. The Islamist Adalet ve Kalkınma Partisi AKP, which has ruled Turkey since 2002, was initially seen by many as an Islamic conservative party, unlikely to impact in a significant way on Turkey's secular nature and pro-Western foreign policy.

Subsequent events, however, have served to temper this early optimism. Turkey under Recep Erdogan has begun to move closer to Iran — defending Iranian nuclear ambitions. During Israel's Operation Cast Lead, when rival Arab summits were held by pro-Western and pro-Iranian Arab states, Erdogan chose to attend the pro-Iranian gathering in Doha. Turkey has also moved closer to other members of the pro-Iranian alliance. Joint military exercises between Turkish and Syrian forces were held in the Turkish–Syrian border area in April 2009, and later that month Turkey hosted pro-Iranian Shia leader Moqtada al-Sadr.

Turkey has by no means yet cast its lot with the pro-Iranian alliance. But the fact that this key North Atlantic Treaty Organization (NATO) state has elected to make prominent overtures towards Teheran is testimony to two things: first, the extent to which the ruling Turkish party does not differ fundamentally from other manifestations of Islamism as was initially thought — and in this regard, the AKP has also begun to abandon its early statements of pluralism, dismiss dissent, and criticize the Turkish media. Secondly, Turkey's actions are testimony to the extent that the pro-Iranian alliance's gathering strength in the region cannot be ignored, and is influencing all aspects of the international relations of the Middle East.

The formation of the Iranian challenge — Iran's shrugging aside of borders as it attempts to flex its muscles across the region, its claim to be a "sunrise power" moving against a crumbling Pax Americana in the region, its framing of its expansionism in the language of dignity and rebellion, and looming over all this, Iran's nuclear ambitions — all are serving to bring together a rival camp of countries with a shared interest in resisting this process. Because of the broad sweep of Iran's outreach, the camp coalescing to resist it is heterogenous. It also consists of countries that have a history of enmity.

Lacking a uniting idea, the anti-Iranian alliance has many weak links, and no real common strategy. Some of its members would prefer to find a way of accommodating Iran rather than fighting it. Only a few are able to pose a real obstacle to the onward march of Teheran's power across the region. But its emergence, and the contest between these two camps, has now become the salient strategic fact in the Middle East region.

Who are the members of the anti-Iranian alliance? It consists of all those states for whom the expansion of Teheran's power represents a direct threat. In this category, of course, is Israel, which has been earmarked for destruction by the rising element in the Iranian elite.

Also included are the two states who have credibly laid claim to the leadership of the Arab world over the last half century — Egypt and Saudi Arabia. The small Arab emirates of the Gulf (with the exception of Qatar), Jordan and Morocco are all members of this alliance, as was Lebanon in the short period between the Syrian departure and the beginning of Hizballah's push for power. The West Bank Palestinian Authority of Mahmoud Abbas is also an ambiguous and uncertain member.

The forces arrayed against Iran differ from the pro-Iranian alliance in a number of important ways. It would be an exaggeration to say that the pro-Iranian alliance is entirely ideologically coherent. It suffers from a series of significant rifts among its members — between Islamist Iran and "secular nationalist" Syria; between Shia Iran and Sunni Hamas, and so on. But there is at least something resembling a uniting idea among the members of this camp — namely, the idea of "muqawama" (resistance), the claim to be representing authentic, defiant regional traditions, identities and interests, the elevation of certain forms of political violence and of ideals of self-sacrifice, the notion that the Middle East has been uniquely humiliated by the West, but that this time is now passing.

This set of ideas is less coherent than it proclaims itself. But the various forces that find themselves arrayed against it have no unifying idea at all, and in many ways are natural enemies. The anti-Iran alliance brings together such disparate players as Jewish Israel and Salafi Saudi Arabia, nationalist Egypt, Palestinian/Arab nationalist Fatah and Arab nationalist 14 March in Lebanon. It is for this reason that the editorial pages of the Egyptian and Saudi media continue to fulminate against Israel, even as the government agencies of all three states cooperate in myriad and significant ways.

The counter-Iranian alliance is held together by basic self-interest. Its two strongest members are Israel and Egypt. It is these countries that are doing the "heavy lifting" in countering Iran. Egypt fears the possibility of being marginalized by the growth of Iranian power. Cairo is also deeply concerned at the possibility of internal Iranian subversion. The current regime has held power for over half a century, but a leadership crisis is beckoning. The Muslim Brotherhood remains the most potent opposition force, and the ties with the West that are the key strategic link of the regime remain controversial and unpopular — in particular the peace treaty with Israel.

Egypt, after a long period of uncertainty, has begun to act in a determined way against Iranian attempts at encroachment. During Israel's Gaza operation in early 2009, Cairo's decision to keep the southern exit from the Strip sealed played a crucial role in the military setback that Hamas suffered during the operation. The calls by Hizballah leader Hassan Nasrallah for the bringing down of the Egyptian regime at that time brought the new regional cold war into its sharpest focus.[14]

The subsequent uncovering and conviction of a Hizballah cell preparing to launch terror attacks within Egypt, and of an Iranian arms trail stretching from Sudan, across Egypt and Sinai, to Gaza, further confirmed the reality of the Hamas enclave as part of a larger regional alliance.[15] But the determined Egyptian action against Hamas and Hizballah demonstrated that the regime in Cairo was unafraid to confront its newly declared enemies. The Egyptian response was also unprecedented in its anger and contempt for Nasrallah, who was derided in the official media as the "monkey sheikh" and a "son of garbage."[16]

In the past, Egypt was quick to abandon the shibboleths of Arab nationalism when they conflicted with the interests of the state and the regime. On this basis, Egypt became the first Arab state to pursue a separate peace with Israel. The events of early 2009 showed that Egypt would be no less ready to puncture the balloon of "resistance" and enter a de facto alliance with Israel, if once again the interests of the state seemed to demand it.

For Saudi Arabia, the rise of Iranian power represents an obvious geopolitical threat in its close geographical vicinity. The institutions of the Saudi state are weak, however, and its population small. The Saudis well remember the chaos engendered in the kingdom in the 1980s by the Iranians because of Saudi support for Iraq during the Iran-Iraq war. Saudi Arabia's largely Shia and oil rich eastern province remains vulnerable to Iranian subversion.

The Saudis, having reached a modus vivendi with the Iranian regime in the 1990s, would like to maintain it if possible. They are as frightened by Iranian nuclear ambitions as they are by the possible ramifications of US or Israeli moves against Iranian nuclear facilities. The instinct of the Saudis is to try to appease and buy off problems, rather than confront them — and this they have tried to do also with the threat of Iranian regional encroachment, notably in their attempts to tempt Syria away from its friendship with Iran.

However, as the dimensions of the Iranian threat have grown more apparent, so the Saudi tone has been hardening. The government-approved media of the kingdom has grown harshly critical of Iran and of Hizballah and its "interference" in the affairs of the Arab world. Still, Saudi Arabia is too fragile an instrument to form anything but a subaltern element in any alliance to block the advance of Iran. Its instinct will be to reach accommodation where this seems possible.

Of course, Saudi Arabia has itself played a far more central role in helping to advance the politics of Islamism in the region and globally than has Iran. Western oil needs and Saudi wealth has not allowed this aspect of the kingdom to interfere with its favored status in the West. The strategic importance of Saudi Arabia is such that it has never been under US pressure either to normalize relations with Israel, or even to desist from the virulent anti-Israeli and anti-Jewish propaganda that is a staple product of the kingdom.

Saudi involvement shows the extent to which the "pro-Western" alliance in the region is a fractured and somewhat incoherent gathering, in comparison to the smaller pro-Iranian alliance, which possesses a sense of common mission and a series of simple unifying ideas.

The small emirates of the Gulf — with the exception of Qatar — occupy a similar space in the anti-Iranian alliance to that of the Saudis. Again, they are in close proximity to Iran, and states with large Shia minorities like Kuwait, or Shia majorities like Bahrain, are particularly vulnerable to Iranian subversion.

Iran also has outstanding territorial claims vis à vis the UAE and Bahrain (in April 2009, Ali Akbar Nateq-Nuri, a senior aide to Supreme Leader Ayatollah Ali Khamenei, described Bahrain as Iran's "fourteenth province," while the ownership of three islands in the Gulf — Abu Musa and the two Tunbs — is a matter of dispute between Iran and the UAE).[17] In Kuwait, more than 1,000 alleged Iranian agents were arrested and deported in 2008.

These states are terrified at the thought of a resurgent, nuclear Iran, seeking to dominate the Gulf region. But, like Saudi Arabia, they also fear the possible consequences of a firm move against it. The position of the Kingdom of Jordan is similar. These fragile states will seek to stay outside of any battle for control in the region, and to accommodate themselves to the victor. Privately, they are concerned at the apparent US and Western weakness in confronting the threat.

Perhaps the two weakest links of all among anti-Iranian forces are the Fatah movement among the Palestinians and the March 14 movement in Lebanon. Both these forces are unable to muster a military response to the threat posed by the pro-Iranian, Islamist formations within their own contexts — Hamas and Hizballah, respectively. Both are able to resist being absorbed by their opponents only because of a Western commitment to their survival.

So, the geopolitics of the Middle East are undergoing transformation because of the meeting of two, directly related processes: the rise to prominence of a radical Islamist elite within the oligarchy that rules Iran, and the broader spread of Islamist political movements throughout the region. Modern communications and porous borders between states are facilitating the link-up between these two processes.

Iran, on the basis of interests as well as sentiment, is attempting to take ownership of the Israeli-Palestinian conflict. Teheran intends to use Israel as a justifying factor for its own encroachments in the region. But the sincerity of the new Iranian elite's commitment to destroy Israel should not be doubted. Should Iran acquire a nuclear capability, the ability of the regime to pursue regional hegemony would be vastly exacerbated.

A counter-alliance of sorts is emerging among states threatened by Iran's ambitions. This counter-alliance is disunited, with many of its members preferring to sit the conflict out and make accommodation with the victor.

Israel and Egypt are the two states prepared and able to perform the heavy lifting in the regional attempt to contain and push back the advance of Iran and its clients. As such, the new conflict being born is not a fight between Israelis and Arabs. Rather, it is the product of the combining of the ambition of a state regime with the spread of Islamist ideas, on the fertile soil of a region whose encounter with modernity and sovereignty has been deeply problematic and which has not yet succeeded in producing stable, representative government.

This new regional cold war is not entirely cold. It has a number of active fronts in which representatives of the Islamist camp and its enemies are engaged in open warfare. From Israel's point of view, there are currently two fronts in which forces of the Islamist alliance are committed against Israeli forces. The first is the Gaza Strip, ruled by Hamas. The second is southern Lebanon, controlled by the Iran-created Hizballah.

The emergence of a regional coalition committed to the Jewish state's destruction is having a profound effect on attitudes also within Israel itself. A more militant, stark, pessimistic outlook is taking hold in the Jewish state, as the country re-adapts itself to the new climate taking hold across the region.

Notes

1. Yossi Melman and Meir Javedanfar, *The Nuclear Sphinx of Teheran: Mahmoud Ahmedinejad and the state of Iran*, New York: Carroll and Graf, 2007: 22.
2. "Iran conservatives to win big parliament majority," *Agence France Presse*, 14 March 2008.
3. Denis Sullivan, "Will the Muslim Brotherhood run in 2010," *Arab Reform Bulletin*, May 2009.
4. Amir Taheri, "Iran fills the void," *Wall Street Journal*, 4 May 2009.
5. Barry Rubin, "Why Syria Matters," *Middle East Review of International Affairs*, vol. 10, no. 4, December 2006.
6. Amal Saad Ghorayeb, *Hizbullah: Politics and Religion*, London: Pluto Press, 2002: 14.

7. Ibid: 15.

8. "Israel, Lebanon: the conflict in Gaza and a possible northern front," *Stratfor*, January 3 2009.

9. Jonathan Halevi, "Hizbullah's role in attacks against US and British forces in Iraq," Jerusalem Center for Public Affairs, vol. 8. no. 9, August 2008. http://www.jcpa.org/JCPA/Templates/ShowPage.asp?DBID=1&LNGID=1&TMID=111&FID=379&PID=0&IID=2509 Accessed: 2.5.10.

10. Michael Eisenstadt and Neri Zilber, "Hizballah, Iran and the prospects for a new Israeli-Palestinian peace process," *Peacewatch* 486, Washington Institute for Near East Policy, 22 December 2004.

11. Michael Rubin, "The Enduring Iran-Syria-Hezbollah axis," American Enterprise Institute Middle East Outlook, December 2009.

12. In January 2010, the Hamas regime in the Gaza Strip announced its budget for the coming year. Of a total budget of $540 million, only $60 million would be raised by taxation. The rest was to be received from "foreign aid" from un-named sources. It may be assumed that the bulk of this is due to be received from Iran.

13. Ramadan al Sherbini, "Egypt's president skips Arab League summit in Doha," *Gulf News*, 28 March 2009.

14. "Egypt refuses full opening of Gaza crossing," *Ynetnews*, 30 December 2008. http://www.ynet.co.il/english/articles/0,7340,L-3647299,00.html Accessed: 5.5.10.

15. "How Israel foiled an arms convoy bound for Hamas," *Time*, 30 March 2009.

16. David Schenker, "The Pharaoh strikes back," *Weekly Standard*, 6 May 2009.

17. Ali Younes, "Iran, Bahrain and the Arabs," *Al-Arabiyya*, 3 March 2009.

CHAPTER 5

Conversations in the Season of Remembrance

The emergence of an Iranian-led Islamist alliance in the region strategically committed to Israel's destruction is changing the Jewish state. According to the script written by this alliance, the proper Israeli response should be one of fear and despair. Predictions of this kind have failed to be realized. But the changed climate of the region is producing a less hopeful, less optimistic Israel, which is doing what most nations under threat in history have done: namely, turning in upon itself, in order to find the sources of strength and the means to survive in a changed region.

The renewed conflict poses an old dilemma for the Jewish state: how is the country to remain sufficiently fierce and committed to survive in a danger-filled environment, and yet still remain the enlightened, open, Western-style society, with its face turned outward to the world, which it wants and needs to be?

This dilemma finds expression both in political trends, and in Israeli society's grappling with the deeper questions raised by a conflict that seems to have an inexhaustible power of regeneration.

Israeli politics has, for 40 years, been divided between trends committed to the idea of peace based on territorial compromise, and those that believed in the retention by Israel of all lands conquered in 1967. Adherents of the idea of the "whole land of Israel," and those who believe in a general willingness in the Arab and Muslim world to accept the Jewish state, on condition that it makes territorial concessions, may still be found on either end of the Israeli political spectrum.

But there is now a growing sense that the passionate divisions between these camps belonged to the period of the country's adolescence, and that Israel is moving toward a certain cautious and disenchanted maturity. This maturity is based on the recognition that the old divide between supporters and opponents of "land for peace" no longer adequately addresses Israel's situation. Instead, a new consensus based on willingness in principle for the re-partition of the country, coupled with skepticism as to whether there is a "partner for partition" on the other side has emerged.

It is in the nature of maturity to be less joyful than youth and to have fewer illusions. But the changed perspectives are coalescing around existing symbols, within the familiar Israeli political culture, rather than in opposition to them.

The result is an emerging political consensus, along with a weary disenchantment, both with the possibility of peace, and with the excitement of nationalist adventure. These aspects reflect themselves in myriad ways, in the deep fabric of Israeli life.

On Remembrance Day 2009, I traveled to the cemetery at Hod Hasharon to take part in a memorial ceremony with other members of my unit. Such gatherings take place all over the country. In Israel, as is well known, Remembrance Day is immediately followed by Independence Day. Because the Jewish calendar is lunar, the end of the day takes place at sundown, so in fact the sorrow of the day of remembrance gives way to the celebrations of Independence Day at some slightly indeterminate point in the late afternoon.

At Hod Hasharon, in the small corner plot where the ceremonies take place, there are two graves next to one another of recently fallen soldiers, which attract the largest crowds on Remembrance Day. One of these is of Alon Smoha, my friend and comrade, who is the reason I go there. The other is of a young man called Steven Kenigsberg, who served in the Givati Brigade, and who was killed at the Kissufim Junction in 2002. Steven Kenigsberg was 19 at the time of his death. His father, Kevin Kenigsberg, is an immigrant to Israel from South Africa, and a friend of mine. Two distinctive military and sociological tribes gather at the graves each year, and, because of the numbers, they become one crowd. Like different families at a wedding.

Around the grave of Alon Smoha are his friends from our unit, representatives of the 188 Brigade and of the Armored Corps, his family and many of his work colleagues from the big Teva pharmaceuticals factory where he worked. Around the grave of Steven Kenigsberg are people from the Givati Brigade, the Infantry Corps, the Betar youth movement to which his family was connected and members of his family from overseas. There are no work colleagues, of course, because Steven Kenigsberg was just out of school when he enlisted.

Shakespeare, in Henry V, talks of a "royal fellowship of death" on the field of Agincourt. This phrase is plangent and disturbing, and sometimes I am reminded of it in the culture of remembrance in Israel. There is no good or ideal way to remember the war dead. Some cultures attempt a sort of prettification of the experience of combat which contains within it a deep lie. It seems to imply that there is something clean and elevated about death in battle. There is not.

In Israel, remembrance is deeply personal. It takes place among small communities of people who know each other and who knew the people they are remembering. When I see Kevin Kenigsberg amid the soldiers in purple or in red berets gathered around his son's grave, what I see mainly is the way that the white has spread a little further in his ginger beard in the last year, and the fact that he has not yet given up smoking.

There are no easy answers. "Too long a sacrifice," said Yeats, "can make a stone of the heart."[1] Is there not something of Moloch in the very nature of remembering the war dead? Must there not inevitably be an element of paganism, or idolatry in it? The Israeli writer Amos Oz depicted death as an aged seducer, spreading illusion to entice disappointed souls into his embrace.[2] Military death has seductive powers too. Its solemnity and ritual and authority give it the ability to silence dissent, to enforce obedience. Societies engaged in conflict need to be on guard against allowing it this power, to which it will naturally tend, because of the intensity of the experiences surrounding it. This is hardly a problem for most Western societies today, which in the main remain less knowledgeable of war than any in human history (though the accumulated experiences of Iraq and Afghanistan are changing this). It isn't a problem for the Islamist and totalitarian enemies of Israel, either, which don't need seducing by death because they openly proclaim their love and loyalty to it.

For Israel, however, the dilemma is a real one. It is issues like these that are the practical side of the project of Israel's enemies. Open, Western societies are not made, they think, for endless conflict. People won't stay. Or if they do, they won't be willing to send their children to fight and die against an enemy with an inexhaustible will for destruction. Or else Israel will lose its moorings to the West as it takes the necessary, inevitably ugly, measures to defend itself, and will become unrecognizable, and isolated.

If Israeli society fails to produce an answer to such cardinal questions, then the country's long term viability as an open and democratic society will indeed be called into question. How may one stay true to a realistic assessment of the nature of conflict and sacrifice, while educating further generations to involvement in the struggle for national consolidation? How can a society remain both ready for war, and uncorrupted by the readiness? When the conflict seemed to be winding down, such things began to matter less. But the conflict is no longer winding down, and the issue is growing in relevance.

The enemies of Israel have placed their central bet on the country proving unequal to this task. The pro-Iranian alliance conspicuously lacks a conventional military option. Their strategy is to hollow out Israel from within — placing before the Jews of Israel a series of unsolvable dilemmas: endless conflict, the necessity of an unsustainable level of self-sacrifice. As the Hamas official Nizar put it to me in Ramallah, if the price of maintaining Israel can be raised beyond a certain point, there will be fewer and fewer willing to pay it. Because in Nizar's view, the Jews came to the country, as is their wont, to "pray and make business." Israeli society is currently in the process of responding to this challenge.

This process, experienced close up, can be depressing and exhausting. For my own part, I wanted for a long period after the events of the 2006 war to withdraw somewhat from the collective. I liked Jerusalem and had no intention of leaving. All the same, I felt a yearning to move beyond the narrow confines of militant Jewish identity, in which I had been wrapped up for two decades.

My study of the Arabic language and my work as a journalist opened doors to other identities, other experiences in Jerusalem and further afield, and I felt a sort of hunger for exploring these. But in 2009, the yearly period of Israeli-Jewish national remembering which begins with the Pesach festival, runs through Holocaust Day and on to Remembrance Day and Independence Day, had the effect of reminding me of things I had forgotten.

It was a year since I had seen Kevin Kenigsberg. I remembered the night in the winter of 2001/2002 when the news of his son's death was announced. It was just after the festival of Purim, and shortly before the commencement of Operation Defensive Shield, in the darkest months of the Second Intifada. I had seen Kevin at a Purim party a few days earlier. He and his girlfriend had been dressed as devils, with little red horns. And there he was on the television screen, and a picture of his son who had just finished his training in Givati, and who was now dead.

Kevin Kenigsberg comes from a Lithuanian Jewish family, as his name suggests. His father was one of the early activists of the right wing Zionist Betar youth movement. The family fled pogroms in the Baltic and arrived in South Africa. Kevin was active in Betar as a young man, and in rightist Jewish politics after that. Separated from his wife, he finally arrived in Israel in 1999, together with his son Steven, who was then 16. Kevin was steeped in the politics and culture of the Revisionist Zionist movement and the Betar youth movement that gave birth to the Irgun Tzvai Leumi military organization, and to the

Herut party and its descendant, the Likud. His son was also involved in Betar, and its stark vision of Jewish pride and defiance was what had led him to the Givati Brigade.

Every year, in the graveyard at Hod Hasharon, I leave the close knit circle of my friends from the Armored Corps and, a little self-consciously, I go over and embrace Kevin Kenigsberg. Kevin, a well-built, ginger-bearded man, has aged a lot since the death of his son, when he seemed younger than his 46 years. Every year, we talk a little and enquire as to each others' affairs, and that's that.

In 2009, however, I decided to prolong the conversation, and arranged to meet with him a few weeks later. I wanted to ask him about his own sense of where the country was headed, as the region entered a new and stormy era. I also wanted, if I could, to talk to him about immigration, parenthood, bereavement, and how one could balance national and individual responsibilities. I had an image in my mind from Steven's funeral. It was of Kevin being led, with his head bowed, from the cemetery at Hod Hasharon, his arms resting on the shoulders of his other son for support. The image had stayed with me.

Steven's death had come at that strange and terrible time when bombs were going off on a weekly basis in Jerusalem. There had been a growing rage in some circles at that time at the perceived impotence of the Israeli government of Ariel Sharon to act against the terror organizations. It was the last stage of self-restraint, a month before Operation Defensive Shield. In all that madness, the death of my friend's son had come as the latest terrible and insane event.

Sitting with Kevin Kenigsberg in his apartment in Hod Hasharon, seven years after the death of his son, I listened as he filled me in on various details of the events of those days. Kevin smoked and his two French bulldogs played and snapped around us. Steven's picture is there on the fridge door. Another one that looks just like his father.

Kevin was in his mid-forties when he and his son arrived in Israel. Father and son fulfilled a joint dream when they arrived at the absorption center in Ra'anana, a center of South African immigrants to Israel. A couple of years later, Steven was drafted and volunteered for the Givati infantry brigade.

Two details of what Kevin told me that evening in Hod Hasharon, concerning how he learnt of his son's death remain in my mind. The first is how he was asked at his work to go the office of the CEO, only to find that his boss was not there. Instead, there were three men in the room whom he did not know, two wearing uniform. They all stood up as he entered. One of the men began to say something to Kevin in Hebrew. Kevin apologized and said that he couldn't understand. So the man switched to English to tell him that his son was dead.

The killing of Steven Kenigsberg, as Kevin related it to me that night, was in one of the dreadful, messy firefights that were taking place all along the border at that time, in the weeks before Operation Defensive Shield saw the IDF going back on the offensive. It was common for lone Palestinian terrorists, or groups of two or three, to seek to engage army patrols. Steven's section had been taking up positions at a pillbox on the border with Gaza. The gunman had arrived, tossed a grenade that didn't explode, and had then sprayed a burst of automatic rifle fire, firing from the hip as the Palestinians do. This first burst had killed Steven.

The second aspect of the talk with Kevin that sticks in my mind is how he told me that Colonel Imad Fares, the Druze officer who commanded Givati at that time, had come to his house. They had talked, and Fares, with the wisdom of the fighting mountain people from which he comes, had said to Kevin "I can see what kind of man you are, and I'm telling you that if there will be peace, you would be willing to shake the hand of the man who killed your son."

Kevin had mused for a moment after relating this anecdote to me, and then said quietly, "I don't know, perhaps I would." Then he had gone on to tell me that a few weeks after the incident, Steven's company commander had called him personally to tell him that the unit had hunted down and killed the man responsible for his son's death. "I don't know if it's true, of course," he added.

Later, our conversation turned to broader issues. Kevin grew up in the Betar movement, and remains loyal to its ideology. The movement was famous for its refusal to accept the first partition of Palestine in 1922, which split Transjordan, modern day Jordan, off from Mandatory

Palestine. The slogan of "shtei gadot le'yarden" — the Jordan has two banks — was one of its famous calling cards, along with its consequent demand for a Jewish state on both banks. Kevin told me that "ideologically, I still believe in 'shtei gadot,'. Practically — that's a different matter." He bridles still at the thought of compromise, "Munich," he tells me when I ask if he doesn't think that perhaps concessions of some kind are inevitable.

But also, and still, he tells me how he was shocked when his stepdaughters spoke in aggressive terms about the people of Gaza during Operation Defensive Shield. "Can you imagine it," he laughs, "me standing up for the other side."

Above it all, very importantly, is a refusal to be a victim. "We're not victims, we're survivors," he says, taking a drag on his cigarette, the picture of his son behind him.

I am happy to meet Kevin in a place other than a graveyard amid the red soil of the Sharon plain. And I am happier still, and impressed, to see the way that he has placed his life in order. Much of the harsher, less grounded stuff has gone, boiled away, I think, in the heat of his experience, which tests, and leaves only real and solid things in place. "When my enemy says he wants to kill me, I believe him," he reminds me, "I don't say it's just talk." No time for hatred nor illusion regarding the enemy, and a suspicion that even he, whose son is dead, might shake their hands if there was peace. In the meantime, suspicion — and resolve.

After the conversation, we walk into Hod Hasharon to eat something at a local shwarma place. I never thought about this nondescript town much, but it has become the central spot for me to try my testing of where we are headed, and to remember the dead. Just up the road from Kevin Kenigsberg's house is the home of the Smohas. They don't know each other, these two fathers, though every year they stand next to each other, by the graves of their sons.

Kevin has become a well-known local personality. The younger ones call him "Mr. Kenigsberg," which seems to suit his proud, slightly aloof bearing. He loves the human, Sancho Panza style of local Israeli politics and is forever involved in some intrigue or other.

He is planning to stand for the municipal council and wants to make the Likud Central Committee. Seeing him in the restaurant on the main street of Hod Hasharon, joking with the owner, waving to passing acquaintances, I remember the words of Yehuda Amichai in his poem "Jews in the Land of Israel": "spilled blood is not the roots of trees — but it's the closest thing to roots we have."[3]

We shake hands and I take the bus back to Jerusalem, my mind full of the sight of Kevin appearing on Channel 1 news that evening in 2002, only hours after the visit of the three unintelligible men to his workplace, two of them in uniform. And how he was led, supported by his eldest son, from the scene of the grave. How his friends from the Betar youth movement had gathered around the still open grave, some in the ill-fitting suits of budding politicians and some in military uniform, and had sung their movement's anthem, very softly.

The events of the last years have made me a connoisseur of funerals. Of parents burying their children. All of that quiet dust was quickened by our conversation. But I gained at least to my own partial satisfaction the answer to the question that I sought. Maturity, tiredness, hatred, long burnt away. And no danger of the price being raised beyond reach.

Nizar from Ramallah is bound to miss the strength in the identity of people like Kevin Kenigsberg, because it bears so little relation to his own sense of strength. The Palestinian and broader Arab nationalist and Islamist narrative is built on a celebration of a particular, specific plot of land and the particular attachment to it made possible by a pre-modern society.

National stories, a long, unbroken national consciousness — the Arabic speaking world has historically been rather weak in these. But there is the attachment of the Fellah (peasant) to his land, from that all else follows, combined with the Muslim militancy and sense of natural overlordship which is now manifesting itself ever more overtly.

How then to understand a system of national consciousness that has been meager in land and the tangible, physical aspects of identity for much of its history, and that nevertheless burns with immense vividness? How to understand an immigrant father, not even speaking the language of the country, who gave his son to the IDF infantry?

Nizar and the others like him are convinced of the inevitability of their victory, in the long term, in any case. Look at the map, they say. Look, how many we are and how few our enemies are. No need to fret over details. But they underestimate their enemy.

Kevin Kenigsberg's sense of location and strength emerge fully formed from a particular Diaspora Jewish identity — rooted in suffering in Europe and fierce nationalism and a stark sense of the likely inevitability of hatred of the Jews. This outlook is one of the pillars of the current mood in Israel. But I think that the underlying pragmatism I heard him express is no less important. To understand the current mood and trend in thinking in Israel, it is necessary to grasp the particular nature of the combining of these two aspects in the Israeli Jewish psyche. A sense of siege is reflected in current reality, informed by the memory of past events and an underlying sobriety. It is an outlook not mainly concerned with legal or divine claims to land. Rather, it is focused on survival through strength.

It also works both ways. The growing pragmatism and disenchantment of Israeli society applies not only to people from right wing ideological backgrounds. Rather, it is a process affecting all sides of the society. "The problem for Israeli leftists," as my friend Ariel Ronen put it to me, one Saturday afternoon as we met at his mother's house in south Jerusalem, "is that they don't find leftists on the other side."

Ariel runs his own marketing business in Petah Tikva (it's going "slowly but slowly," he tells me, when I ask how the business is doing, in the midst of the economic downturn). He is another of the old, tight knit crowd in our reserve unit, going back to the first days in the early 1990s. I think of the political developments of the 1990s, and for most of the key events, I have a corresponding memory of taking part in a heated but good natured argument about the subject in question, in a military setting, with Ariel.

The memories also trace my own process of absorption into the country. I can remember when I first began to feel confident enough in Hebrew to begin to intervene in the discussions, rather than simply listening in. I remember relishing the role of the prophet of doom, when we were on a training exercise in Tze'elim in the desert, shortly after the withdrawal from southern Lebanon in May 2000.

Ariel and I walking back from the shooting ranges in the dark, going this way and that on deterrence, retreats under fire, Islamist ideology, projecting strength. And he and I sitting in a tent in Gush Etzion, with the same non-stop discussion of Oslo and naïveté and illusions and listen-brother-we-need-to-give-things-a-try, and this-naïveté-will-get-us all-killed. The fractious, endless Israeli argument in miniature.

It continued through the years that followed. The terror attacks in Jerusalem, and the weeks of reserve service in the Ofer jail. In the meantime, Ariel married and had a daughter and we all grew up and grew a bit older. He was no longer the cool young student from the Hebrew University of Jerusalem, blasting trance music out of a car stereo as we moved into the base in the Gush. All that was years and years ago. How the time goes by.

We talked a lot before south Lebanon too, but then, for some reason, there was little energy for political discussion, so we focused on quieter matters. And as the days of fog and cancellation and confusion continued in the time before we went in, our conversations grew less pleasant.

He was the last person I spoke to before we boarded the tanks on the way to el Khiam and Marjayoun. And what he told me then was very brief and very prescient, above the engines of the tanks roaring into life. He said, "We aren't ready for this. Not all of us will be coming back." At the entrance at Metulla, as the darkness came down, we gave each other the thumbs up, standing and smoking on the hulls of our tanks backed up next to each other.

Much of what is supposed to be military comradeship turns out to be lies. Not quite all, though. There is a small percentage left which remains to convince you that this is the reason why war remains a perennial part of human affairs. This is hard to quantify.

Anyway, it was clear to me that my conversations with Ariel over the previous decade and a half were an important part of the jigsaw. Ariel Ronen is the Jerusalem-born son of a native Israeli father and a

Belgian-born mother. He has thick, unusually blond hair for an Israeli, and fair, delicate skin. It used to be a matter for hilarity in the unit that he would turn up for duty with skin creams, which he would begin to apply to his skin as the harsh sun turned it pink, then red.

We would meet sometimes for drinks on Fridays, and like the rest of us, Ariel has been on a journey these past years. He was a member of the Meretz youth in the 1990s,[4] and his roots are all in the Israeli left. His father was a senior IDF officer, and he personified perfectly the public that combined secularism and leftism with an intense Israeli patriotism, and that was the backbone to Israeli public support for the peace process of the 1990s.

Like Kevin, his basic principles remain the same. And all the same "for me, the watershed, the tipping point, was the lynch in Ramallah," he told me, when I asked him where his thinking was these days on the conflict? "It put me in a position of remembering with whom we were involved." The lynching in Ramallah of two Russian-born IDF reservists took place in the opening days of the al-Aqsa Intifada in autumn, 2000, as we've already observed.[5] An Italian journalist surreptitiously filmed the scenes.

They were broadcast on Israeli television, and the journalist was threatened by Palestinian militants and had to leave the country in a hurry. There is an unforgettable image there of a young man, one of the mob, turning his bloodstained hands to the camera, yelling with delight. The images had a profound and sobering effect on many Israelis, and may signal one of the moments when the bright hopes of the 1990s died, and the grimmer mood that pertains today began to be born.

"At that point," Ariel continued, "I said 'enough,'" and he grimaced and added, "and I thought, what a garbage tip." His underlying senses of the conflict and the rights and wrongs pertaining to it have not changed. It is the sense of what is possible, and the time frame, which have changed. And in the meantime, in the interregnum, the question then shifts for this son of the Meretz youth also — to the issue of the relative strength of Israel, and its ability to live out the political and strategic ice age into which the region seems to be descending.

In this regard, too, he has little doubt. "Their failure, the failure of the Palestinians, is that they can't bring us to our knees, with everything they've thrown at us. It's like stings, that you first of all scratch yourself and after a while you build up immunity and hardly notice. So if buses are blowing up, you put security teams on all the buses, and when you don't need them anymore, you remove them. People now want security, they want quiet, and they don't want to ask too much detail about how they got it. Once people used to demonstrate outside the Defense Ministry. I was the same when I was in high school."

"It's clear to everyone today," he told me, "that we have to reach some sort of compromise on territory. But things have changed. When we were young, you know, we grew up on that stuff. 'I was born for peace' and the peace with Egypt, all that emotion. You won't see that kind of emotion here again. Now it's more like — OK, this is the only bride I have, stuck on a desert island, so I'll marry her, even if she's ugly."

"We've been through a process," he continued, "from Golda Meir who said there were no Palestinians, then it was — we won't speak to the PLO, and now we're discussing the precise dimensions of the two states. All in 40 years. Processes of change that could have taken 200 years."

And what about the region? I ask him. What about the other side? Are they going through a similar process? He knows the answer I want, and for a moment we are back in our sparring matches in remote and dusty military outposts. "I don't know," he says, simply, "Don't know if they're going through a similar process. It can go both ways. Now all this talk of an Islamic Middle East — and it's working, like you said. Iran, Pakistan, whole areas of Pakistan run by the Taliban."

And where does that leave us, long term? Are we winning? I press him, not quite sure of why it seems so important for me to hear his opinion on this. I guess because Ariel has a brand of patriotism which is non-declamatory and non-emotional, so I know that any response he gives on this will be considered, and reflect his true opinion, not the reflex response deriving from a sense of a verbal call to arms.

He pauses a little, and then says, "Of course, we can't rule out the possibility that in two or three hundred years this country might not exist." His mother, from the kitchen, registers a note of protest, but he continues, "What's certain is that this state will not cease to exist of its own free will. There won't come a certain point where we say, 'OK, you know what, it's all been a big mistake, bye bye, we're going to Canada. If it happens, it will happen in a terrible war, which will take half of the Middle East with it.

"And you know what? Maybe we are winning, or at least not doing so bad in the ongoing series of tests of which the conflict consists. Let's remember, he reminds me, what happened in Gaza — and what was supposed to happen. "They're arming no doubt. Still, the Iranians must have noticed that all their theories failed in Gaza. They set traps and we were supposed to be digging the bodies out by the shovel-load — and they ran away."

And I am reminded of a garden party at the house of a prominent European diplomat in east Jerusalem which I attended a few months before the Gaza operation. And how, in the sweltering sun, a senior European official, a former military officer, had regaled the journalists present with details of the military machine that Hamas was creating in Gaza.

The levels of training, and the tactics, that would make it impossible for Israel to operate effectively in the Strip. Once again, it was the will for sacrifice that was supposed to achieve this. Hamas, the official told us, as we drank our ice cold beer in the afternoon, has calculated that they could kill 12–20 IDF soldiers per day in any Gaza operation; a rate which Israel could not sustain. By ensuring this, they achieved strategic deterrence against Israel.

Such a statement reflected a certain awe that some feel towards Islamist fighters, which represents in itself a major moral victory for that cause.

The matter was put to the test in Operation Cast Lead. And, as it turned out, Hamas's propaganda abilities outstripped the ability of its fighters, and the IDF had indeed internalized some of the lessons of the 2006 War. All just a beginning, of course, with many more tests to come.

Thus did we pass our pleasant afternoon, at Ariel's mother's kitchen table in Gilo. In recalling our long mutual journey, conducted mainly in places of sweat and dust and noise and sand, during the festival of Shavuot, and a few days before a very large civil defense exercise.

The silence here is always deceptive. I remember the tanks heading for Gilo at the start of the Second Intifada, in the transition moment from what had gone before. How we watched them in wonder. And the noise of blast and counter blast that we used to hear from the south in those years. But how pastoral it was on that afternoon in the early summer of 2009.

Ariel has not given up his rationalist view of things, nor his strategic optimism. It is a matter of lasting out the moment of ideological fury and energy emerging from the Islamists. And then, after all, maybe we can talk with them. The bottom line is that Islamism doesn't appear to be going anywhere, and neither is Israel. So "maybe in ten years they'll come back, a bit fatter, with a bit of the passion gone, and with something to lose, and then we can have a different kind of conversation." He looks at me after saying this, and smiles a little ruefully. "It's a theory, of course. I don't know if its right."

After the remembrance ceremony in Hod Hasharon in 2009, I drove back with Menash, our deputy company commander, to Jerusalem. It was the first time we had spoken properly since the war. We talked compulsively about details of the various operations we had taken part in, and about the rushed military investigation of the Marjayoun-el Khiam incidents.

I told him that I spent most of the year supposing I was the only one of us still thinking about all this stuff. Then when I met up with other people from the unit, I realized it was still burning in all our bones. Anger and resentment and a sort of strange nervous energy that found no outlet. Menash still has the scar on his neck where a piece of shrapnel cut into him from a missile that landed on the hull of his tank in the valley between el Khiam and Marjayoun.

He dropped me off in the center of west Jerusalem, and I wandered around in the late afternoon. It was that curious time of transition when Remembrance Day has not yet finished and Independence Day not yet started. I cursed the pedagogues of the first days of the state again, for their decision to stick the two unlikely partners together. Remembrance and sovereignty. How good the idea must have looked on paper.

It was too late to go home, so I decided to have an early evening drink. In the bar, a young couple who looked like students were having a furious row with each other and with the girl serving. In the background, the melody of "Ammunition Hill" was playing. This strange and staccato song commemorates a bloody battle that the paratroopers fought in Jerusalem in June 1967.

The couple were arguing about the song, and what it meant. "These songs we have celebrating war," the young woman was saying, "listen to these lyrics, all making it into something glorious." And the young man was trying to defend the song, saying "No, not glorifying it, but in a country like ours, you're bound to have songs which are about trying to recall things, and show respect to the people who . . ." "Yes, and what for?" The girl behind the bar interrupted, "so they can send more people off to die in the wars, so they can get more young people to go off and get killed."

It was a good Israeli conversation in which no one, heaven forbid, was to be permitted to finish their sentence, and it continued in a similar vein for some time. A British photographer of my acquaintance, who was also at the bar and who knew no Hebrew, asked me with concern what they were arguing about.

"Oh, just relationship stuff," I said, and he expressed a smile of recognition. The conversation faded away a few minutes later and the young couple went out to smoke together.

I raised the subject with the girl behind the bar after a couple of minutes. I said it interested me how in Israel, everything came back to the big issues, which couldn't be ignored. "Personally, I hate it," she said with a smile. "You want to know why?" I said I did, and she told me; "The first time I kissed a guy was on the day the Second Intifada broke out. I was excited and I wanted to tell everyone about it. But I couldn't, because it seemed ridiculous. All around the Intifada was happening and everyone was wrapped up in all that. No one was interested in hearing that I'd just kissed someone. That's why I hate that garbage."

And she smiled and went back to pouring beers. I was taken aback at the idea that people who were children when the Second Intifada started were now working in bars. This made me part of the same phenomenon she was saying she hated. I am now apparently measuring the entirely normal process of aging, and the consequent sense of wonder and trepidation at the existence of younger people by using Middle East disasters as my landmarks.

Within an hour or so, darkness had come down and Remembrance Day had been defeated, and the wild celebrations of Independence Day were getting under way.

Spilled blood is not the roots of trees. But to misquote another famous poet, the point to note about Israel is that things have not fallen apart, and the center has held. So far, at least. The view of the conflict held by the greater part of the regional public, and by powerful and growing political-military forces in the region is that held by Arab nationalism since the Balfour Declaration: namely, that Jews possess no national rights in the land west of the Jordan River, that the consequent existence of Jewish sovereignty in the area is an affront to natural justice, and that the logic of history and the balance of forces is such that the Jewish state must eventually be washed away.

As a result of this, Israeli history has consisted largely of foundation and resisting siege. A new chapter of this process is currently in the process of opening up. The enemy is waging the old war in a new way. It is trying to play to the supposed weaknesses of Israel and to the strengths of its enemies.

Ongoing, never-ending warfare, the looming threat of a nuclear Iran, the prevention and frustration of all peace processes. These are the weapons to be utilized. The attempt to isolate and delegitimize Israel internationally, and particularly in the West is also part of all this. A key feature of the new conflict is that it is not taking place within limited geographical borders. The cities of the West, the international media, and public opinion are all key arenas. Trans-national communications have helped to make the conflict one of the iconic frontlines and faultlines in the clash between east and west.

In the meantime, Kevin Kenigsberg is married again and living with his new wife in Hod Hasharon, with the picture of the son who looks so very much like him unobtrusive on the fridge door. And Ariel Ronen is cursing the effects of the credit crunch on his business and employing all his rhetorical skills to make sure the reserve army lets him out on the right days to do something about it. And the questions of how to strike the right balance between freedom and responsibility, between remembering and healing, between yesterday and tomorrow, remain endlessly discussed and never finally answered. For as long as the conversation and the argument continue, I think, there is room for optimism.

Israel is changing as a result of renewed conflict and declining hopes for peace. A large, disillusioned center has emerged, which includes people who were part of both the old left and the old right ideologies. In the manner of the times, political loyalties are more fluid, less mobilized, less ideological and less naïve than was once the case. There is no sign, however, of a general breakdown in the country's view of itself and the justice of its cause.

On the other side, too, in the large and trans-national camp arrayed against Israel, there is a sense of a rising trajectory, and of a new type of warfare, utilizing new tools, which it is believed, will bring the victory that has for so long proved elusive.

Notes

1. William Butler Yeats, "Easter, 1916."
2. The comparison was made in Amos Oz, *A Tale of Love and Darkness*, London: Random House, 2004.
3. Yehuda Amichai, "Jews in the Land of Israel," in *The Selected Poetry of Yehuda Amichai*, London: University of California Press, 1996: 87.
4. Meretz, an alliance of three left wing Israeli parties, remains the main party of the Israeli Zionist left.
5. See Chapter 1.

CHAPTER 6

Broken Borders

In the face of such an adversary, the solution may only be "Flank Protection" to be carried out upon the soil of all interfering nations. The indigenous Believers that reside in these meddling countries however can only do this. For it is they, the locals, and not the foreigners who understand the language, culture, area and common practices of the enemy whom they co-exist among ... Terror works, and that is why the Believers are commanded to enforce it.

Dhiren Barot, "The Army of Madinah in Kashmir."[1]

In the 1990s, in the high days of the peace process, it was common to hear the Israeli-Arab conflict described as a disagreement over "real estate." This expression was intended to suggest that the dispute, while it might be submerged in ideological and religious argument, was actually quite a simple affair. It consisted, the argument ran, of a clash between two national entities over the fair parceling out of a disputed area between them.

This depiction of the conflict hid more than it revealed.

Many other ideas were built upon it. If the dispute was about real estate, then why had it proved so intractable, bloody and long-lived?

The answer given was that while this was in essence what it was about, the problem was that many participants in it thought that it was about something else. So that over the relatively simple base of the conflict had been erected vast superstructures of ideology and religion and identity and nationalism. These had come to obscure the true, more humble contours of the argument. What was necessary, therefore, was to find a way to clear away these superfluous structures, in order to make possible a rational discussion about the concrete issues at the heart of the matter.

This conceptualization gets the situation precisely the wrong way around. The essence of the conflict between the Zionist Jews and their Arab and Muslim enemies is not a dispute centering on tradeable, physical things, and therefore subject to a compromise solution. Or at least, insofar as it is that, it is not hard to solve. The thing that prevents a solution is quite separate from discussions about land allocation. The conflict is about a clash of ideas and symbols, based on the fundamental rejection on the part of the Arab/Muslim side of the right of the Jewish side to sovereignty in any part of the area in question. That is, insofar is it is about real estate, it is about the right of a particular structure not to be completely demolished, or the absence of that right.

This point was obscured during the latter period of Arab nationalism's clash with Zionism, though it was very clear at its outset. Arab nationalism in its early days was unambiguous in rejecting on principle the right to existence of a Jewish state. The existence of such a state was seen as a remnant of the period of European domination of the Arabic-speaking world. As such, the conflict pitted the desire of Jews to create and maintain sovereignty in what they regarded as their ancient homeland, and the desire of Arab nationalism, embedded in the Islamic heritage of the Arabic-speaking world, to maintain what it regarded as a section of its own patrimony. A clash of rival ideas made flesh.

Arab nationalism, though, was eclipsed in June 1967. After this it began to decline as a living idea capable of marshaling the will and emotions of masses of people. As its tide receded, it left behind real people, and real, mundane interests.

The basic idea of the illegitimacy of Israel was not renounced, and did not disappear. But in much of the Arab world, it was relegated to the world of culture and media, where it burned on with unflagging strength.

With the fading of ideological intensity, the argument that the dispute was evidently a limited clash over "real estate" began to be feasible, and began to be asserted. The peace agreements concluded between Israel and the post-ideological regime in Egypt and the non-ideological one in Jordan were made possible on this basis.

But what has happened over the last decade is that the original, white-hot convictions of Arab nationalism have returned in new garb. The destruction of Israel is no longer seen as part of returning to the Arab nation its patrimony. Rather, it is the Islamic "Umma" which is located as the historical actor that will defeat the Jews. The conflict has therefore been re-generated by an old idea presented in a new form.

The conflict between Israel and those who seek to destroy it is the fruit of ideas. The breakdown of borders and reduction of distance has enabled those ideas to reach new listeners. The basis of the conflict is today more clearly about thought, not about tangible, solvable matters, than at any time since Israel's creation.

For those intimately acquainted with Israel, this has a curious effect. The conflict argued and agonized over in the West and the Islamic world often seems to bear hardly any resemblance to the familiar, daily reality of life in the country. But again, it would be naïve to assume that the other worldliness of an idea will prevent it from impacting on reality. Delusions can be great incentives to action.

The result is that a kind of mythical Israel has been born, in the minds of the country's opponents. This mythical Israel emerged first in Islamist circles, but has now migrated to the minds of large numbers of Israel's Western, secular enemies. The mythical Israel is a place of uninterrupted darkness and horror, in which every human interaction is ugly, crude, racist and brutal.

The battle against this monstrous, imagined entity has become a central rallying cry for the global jihadi movement. It is also a key motif for what remains of the far left. These two trends have formed unlikely political partnerships in some European countries, and to some degree in the US. The conflict has thus broken its borders. This aspect of "broken borders" is crucial in understanding the nature of the current clash. The Israel-Islamist conflict reflects larger trends, and has indeed become a key front in a larger ferment between radical Islam and its allies and the liberal West.

The process has taken many forms. At its most dramatic, there has been the involvement of foreign jihadis in front line combat and terror activity against Israel. These have included European-born Islamists. But this most extreme manifestation is part of the larger trend of the penetrating of Middle Eastern Islamist ideas into wider public consciousness, which itself is partly a product of the growth of the popularity of Islamism among Muslim communities in the West.

The process of re-symbolization of the conflict was already under way in the 1990s. At the height of the peace process, it proceeded largely unnoticed, out of sight and out of mind of the media, in mosques and meetings and study centers. The United Kingdom has been one of the societies most affected by this process. British-born Islamists have been over-represented in the various fronts of the global jihad. Indeed, the Pakistani-British jihadi, lurking in some obscure English town, has become a staple figure in depictions of Sunni Islamism in the West. This does not, however, mean that the UK is the only, or the most important, center for this process. Parallel processes are underway in the other countries of Western Europe, and in a different form, in the US.

What has happened is that Middle Eastern political ideas have found their way into the Western political discussion. In the first instance, they have entered via that section of local Muslims sympathetic to Islamist ideas. From there, because of the crossover between Islamist movements and the radical left, these ideas have taken up residence closer to the political mainstream. The cross-pollination of ideas between the Middle East and the West is a matter of strategic importance, in understanding the Israel-Islamist conflict.

I happened to be a spectator to an aspect of this, at a fairly early stage of its development, in London in 1995. Of course, I couldn't know where it would all lead, and it is easy in hindsight to invest scenes with a greater drama and significance than they really had. But I don't think I'm exaggerating when I say that at Islamist meetings in London at that time, there was a strange élan, a sense of getting ready for something, with not much time left.

In 1995, I was in the UK studying for a masters degree in Middle Eastern politics, at the School of Oriental and African Studies in London. I had an interesting year. The college was filled with young people from all over the world. It was a time of optimism — both for our region and more generally.

Among the kaleidoscope of different nationalities at the college at that time, there was a student society that was called the 1924 committee. Its members consisted of young, British-born men of Pakistani origin, and they were often to be found giving out leaflets and fliers at the entrance. The leaflets were long and wordy, and concerned with various social and political issues. They bemoaned the abolition of the Islamic Caliphate by Mustapha Kemal Ataturk — they were named after the year in which this had taken place. Because of my dark skin and black hair, these young men took a friendly interest in me, assuming that like them I was a British Muslim.

I would take their leaflets and read them at home. It was two years after I had been demobilized from the IDF, and their friendliness would not have survived finding out who I was. It was fascinating and unexpected for me to discover Middle Eastern political ideas gestating and growing in the heart of London. I had become acquainted with such ideas in Israel — in Jerusalem, and in army service in Gaza, Nablus and Hebron. But for me, Israel and Britain had always seemed like two separate universes, contrasting with one another in almost every conceivable way. So to discover the familiar slogans and attitudes of Mid-Eastern Islamism close to the University of London Union building on Malet Street was bizarre.

I enjoyed the fact that the 1924 Committee — which turned out to be connected to a radical Islamist party called Hizb ut Tahrir, was taking such an interest in me. So, as a rather childish game, I would sometimes approach the stall they kept outside the college entrance, take a murmured interest in this or that leaflet, and listen as one of the young activists would commence a long, calm, and certain address on the issue at hand. Inevitably, after a few rounds of this, one of them asked me a little about myself. Without any prior planning, I heard myself inventing a story about an Egyptian father and an English mother, and an interest in discovering more about Islam.

The result was that I began to be informed about the regular meetings that Hizb ut Tahrir was holding among students in London, and I was exposed to a fascinating world which combined much that was familiar to me with much that was deeply strange, and disturbing.

I began to attend the meetings on a regular basis. They took place on campuses, usually of colleges in the south and east London area. Hizb ut Tahrir's strategy was to focus on places with a large population of students from Pakistani families, and this was reflected in the people attending their meetings. The majority clearly had origins in the Indian sub-continent. There was also a noticeable smattering of Afro-Caribbean and African people, and a very small number of whites. The majority of attendees were men. But there were young women, too, all wearing the hijab. The subjects of the meetings varied from international affairs — with a stress on oppression of Muslims by the "Kuffar" (unbelievers) — to more philosophical issues, in which the stern clarity of "HT" (Hizb ut Tahrir)'s brand of Islam was contrasted with the supposed moral flabbiness and decadence of the West.

I discovered a whole flourishing subculture existed around this party. There was even a sort of dialect that the activists seemed to use — a unique combination of Asian-London peppered with Arabic words and the occasional Urdu phrase — all delivered at top speed. This was the sound of emergent British Islamism.

The movement used a variety of speakers, but it was immediately obvious who the real boss-men were. There were two of them, both from the Arab world.

The first was Farid Kassim, a slim and bearded man of Syrian origin. Kassim was disabled, which for some reason seemed to add to his charisma. Although he was an Arab, he would throw in Urdu words in his speeches, to the delight of his audience, almost all of South Asian origin. The other major figure was Omar Bakri Muhammad, another former Syrian, of stockier build and with a long, prophetic black beard. Omar Bakri was a somewhat comical figure, not as impressive as Kassim. This was partly because his spoken English could be placed somewhere between Beirut and Tottenham, and sometimes veered wildly from the one to the other. Also because he had a way of working himself up into a lather, and beginning to roar and bellow when speaking on a platform. This was in contrast to other Islamist speakers, who were impressive precisely because of the air of absolute calm and serenity they projected.

So, I found myself quite liking Bakri, in spite of the strange circumstances in which we came into contact. I don't know how he would react if he knew that he was sometimes standing a few inches from an Israeli masters' degree student (and erstwhile IDF tank driver) on the many evenings in mosques and rooms in polytechnics in which he called for the destruction of Israel and the downfall of the West. But for all the slightly buffoonish aspects of Omar Bakri, there was nothing comical in the feelings he was able to inspire in his young followers.

The young men who attended the meetings, with whom I'd sometimes chat, had grown up in London, like me. It took me a while to get the measure of their thinking. Initially, I made the mistake of assuming that their anger derived from racism, and the response to it. My upbringing in the sometimes very racially-prejudiced London of the 1970s and 1980s had conditioned me to assume this.

But I was out of date. When I tried to raise this issue with them, my ideas provoked amusement. They had long ago left behind such questions. Of course the "kuffar" despised and feared the "Muslims." This was inevitable. But it was certainly not anything to get excited or upset about — it was like the noise made by children. People find all sorts of outlets for their anger, and I still think that the experience of racism is one of the reasons for the popularity and growth of groups like Hizb ut Tahrir. But the point is not only what brings people in, but also what they find once they enter, and how that goes on to shape them.

I missed their thinking because I wasn't used to seeing things through a religious mind-set, with all the changes such an attitude brings. I expected these young Islamists to be similar to nationalists in their outlook, with a thin theological layer on top. But they were not. The linking of their project, in their minds, to the creator of the universe created something quite different. It gave them a sort of patience, and an ability to take the long view on the struggle in which they were engaged.

What it also did was to remove the basis, however flimsy, for locating the common ground that existed between people claiming allegiance to projects ultimately based on ideas developed in the secular West. My uninvited attendance at Hizb ut Tahrir meetings continued throughout my year in England.

In the spring of 1996, at the entrance to SOAS, I was handed a leaflet inviting me to attend an inaugural meeting of a new group, to be held at a mosque in south-east London. The new group was called "al-Muhajiroun" (the emigrants). This name related to the earliest days of Islam, and to the small group who accompanied Mohammed from Mecca to Medina, in the early days of his mission. The group, I quickly learned was the result of a split that had taken place in Hizb ut Tahrir, between Omar Bakri and Farid Kassim. It was forming outside the framework of HT. There was a general whisper that that it was likely to be taking a more direct role in the prosecution of jihad. A Saudi dissident, Mohammed Masari,[2] was said also to be involved. The meeting was to take place on a Sunday. I decided to attend.

My attendance at the meeting began in farcical fashion when, on arriving at the mosque, I accidentally entered the women's section, and withdrew, amidst much amusement from the hijab'ed female supporters of the new movement gathered there. Hoping that none of the "brothers" had noticed, I hurried downstairs to where the main meeting was to take place.

The meeting room of the small, out of the way mosque was packed, and stuffy. There was an old, threadbare carpet. Omar Bakri was sitting near the front, and I found myself seated immediately behind him, close enough to be looking straight at his neck and his hairline, and the back of his jacket. Masari, a tall, thin, and instantly more impressive figure than Bakri, was seated at the back. After a while, the speeches began, with Omar Bakri being introduced. The speech was more openly militant than anything I had heard from Hizbut Tahrir.

There was something more Middle Eastern about it. Omar Bakri didn't spend time on any of the esoteric civil issues that I had heard sometimes at HT meetings. He didn't seem concerned with persuading his audience of the moral superiority of Islam. Rather, the speech was directed at concrete support for forces in the Middle East directly engaged in jihad. "We will be their eyes and ears here," he promised the audience, to applause. After Bakri's speech, Mohammed Masari got up and spoke from the floor for a few minutes. He was smiling as he spoke, and his style was very different. He made a few mild remarks about the process of building and establishing the movement, and sat down again.

I wonder if I was the only one watching that evening under false pretences. I think I probably was. Public awareness of the issue of the birth and growth of pro-jihadi circles in British cities at that time was non-existent. And I was just a British-Israeli graduate student with an interest in Mid-Eastern political ideologies. We were in the middle of the 1990s and in the high days of the end of history.

On the way out, a bearded young man with a red and white keffiyeh started up a conversation with me. At first, I was worried that he had spotted that I didn't belong, because he asked me how I had heard about the meeting. When I told him that I was at SOAS and had received a leaflet about it, he began to ask me some more questions about myself. I recited the usual litany about my absent Egyptian father, ignorance of Islam and growing interest in it. As we boarded the tube train together, I began to realize that my new friend wasn't suspicious of me at all. Rather, he wanted to share a warm, glowing moment of jihadi solidarity. All my statements concerning my interest in Islam were greeted with a happy "hamdulillah," delivered in that half-Arabic, half-Pakistani, all-London accent which I was rapidly coming to realize was one of the distinguishing features of the supporters of HT and its various sister organizations and split-offs.

He was a big, powerfully built young man, and what struck me most was the absolute self-confidence he had — talking in a loud voice about the kuffar and the Muslims and hamdulillah, entirely indifferent to the other passengers, who were entirely indifferent to him. They, I suppose, were convinced that this half-comic figure, with his wild beard and his keffiyeh wrapped around his head, might well have been a problem for someone, but surely had no reason to concern them. We were, after all, on a tube train in London. What possible interest could Muslim extremists have in the mundane familiarity of the London Underground rail network?

The al-Muhajiroun launch was the last jihadist meeting I went to in London. I returned to Israel in the spring of 1996, and thought little more about the episode, or my excursion into the curious London Islamist subculture of which it formed a part.

In the 2000–2004 period in Jerusalem, suicide bombings were part of everyday life. The initial shocked reaction to them turned into a kind of numbness. The bombing of the Mike's Place Bar in the summer of 2003, however, was different. It was the first evidence of the blurring of borders between the conflict between Israelis and Palestinians and the flourishing jihadi subculture in Western Europe.

On 30 April 2003, two young men of Asian appearance approached the Tel Aviv branch of Mike's Place. Their names were Omar Khan Sharif and Asif Mohammed Hanif. Each had an explosive charge strapped to the small of their back, and a hand-held detonator attached to their belt. Hanif, who was 21 years old and the bigger of the two men, tried to gain entry to the bar. A security guard, Avi Tabib, had decided that there was something suspicious in the demeanor of the two, and blocked Hanif. Hanif then detonated his explosive charge. In addition to Hanif, three people were killed in the blast. Their names were Dominique Hass, Ran Baron and Yanai Weiss. Dominique Hass was a waitress at the bar, the other two were musicians. Sixty-five other people were wounded. Tabib, whose actions undoubtedly prevented a much worse death toll, was badly wounded but survived.

Sharif attempted then to detonate his own explosive charge, but the bomb apparently failed to explode. He fled the scene, ditching the explosive belt in a bin. A manhunt for him began, and his bloated corpse washed in from the sea two weeks later. The circumstances of Sharif's death have never been made clear. Perhaps he was killed by his Palestinian colleagues for failing to carry out his mission. Or maybe the Israeli security forces did away with him. Or perhaps he simply drowned as, panic stricken, he swam out to sea in the vain hope of eluding those chasing him along the shore. Impossible to know.

The Mike's Place attack was the first suicide bombing in the context of the Israeli–Palestinian conflict to be carried out by non-Palestinians, and non-Arabs. Asif Mohammed Hanif and Omar Khan Sharif were British-born Islamists of Pakistani origin. And Sharif, the older of the two, had received his introduction into Islamism while a student at Kings College in London in 1994. He had been a close associate of Hizb ut Tahrir. It became clear from reports that surfaced in the weeks following the attack at Mike's Place that Omar Khan Sharif was one of the people who had followed Omar Bakri into al-Muhajiroun. Sharif was a native of Derby, and the son of a relatively prosperous, self-made Pakistani-born businessman.

He had remained in close contact with Omar Bakri, and had been seen giving out leaflets for al-Muhajiroun on the streets of his native Derby just two weeks before the Mike's Place bombing. He was also a regular attendee at lectures and talks given by Bakri in Derby. The last one he attended took place on 14 April, just two weeks before the attack. Bakri, of course, was quick to deny any organizational link with the Mike's Place bombing. He admitted to knowing both men. Sharif, he noted, had studied at a movement school, taking a course on Sharia law. But he denied any prior knowledge of their plans.[3]

Omar Bakri was probably telling the truth. Hamas claimed responsibility for the bombing. It is highly unlikely that Bakri and al-Muhajiroun possessed the ability to bring explosives and detonators into Israel.

But this isn't really the point. Bakri and those around him in London in the 1990s had taken ideas generated in the Middle East, and British laxity and complacency had allowed them to spread these ideas in quiet corners, undisturbed, throughout the years of plenty of the 1990s. The result was the creation of the people of whom Omar Khan Sharif was the first example. These were people who returned to the place from which the ideas that had inspired them had come — now as fully-fledged participants in the jihad.

The mechanics of Sharif and Hanif's odyssey from Omar Bakri's lectures to the Tel Aviv beachfront were in themselves fascinating and illuminating. They arrived in Israel from Jordan, via the Allenby Bridge, using their British passports. They then traveled down to Gaza, where presumably they met with their Hamas contacts.

They entered Gaza in the company of an unwitting journalist, whom they had befriended. The two also attended a memorial event for Rachel Corrie, the American pro-Palestinian activist crushed beneath an Israeli bulldozer a year before the Mike's Place bombing. They left Gaza in the company of their journalist friend. None of the various human rights activists and others with whom Sharif and Hanif were in contact during their time in the West Bank and Gaza volunteered any information after the bombing.

The saddest and strangest aspect of the whole affair, for me, was the very great similarity, in so many ways, between the backgrounds of the perpetrators, victims, and unwitting helpers in this bombing. All were products of the West, and of the open society. All were beneficiaries of its abundance and possibilities. Yet, when Omar Khan Sharif of Derby and Asif Hanif from Hounslow approached Mike's Place bar at the beachfront they didn't see an innocuous place of entertainment, filled with Westerners, culturally similar to themselves. They saw "kuffar," who had forfeited their right to live. Thus, did two British men kill Dominique Hass, a Jewish immigrant from Paris, along with some Israeli blues musicians.

Someone had created those feelings and responses.

A year after the bombing, Hamas released a video of Sharif and Hanif, taken in a flat in Gaza shortly before the Mike's Place bombing.

In it, the two men resemble Hamas men in every way. They are holding M-16 rifles, laughing and joking, bearded, with green and white headbands wrapped around their heads. They are speaking a mixture of Arabic and English. The phrases are very familiar. They are the usual slogans of the suicide bombers' videos that spread like a virus in those years. But the two are speaking in that other accent, that I remembered from the mosques and meeting places of HT and al-Muhajiroun. That same unique London-Pakistani-Arabic mixture that was their vernacular of choice.

Once, some years after the Mike's Place bombing, I happened to walk past the small hostel at Hayarkon 48 where I knew that Sharif and Hanif had spent the night before the bombing. It is a cheap but orderly place, catering in the main for transient young travelers. Hanif and Sharif were able to blend in easily among this most open of publics. Their English accents placed them immediately in context. There are stone steps that smell of floor cleaning fluid, mixed with the aroma of the salt coming in from the sea. Tel Aviv is all around. A sensuous, physical city, like others up and down the Mediterranean coast. The Mike's Place bar on the beachfront is a few minutes' walk away. Sharif and Hanif's guilt is their own. The waste is their own. But the production line in poisoned minds that Farid Kassem and Omar Bakri were running in London in the 1990s, under the indifferent noses of the authorities, also has its share in the responsibility.

There were others who chose a different destination: namely, to take the jihad into the very heart of the lands of the "kuffar" themselves. Their most infamous and paradigm-changing deed was the suicide hijackings of 9/11. And they struck again in London on 7 July 2005.

There is a direct connection between the July 2005 bombings in London, and the Mike's Place bombing in 2003. Mohammed Sidique Khan, the ringleader of the group that committed the 7/7 bombings, knew both Asif Mohammed Hanif and Omar Khan Sharif. He is thought to have been linked to the same British jihadi cell as them, though few in-depth details of this cell have reached the public eye.

A Manchester businessman, Kursheed Fiaz, later related how he met all three men, together, in 2001, as they sought to recruit young British Muslims for training in Afghanistan.[4] There is also a common al-Muhajiroun link. Sidique Khan and Shezhad Tanweer, another of the 7/7 bombers, were both members of the organization. It was through his links to the organization that Sidique Khan was drawn into the jihad, staying at the offices established by al-Muhajiroun in Lahore, Pakistan, before going on to train at the Malakand training camp in the North West frontier.

The circles of al-Muhajiroun in London have provided many of the other well-known names of the British Muslim contribution to the jihad, including Richard Reid, the "shoe bomber," and the five man cell led by Omar Khyam that planned a bombing campaign in London in 2007, but were caught before they could begin work.[5]

7/7 was a further example of the process whereby Middle Eastern political ideas and processes have broken beyond their geographic constraints. Suicide bombing by Islamists is an invention of the Middle East. It is the spreading of Middle Eastern ideas and practices to places far from the region that underlies the terror attacks in the heart of Western cities of the last years.

This grim fact was perhaps best encapsulated in the sight of the red London bus at Tavistock Square, blown apart and reduced to a metal skeleton in a manner familiar from dozens of Israeli buses in the preceding decade.

Among the people killed on bus 70 on 7 July 2005 was a woman from Jerusalem whose name was Anat Rosenberg. I knew Anat in Israel in the late 1990s, before she left for London, and for me her story completes the circle that began with the Islamist agitation in London in that decade, and continued with the beginnings of British Islamist involvement in the hottest fronts of the jihad.

Like Omar Khan Sharif and Asif Mohammed Hanif, Anat Rosenberg traveled between center and periphery — between a place of strife and premature death, and a land of plenty. Unlike them, hers was an eminently sane journey, in the opposite direction from theirs — away from violence and suffering and in search of meaning and beauty.

I met Anat — the symmetry is odd, I know — in the Jerusalem branch of Mike's Place in 1997. It was about 1 in the morning. I was a little the worse for wear. Anat came in with a friend of hers. She liked me because I was from London. For Anat, Britain represented most of the things she was looking for: irony, and art, and blessed privacy. A chance to live in a place not weighed down with history and ancient dust. A place where one could make one's own private search, unmolested by huge and intrusive ideas.

We saw each other a few times after that. We used to meet in the bar of the Jerusalem Cinematheque, sometimes just the two of us, sometimes with other friends. Anat was a dizzy, loquacious, immensely warm person. We were friends for a couple of years. We lost contact after she fulfilled her ambition and moved to London in 1999, I guess. In the weeks before she left, she began shyly to ask her friends to call her "Annette."

She sent me her contact details when she arrived in the UK, but we lost touch. I would never have seen her again, I suppose, were it not for Hasib Hussein and his bomb bringing us back together on 7 July 2005. I remember when the news of the attack began to come through on the internet. I was working in my apartment in Jerusalem, and I began to call family and friends in London to make sure that they were okay. This was a familiar ritual in Israel in the days of the suicide bombings. It was strange to be doing it in reverse.

None of my immediate family was in the area. Later in the day, on the BBC website there appeared the names of some people who were missing, and who the authorities feared might have been caught up in the bombing. One of the names was a woman called Anat Rosenberg.

The sight made me start and pause. But of course, it was possible that there was more than one person of that name. Then, a few hours later, a picture appeared on the website. This ended all doubt. It was Anat. A few years older, to be sure, but unmistakably herself. Her black, shiny, straight, bobbed hair and angular face and porcelain pale skin.

I knew, again from the experiences of Jerusalem, what it meant when they weren't sure if a person had been caught in the bombing or not. It meant that they had discovered remains that were too badly damaged to be identified, and there was a person who had not yet made contact with their partner or family. So they were waiting, to see if the person made contact. Or if they were never going to make contact again, because they were already found.

The media took a great interest in her story. They saw an irony in it: Israeli woman leaves her homeland because of suicide bombings, only to be killed in a bus bombing in Tavistock Square in London. This representation was simplistic, however, and not entirely accurate.

Anat had decided to leave Israel already before the bombings began. I'm sure she was afraid of bombings, but this wasn't the only, or the central issue. She wanted to live with the constant presence of art and dance and music in her life. She wanted to distance herself from communities and history and religion, and live in a city of individuals. Jerusalem is never quite like that. So she left in search of it. From communalized Jerusalem weighed down with identity and grudges, to atomized, post-modern London, where a person may make an untroubled and private journey.

They brought her back to Jerusalem to bury her. It was high summer, blazing July sun. I was in the army reserves at the time, stationed near the village of Beit Sahour. The country was roiling with discontent in the weeks leading up to the disengagement from Gaza. They gave me leave to go to the funeral, which took place at the graveyard in Givat Shaul.

The funeral was a quiet and restrained affair. I was exhausted, my bones aching from practicing section attacks in the ground around Lachish. They had wrapped Anat in a black velvet shroud with golden Hebrew lettering. She was on the stretcher with which they bring you to burial in Israel. A Sephardi Rabbi spoke. He tried to make of Anat's very free life something which could respectably be discussed in a religious setting. Then the Israeli journalist Yoni Ben-Menachem, who was a cousin of Anat's, delivered a eulogy, with a sort of precise, controlled fury. Then a relative read a little poem. I remember the short, stocky bodies of Anat's relatives, as they carried her on the stretcher. Where were all the people with whom we had sat around bar-room tables in our summer years in the 1990s? Absent. An old crowd of tired family members, roasting beneath the sun.

On the way back, I traveled in a taxi with an Arab driver in his fifties. He asked me if this life that our Jerusalem had been living in the last few years was worthy of the name. I told him I was coming from the funeral of a friend killed in a terrorist attack in London. He expressed his regrets. He was a religious man, a Muslim, and he said that everything was in the hands of God. Everything came from God, and therefore had to be accepted. We shook hands as he dropped me off back in the center of town.

Anat Rosenberg's death completes the pattern. The floating of ideas, detached from their original context, into new areas with unpredictable results. Middle Eastern dissident Islamists make their homes in a Western country. They make contact with local disaffected young people of a relevant cultural background. Some of the most committed of those young people travel to the places where the ideas that had inspired them sprang from.

The young men discussed here had no personal, biographical stake in the war in which they involved themselves. But thanks to the preaching of Omar Bakri and his friends, they had become convinced that the body to which they owed allegiance was the Islamic "Umma," the totality of the world's Muslims, imagined as a single people. This new loyalty proved enough to cancel out both any allegiance they might have had to the land of their birth (the UK), and any cultural connection to the more moderate Islam which their parents had brought with them from Pakistan.

Mohammed Sidique Khan, Hasib Hussein and their friends of 7 July 2005 represent an arrow traveling in another direction. They were part of the same "school" as Sharif and Hanif — the al-Muhajiroun organization. They traveled from their homes in Europe on behalf of the jihad too. In their case, the traveling was to the Malakand training camp, in Pakistan. And of course, they chose to put their training into practice in the heart of one of the lands of unbelief. The more modest journey of my friend Anat, who wanted to live in the land of tolerance and privacy, was interrupted through collision with this larger process, and was ended forever.

All this is very much of the world that has come into being since the collapse of communism brought the twentieth century to an early end. The true contours of this new reality are still only now emerging. One of the very characteristic aspects is the collapse of the power of states to control information, and hence to shape the minds of citizens. Propaganda films from the Cold War seem to belong to an ancient time now. What appears chiefly archaic about them is the idea that alternative sources of information for people could so easily be prevented from existing — and the state could with such ease create a kind of sound-proof aquarium effect, within which its citizens could be shaped. That idea was once the epitome of sinister dystopia. Now it seems like absurd anachronism. We all, at least all of us in the West, can cross state borders with graceful ease, without even leaving our desks.

This possibility, in the 1990s, was assumed to be leading to greater understanding between people. And to some degree, it has done. People like Anat Rosenberg — with their broad cultural horizons, and their picking and choosing of items of allegiance — are made possible by it. What it has also done is to create the possibility of trans-state and trans-national communities, some benign, some virtuous, and some very evil. The international networks of the jihad are one of the products of this process — though their existence has also been made possible by imaginative failure and complacency on the part of Western governments.

In the international subculture of the jihad, the conflict between Israel and the Arabs is seen as a straightforward fight of good against evil. The religious case against Israel — namely, that it represents the unacceptable situation of a once Muslim land falling back under the control of the "kuffar" — is seamlessly intertwined with a broader, leftist or third world-ist case, according to which Israel constitutes an unjust imposition by the West of a "settler state" on a part of the Middle East.

The latter idea was a staple of the Arab argument against Israel in the first decades of the conflict. It never disappeared. But in the time of the growing Islamization of the politics of the Arabic-speaking world, it has returned with increased power. It is an idea that, as we have seen, is not connected to any particular political context, nor can it be appeased or compromised with at the point of its ascent.

The last years have witnessed a broader combining of Islamist ideas with those of other radicals in the West. Britain, France and Belgium have seen attempts to create joint far left-Islamist political parties, with limited success. The movements against the Iraq war offered a further example of the process. The Stop the War movement in Britain, for example, was created jointly by the Muslim Association of Britain, and the Trotskyist Socialist Workers Party. The former was a front organization for the Muslim Brotherhood, and included Hamas men among its senior officials.

The extreme, later murderous, sects that I stumbled across in mid-1990s London represented only one, particularly radical, stream in burgeoning British and European Islamism. There are more sophisticated trends that would deride al-Muhajiroun and Hizb ut Tahrir as primitive and simplistic, and that would not support terror attacks in Europe (though most would support them in Israel). Al-Muhajiroun is now a banned organization in Britain. Omar Bakri has been deported to Lebanon, and is active among radical Sunni Islamists in the Lebanese city of Tripoli.

But the alliance of radical Islam and the radical left in Europe and the United States has become a permanent and accepted part of the political landscape. The Palestinian cause is, of course, central to Islamists, and is of great importance for the radical left. As a result, unsurprisingly, solidarity on this issue is one of the central meeting points between these two very different political/cultural systems.

However, very noticeably, what is happening is that it is the Islamist conceptions that are "winning" in the encounter, and that are gaining acceptability, first among the more radical leftist circles, and then on a broader stage.

The Islamists bring a cultural authenticity and willingness for violence that thrill many on the European far left, who have been rather homeless since 1989. The mobilizations in European capitals at the time of the Lebanon War of 2006, and Israel's Gaza operation in late 2008, demonstrated the extent to which the Palestinian issue had become the central symbolic meeting point for these two unlikely bedfellows. Somehow, the centrality of this cause enables leftists and feminists to feel comfortable marching alongside Islamists who believe in the death penalty for adultery, and the legal inferiority of women.

It is the Islamists who have the vivid, exciting ideas. Their allies are drawn along beside them. The result of this coming together is that traditionally fringe and radical "solutions" to the conflict between Israel and its enemies are now becoming more mainstream in the West.

Islamism supports a version of what would nowadays be called the "one state solution" to the conflict. This term is a euphemism for proposed solutions that include the nullification of the Jewish right to self-determination, and the consequent disappearance of the Jewish state. The European and American far left supported a different version of the same basic idea in the 1960s and 1970s. For a long period, this notion seemed to have faded into history, rendered impractical by the self-evidence of Israel's existence and apparent viability. This is now changing. This slogan is the means by which Western leftists are able to rationalize their support for the disappearance of Israel. Of course, in the Western left, this slogan comes wrapped in the packaging of opposition to ethnic nationalism in all its forms. It is noticeable, however, that the particular ethnic nationalism whose disappearance is deemed most urgent is that of Israel and the Jews.

As Islamist movements rise in prominence in the conflict in the Middle East, so it is their conceptions and proposed solutions that are coming to occupy a more and more prominent place among their cohort of supporters in the West. Among those Western supporters are a large complement of locally-born Islamists, who are in any case in favor of a more radical approach.

It is not only the proposed solution that is changing. The paranoid, conspiracy-laden world of Middle Eastern politics has also found a home among these circles. The alliance of the radical left and Islamism on the national stage remains a negligible force. But in media, civil society organizations and the universities, the curious, hybrid outlook that characterizes it has gained prominence.

This is the strange nexus in which Israel is transformed from a small people and a medium sized Middle Eastern power into a nefarious presence at the root of everything. That peculiar Middle Eastern style in which everything has a hidden answer, unseen forces control the puppet strings of governments and a vast, Jewish-led conspiracy is the real power in human affairs is surely familiar to anyone who has spent any time in a Middle Eastern capital, discussing international affairs with local students and intellectuals. It has now found its way to pockets of the West.

At the most extreme end, in which commitment to the jihad shades into the fire and smoke of involvement in active violence, are the Islamist sectarians of al-Muhajiroun and their like. Here are Omar Khan Sharif and Mohammed Sidique Khan, and the others, primed by Mid-Eastern ideologues, then taught their trade in remote and dusty training camps.

On the other extreme, tapering gradually into the mainstream assumptions of society, are voices that have adopted the Middle Eastern view of the utter centrality and unique nature of the Israeli-Palestinian conflict, and the accompanying, increasingly mainstream view that the conflict can only be solved with the disappearance of Jewish sovereignty. And beyond these, supposedly of no camp, are the people who believe that for social stability and peace, compromises will have to be made with those described here, their "anger" understood and met half way, their "resistance" acknowledged.

All this has resulted in the peculiarly exalted place that the conflict now has in the political consciousness of the West. Other disputes may claim vastly more lives, and may involve suffering on a much larger scale, but, as if by osmosis, many in the West have imbibed the view, prevalent in the Middle East, that Israel's actions against the Palestinians occupy some other category, some uniquely nefarious evil — regardless of statistics of lives lost and levels of suffering that suggest that this is not the case. This, combined with the breaking down of neat geographical boundaries, and the absence of any viable competing radical ideology has allowed old ideas to undergo a strange rebirth and has led the conflict, in both words and deeds, to break its banks and spread across state borders.

The movement of ideas deriving from radical Islam into the mainstream debate is not a process that has happened unaided. In this regard, the bombers and the small, noisy organizations from which they emerged are only the visible tip of the iceberg. Moving along beneath the water line are larger, supposedly more "moderate" groups. These groups, some of whom proclaim their opposition to the "extremists," are having an equally profound effect on the public debate in many Western countries. Shifting Western policy on Israel is one of their concerns. Organizations associated with the international Muslim Brotherhood group have proved the most effective in this task.

Since Britain is the example I have focused on until now, it is worth completing the picture. The UK today plays host to a number of extreme examples of phenomena observable in other Western countries. In Britain, a combination of fear deriving from the bombings of 2005 and a consequent desire to appease the resident Muslim community have created a space in which radical Islamists have been able to begin to exert an influence on policy.

The bombers and those Islamists who profess opposition to them in fact play a complementary role. The bombers succeed in creating fear. The "moderate" Islamists promise to assuage this fear. The result has been that in the first years of the twentieth century, supporters of Islamist positions — on Israel and the Jews, certainly, but also on other issues — came closer to the centers of policymaking in Britain than at any time in the past.

The policy of the British Foreign and Commonwealth Office, as revealed in a series of documents leaked by an FCO official, Derek Pasquill, in 2006, was to deliberately court non-violent Islamists. It was thought that they would offer a counterweight to the men of violence. What was missed was that the violent Islamists and the non-violent ones differed on tactics. Their ultimate goal of the creation of an Islamic state that would implement Sharia law, however, was the same. So the British policy achieved precisely the opposite of its intention. It intended to marginalize the extreme Islamists by cultivating the "moderate" ones. What it succeeded in doing was to admit into the realm of mainstream debate individuals and organizations no less opposed to the West than were the bombers.

Organizations such as the Muslim Association of Britain purported to represent the interests and points of view of British Muslims as a whole. In reality, they were founded by activists of the Muslim Brotherhood and in at least one case Hamas (Mohammed Sawalha),[6] and followed that movement's agenda of a slow, patient transformation of society in the direction of Islam.

The British government appointed civil servants who were themselves Islamists. These included one Mockbul Ali, who headed a group in the Foreign Office called the "Engaging with the Muslim World Group." In this capacity, Ali promoted connections between the British government and some of the Middle East's most well-known Islamist figures. He encouraged relations with such figures as Sheikh Yusuf Qaradawi of Egypt and the Bangladeshi Islamist Delwar Hossain Sayeedi, both of whom have condoned violence.[7] The Director of the UK's Crown Prosecution Service appointed a known Islamist, Azad Ali, to sit on a "community involvement" panel advising him on incitement to religious and racial hatred. Ali had written in praise of Anwar al-Awliki, an al-Qaeda aligned radical Islamist preacher based in Yemen.[8]

Some of the sentiments and positions revealed in the documents leaked by Derek Pasquill have a near surreal nature (it's not so comic when one remembers that Pasquill was fired and ruined as a result of his revelations.) One official suggests "channelling aid resources" through Islamist organizations in the Middle East, because they are known to be less corrupt than their secular counterparts. Another notes that engagement with the Egyptian Muslim Brotherhood "may help in discouraging radicalization." A third, a senior intelligence official at the British Foreign Office, is to be found in a letter leaked by Pasquill advocating the covert promotion by the Foreign Office of anti-Western but non-terrorist messages to "potential recruits to terrorism."[9]

The idea common to all these statements, and the wider policy of which they are a part, is that there is an easy and obvious division between the violent men at the outer edge of the Islamist world, and all the other inhabitants of it. But no such division exists. The key danger of Islamism is not only the near term use of explosive devices — devastating though this can be. Rather, the danger is that Islamist thinking is by its very nature militantly anti-Western. Where it is allowed to grow, strife will therefore inevitably follow. This may be seen in Hamas-controlled Gaza, in Hizballah-dominated Lebanon, in Iran, increasingly in Turkey. The instinct to appease, to engage with the less obviously terrible adherents of it will serve only to pile up problems for the future. It will also produce, as it has produced in the British case, policy choices which would be ludicrous if they did not contain within them the seeds of tragedy. The British experience offers a salutary warning to other Western countries.

The result of all this has been to make the battle for public opinion, and thence political influence and power in the West, into a key front of the Israel-Islamist conflict. During the period of the Cold War, Israel could confidently assume a modicum of understanding in similarly democratic Western countries, faced with similarly autocratic enemies. In its current strategic assessments, the country can make no such easy assumptions. The Islamists have made alliances and sunk roots deep into the mainstream of Western societies. Their project goes beyond Israel, of course. But the demise of the Jewish state is a key way station for them on the road to success.

So, Omar Khan Sharif and Asif Mohammed Hanif, Hamas suicide bombers from England, were the first. But they weren't the last. Between Hayarkon 48 and the Mike's Place bar, they announced the arrival of a type of war that refused to fit in with the convenient categories of the past. A war of armed ideas and symbols, limited not by citizenship, nor geography, nor state authority, nor divisions between political and military activity.

The tragic fate of Anat Rosenberg seems to me to epitomize the transformation. Isn't it meant to be about land, real estate? Then shouldn't there be a front line that one might retreat from? But it is no longer easy to locate the front line. It shifts and may yet find you even when you think you have escaped it. Fighting such a war required a radical re-think as to the meaning of that word. It meant introducing into the frame of conflict such issues as the domestic political culture of other countries and the outlook and level of fortitude of one's own civilian population.

It suggested the frightening prospect of a war of society against society, rather than state against state. Igniting such a war was certainly the aim of many of the Islamists, who believe that this will be their road to success. The first example of what all this could mean for the shape of the conflict between Israel and Islamism took place in Lebanon, in the summer months of 2006.

Notes

1. Dhiren Barot (Esa al Hindi), *The Army of Madinah in Kashmir*, Maktabah al Ansar Publications, 1999.
2. Masari, a former physics professor, set up the "Committee for the Defense of Legitimate Rights," in London. He was later found to be in contact with senior figures in al-Qaeda.
3. Shiv Malik, "Profile: Omar Sharif," *New Statesman*, 24 April 2006.
4. Shiv Malik, "My brother the bomber," *Prospect Magazine*, 30 June 2007.
5. Jamie Doward and Andrew Wander, "Is the Islamist group al-Muhajiroun waiting to strike again?" *The Observer*, 6 May 2007.
6. "Faith, Hate and Charity — Transcript," BBC Website, 1 August 2006. http://news.bbc.co.uk/2/hi/programmes/panorama/5234586.stm Accessed: 17.5.10.
7. Derek Pasquill, "I had no choice but to leak," *New Statesman*, 17 January 2008.
8. Duncan Gardham, "Controversial Islamist advises Crown Prosecution Service," *Daily Telegraph*, 1 November 2009.
9. Nick Cohen, "The High Price of Patriotism," *Standpoint*, November 2009.

CHAPTER 7

A Grave Missed Opportunity

The Lebanon War, 2006. Israel performed poorly. Failure, as is well-known, is an orphan. For this reason, the war has largely been rubbed from the Israeli public consciousness, to be discussed only when absolutely necessary. This is wrong, because the wounded and the veterans don't have the luxury of forgetfulness. But it is doubly wrong because the war is full of lessons, which can only be located through a long and unsparing process of reflection. I want to consider some of these.

But let me first of all continue my own story of the war. Taken up from the hour we crossed the border for the first time.[1]

After we closed the hatches of the tanks and crossed the border line, it took a while, down a silent descent, until we were in the first fields of southern Lebanon. We were heading towards el Khiam ridge. Itzik said the traveler's prayer through the intercom as we entered. Darkness and silence all around us.

Our mission was supposed to last three days, and to leave us deployed north of el Khiam and Marjayoun. The Syrians had made

165

clear that if Israeli forces in the eastern sector advanced beyond a certain point, this could be seen as a reason for war. But the open areas north of the two towns had been put to good use by the Katyusha missile teams, so we were going to try and capture the ground north of the two towns and make it harder for Hizballah to operate there.

We weren't thinking about any of that at the time, though. There were more immediate issues. Once we got started I didn't remember the mines anymore. Being rocky and hilly, south Lebanon is not ideal country for armor. And maneuvering tanks at night is an imprecise business at the best of times. So, my main concern was not getting lost and separated from the rest of the company. The summer night was clear and I had to make sure that the platoon commander's tank, somewhere in front of us, was still visible. It wasn't a matter of sentiment. The Hizballah anti-tank teams didn't operate at night, we were told. But it wouldn't have been a sensible idea to have been driving around alone in a Merkava 3 on that night.

The unit had its first contact on the streets of Marjayoun. The brigade commander's tank was hit with an RPG 29. No one was wounded. The people doing the firing weren't from Hizballah. They were the local branch of the SSNP, a strange, Syrian nationalist grouping with clan loyalties in parts of south Lebanon. The tanks returned fire and the RPG team were killed.

The hours passed. All round el Khiam, things were quieter than we expected. Our job wasn't to enter the town. We circled around it, firing at certain, selected targets. There was a fire spreading in the fields, set off, I suppose, by a stray Israeli shell. As the hours went by, I began to feel sleepy, the fire in my left periscope, the green of the night vision, and the earphones pressing in my ears. I was drinking as much water as I could, but after a while, a kind of disconnected, other worldly feeling began to descend. The fire burning in my left periscope, and the helmet pressing in on my ears. I was keeping the little symbol of the platoon commander's tank somewhere just in front, but not too close.

Things began to go wrong shortly before first light. We got the order to move out, back in the direction of Israel, about an hour before the dawn. We were seven kilometers north of the border, and this would have been ample time. But then, we received word that the company commander's tank had developed a problem with its steering mechanism, and couldn't move. We maneuvered toward where he was waiting, in an olive field.

The light had begun slowly to come up. First of all, a sort of dirty bluish gray replaced the clear black and silver of the night. But this wouldn't last long. Within an hour or so it would be broad daylight. This was the time when all sensible armored units would be well under cover for the day. It was the time when the Hizballah anti-tank crews, who were waiting in Iranian-built bunkers through the night, would begin their morning's work. We were very far from being under cover. Someone had decided that we should try to drag the disabled tank back across the border using cables.

Towing a tank is a laborious, slow business. It limits speed to about 5 km/h, and we had at most just under an hour of something resembling darkness left.

I remembered that I had read somewhere that when an airliner crashes, it's usually not because of one mistake, but rather because of the unfortunate piling of error upon error. Some little ghost of a thought crossed my mind that perhaps we would not make it back across the border.

For some reason, the thought did not induce anything like panic. Rather, I felt a kind of mild and neutral surprise, combined with a sort of curiosity as to how things would turn out. The sense of being somehow not connected with what was going on — it's a sort of defense mechanism, I suppose, whereby the mind deludes itself that the chances of its imminent extinction are an illusion, in order to enable the system to function.

We got the cables strapped on, and began the slow, painful journey back. After about half an hour, the light was getting stronger. We were still five kilometers north of the border. I had hoped to steal across with the night vision still on, but that was clearly now impossible. This presented a dilemma.

We were trying to get back to Israel through the valley between el Khiam and Marjayoun. El Khiam, though we didn't know it at the time, had not been taken by the infantry, so it was still bristling with its 300 Hizballah men, which meant that we were making something similar to a suicide run in the broad daylight, at snail's pace.

But there was something worse. I had miscalculated, and thought I could make it across the border before the sun came up. But it was now broad daylight, which meant that with the night vision still on, we were almost blind. So, I now had to ask the whole convoy to stop, while I performed the fiddly and uncomfortable task of changing the night vision equipment for the regular periscope.

Here's why this matters. The last time we had taken part in a full-scale armored exercise before the war of 2006, was in 2002. The time before that was 1999 which meant that we had been on tanks once in the seven years prior to the war, which meant that performing minor but important drills, very quickly, and with the distinct possibility that an anti-tank missile team was getting into position in the hills above was not a very pleasant prospect.

It meant that my miscalculation was holding seven other men in a position of forming a perfect daylight target. So with mad speed I began changing the night vision. Sometimes the damn things don't close properly, and you have to start all over again. I was praying that this wouldn't happen, and that I wouldn't fumble it. And it worked. I clicked the last two clips into place, and we started moving again. But we were still miles from the border, way down in the valley, the sun coming up.

The dragging process was an excruciating, draining business, with the two tanks bumping and lurching against one another. It was Alon Smoha in the driver's compartment of the other one. The rising sun above, snail's pace, and we were bobbing along like a procession of ducks way down in the valley. Obvious disaster.

Both the tanks were sending out as much smoke as we could manage, in the hope that it would confuse the enemy. That was what they had told us before we went in. Keep moving and lots of smoke, to make it harder for them to aim.

Then an unfamiliar, girl's voice came through the external

communication. She said that the brigade had information that within ten minutes, we would come under missile attack.

It was broad daylight. Still too far from the north of the border. The Hizballah men had seen out the night and were going to work. This wouldn't have mattered if we'd covered the necessary ground in time to beat the dawn. But we hadn't. There was nothing much we could do except keep going, at an excruciatingly slow pace, and hope. We were dragging the tank from a reverse position, so I was looking at the company commander's vehicle in front of me.

Then there was an almighty crash into the tank we were dragging, and flame was coming out of the engine grille. The crash confused us for a moment, because it sounded similar to the sound that a tank makes when it is firing off a shell.

I heard the company commander shouting "Missiles, missiles," through the radio, which left no more room for doubt. Calm, I don't know why but still with absolute calm, it occurred to me with the same mild surprise that very possibly I wasn't going to be getting back across the border.

Then, suddenly, a similar crash and jolt sending shudders all across our own vehicle and I had no brakes left. Tried to brake, couldn't, nothing left. We coasted along for a few meters and came to a halt.

Everything was quiet. Peaceful, for a moment. After the engine running in our ears for 12 hours straight, suddenly complete silence. We could have been flying in a glider. But the internal radio was working, and I heard the order to get out of our dead tank, which had just caught a Kornet missile in the engine, and which was about to turn into a death trap. The engine would go up in flames, and the flames would spread to the turret, and begin setting off ammunition. There wasn't much time. The strange, silent moment was death making itself seem peaceful and welcoming. But we tore through it.

I grabbed my rifle and an ammunition clip, and pushed back the driver's chair, crawling into the turret area. The boys were waiting there, and Itzik opened up the back door. We were fairly calm, through the whole thing. The fact was that though we didn't think about it at the time, we had already been very lucky.

The anti-tank team had known what they were doing, and had aimed carefully. The missiles they had fired were aimed at the front part of the tank, that is, at the engine, with the intention of immobilizing it. It's also possible that they knew how to read Hebrew tank markings, because they'd fired first at the company commander's vehicle, then at ours.

What happened in most of the cases in the war where tank crews were burnt alive in their machines was that after the first missile immobilized the tank, the anti-tank crew fired additional rounds into the body of the vehicle, destroying anything within. But in our case, for whatever reason, they didn't. So we got out — into a lush cornfield, the plants coming up to our knees.

Itzik, our loader, is the formerly Ultra-Orthodox son of a prominent Jerusalem rabbi. He told me later that some of the leading rabbis of Jerusalem were praying for us that night, at the request of his father. It's as good an explanation as any other, I suppose.

There were mortar rounds landing all around. Dangerously close. Maoz spotted an irrigation ditch close by, and shouted for us to take cover there. We sprinted for the ditch and into it. Up to our knees in muddy water, we splashed and sloshed our way along it, through grass and thorns. Behind us, we saw the company commander's crew also making for the ditch. But one man was on a stretcher, jolting and motionless, and even though I could only see his boots, I knew he was dead. Someone shouted "the company commander's dead," and I thought for a moment of that thin youth, in his mid-twenties, who had only recently taken over and who had now been killed.

But, then I saw him entering the ditch, and had to re-adjust again. So it wasn't him. But who was it then? Who was the dead man? With a round chambered in the rifle, I peered up to have a look. It was Alon Smoha on the stretcher, lying on his front, with a very deep wound in his right side. He wasn't burnt or blackened. His feet were crossed over one another. The missile itself must have torn into him.

My main worry, as I stared out across the ditch, was that the Hizballah in el Khiam would now send down a squad to have a look at the handiwork of the missile team. I strained my ears to hear the sound of Arabic voices, or the crackle of footsteps. That would be the beginning of the final bloody act. There would be a firefight, and I imagined my own body crashing back into the muddy water. I looked down at the rifle, and imagined a bearded Arab face coming over the edge of the ditch. Would I give him a bullet between the eyes? We would see.

Yuval had a communications radio with him, and he tried to radio in, but there was no signal. Yet more wonderful news. "So call with a cell phone," I said to him. We had been ordered to hand our cell phones in prior to the operation to discourage idle chat. For some reason, I had decided to ignore this order, and had turned my phone off and put it in my pocket. Now, this looked like a wise decision. I took the little blue thing out of my pocket and, again with the sort of mild, half-amused curiosity that had taken hold of me since we had entered into this mess, I pressed the button to turn it on, wondering if we were close enough to the border to pick up an Israeli signal.

After a few moments, the thing gave out its little optimistic chime, as it bleeped into life. Something utterly absurd about the scene. Seven men up to their knees in water in a ditch, with their dead comrade lying next to them, rifles in our hands, our faces black with dirt and sweat. And the little chime of the cell phone, with its bland mass-produced electronic optimism.

When I looked up, I saw that Yuval had brought his cell-phone along too, so I wasn't the only one. He called in, and got an answer. "Udi," we heard him say, and then he began to explain our situation to the logistics company commander. I learned later that they'd assumed that we were dead or had been kidnapped. When he finished, he explained that they were onto the situation and would be coming for us.

Not in any great hurry, however, we were thinking as the half hour mark passed. I had always imagined that if soldiers were lost in the field, complex, efficient systems, perhaps involving the air force, would spring into life. Instead, we crouched in the ditch, and waited. Either the Hizballah or our own guys were going to find us. But then maybe we were too close to the border for them to try it. I hoped so. I had stupidly, in my haste to get out of the tank before it caught another missile, taken only one ammo clip, instead of my full webbing.

I looked down at the water, and noticed that it was full of tadpoles. Strange to see them flitting easily in the murky swamp. All quite indifferent. And the body of Alon Smoha lying at the edge of the ditch.

We all accepted the death, at that moment, with complete matter of factness. Different thoughts would come later. But I suppose there were old evolutionary systems in us which stopped any further reaction at the time. The fact was that we were still in a context of extreme danger from a military point of view. The battle wasn't over yet, and so the distance between living men and dead ones was much narrower and more flimsy than we most of the time persuade ourselves that it is.

Then we heard a loud crack from where the tanks were. This was it. The Hizballah were here. I strained my ears in the absolute silence for a moment; another crack. But someone announced after a long moment that it was only the pop of ammunition cooking up and going off, as the two tanks went up in flames. More time passed. The moths and the tadpoles, the filthy water, the rifle, with a round in the chamber, heavy in my hands.

Itzik was standing next to me, muttering what sounded like a prayer to himself. Amiram, our gunner, had placed himself out of the ditch, to improve his visibility. The two surviving members of Yuval's crew, who had extricated Alon's body from the driver's compartment in which he had been killed, were standing further down. Both of them were quite silent.

I looked at my watch. Forty minutes had passed since we had entered the ditch. Where the hell were they? Had they forgotten us? We couldn't hear any artillery, or anything from the air.

After 50 minutes, we heard the rumble of tanks in the distance, and machine gun fire and shells. It looked like they were laying down a carpet of fire on el Khiam and its 300 Hizballah men, which was thoughtful. Once again, the look of everything changed. It meant there was a chance, after all, that we might get out of this. But the tanks were very far off. It would take some minutes before they reached us.

I strained everything in my heart willing them to get a move on.

Then suddenly, much closer, and out of nowhere, a different sound. And someone shouted, "It's a Puma, it's the engineers." We all scrambled over the ditch and, there, like manna from heaven, was a Puma armored vehicle of the engineers, with a frantic soldier motioning us to get in fast. I began to make for the Puma. But then Maoz called me back, and I realized that they needed to bring the stretcher and the body of Smoha over the ditch. I ran back, jumped into the ditch again, and took hold of one side of the stretcher. Cursing, up to my knees in water again, we managed to maneuver it over to the other side. We fixed the stretcher up on the Puma, and all dived in. There was gunfire all around, and I didn't know what was theirs or ours.

In the Puma, we were packed like sardines. I was next to Amit, the gunner from Alon's crew. I knew they'd been close friends. He was half in a daze, and he asked me "Where's Smoha?" "He's dead, Amit," I said and I saw he was close to tears. I was nowhere near weeping. Rather, I felt something close to a sort of grim exhilaration that is very hard to describe or precisely locate. Finally, after endless minutes of blind bumping and lurching over the ground, someone said, "OK, we're over the border. We're in Israel." There were still explosions everywhere. There was still the dead man, on the stretcher, with his cruel, gaping wound. But at that point, I realized that death, which had seemed to be bringing its huge, empty face very close up to me and the rest of us, was receding back again to its own realm.

Once we were over the border, there were medical crews waiting, and they took Alon and laid him out and covered him with a white plastic cover, within minutes. The noise of the artillery all around was still deafening. But we were back in Israel.

Thirteen hours was the time of the whole thing. From leaving the avocado field to making it back across the border.

Afterwards, there would be the accusations, the recriminations. Why had we been left to drag the tank back in broad daylight? With a clear view of us from the ridge. Crawling along in a valley six kilometers north of the border. Why had we been left to carry out a suicide mission?

But at the time, there was deep, animal fatigue. We had a strange desire to stay close to one another, I remember. Amiram and I sitting at a bus stop at the entrance to the base, among a crowd of our comrades. Filthy, silent and very tired, some men smoking, others drinking from plastic bottles of Coke.

A British journalist of my acquaintance from the Guardian passed by. I knew him from the bars of Jerusalem. We had argued heatedly on more than one occasion. I waved to him, and realized that he didn't recognize me. At the time, this seemed strange. I had no idea of how we looked. Faces blackened with sweat and dirt, tatty uniforms and boots, matted hair. He tried to ask us some questions, and Amiram answered "I've no idea why they send tanks to fight against anti-tank units. No idea. You better ask our commanders." That was all. The quote appeared in the Guardian the next day.

We were confused and we wanted to sleep, but already the recriminations and the anger were beginning. People wanted to know what exactly the mission had been all about. What was the point of sending us in, after all the stops and starts and delays, only to pull us out again 12 hours later? And the Katyushas screaming overhead through the blue in the harsh summer sunlight were an adequate reminder of the failure of the mission.

There were people who said we shouldn't agree to go in again, until some adequate explanations were given. There were those who said that we were being asked to go and die for an army that hadn't trained properly and whose commanders didn't know what they were doing. Yuval himself was dog-tired, and quiet, and I could see that he was asking a lot of the same questions.

Menash, who would have known how to pull everyone back together again, was in Beilinson hospital. His tank had caught a missile on the hull. He, the brave fellow, had his head out of the turret at the time, and had taken fragments of shrapnel in his neck and arm, which would leave him temporarily disabled. So he wasn't there.

In my own mind, what I mainly felt was disgust at how it had turned out. At the looseness and lack of organization and competence which had led to three tanks from the company being destroyed. We had been sent inadequately prepared and trained, into the killing zone.

There is a kind of Israeli cynicism and knowingness that takes a sadistic pleasure in the mishaps and pratfalls of suckers. Former Prime Minister Ehud Olmert personified this version of Israeliness. It is a post-heroic, shrewd and sophisticated outlook, with few illusions about human beings. The people it admires are those who know how to get ahead, sophisticated men and women of the world, with a taste for luxury and the good things in life. There is an arrogance to this outlook, and it comes with a certain contempt for those unable to win in the game. For those held back by naïveté, slowness, outdated ideas, for the "losers."

This outlook has a pervasive presence in Israeli popular culture. It helped to drive my own fury in the hours following the operation in Marjayoun, and the fury of my comrades. We thought of the politicians and the generals, and we imagined them with their clever smiles and their winks, never quite meaning the words they said, always winking to someone just out of your sight, always cleverer, always one step ahead, the ones who really knew, the ones in control. And then we thought of ourselves, poor dolts, in ragged uniforms on the Lebanese border, with Katyusha rockets screaming overhead.

Men in their twenties and thirties, many heads of families, students, small businessmen, employees. And many of us felt like the fools, the suckers, the fall guys, the sacrifice which a short-sighted, satiated, hedonistic society would send into the grinding-machine, soon to be forgotten.

Because, while they were busy, being Israeli know-it-alls, the politicians and the generals had forgotten the basic rules that their quieter, more modest fathers and mothers knew, and which had created and sustained Jewish statehood in the first place. So that was the situation that confused Thursday morning, as we prepared for the funeral of Alon Smoha, and then for the continuation of the war. "There is no state, don't you get it?" One guy said to me, "What state? There are a few corrupt families at the top, none of whose sons are here. There's us, and there's Arkady Gaydamak."

Gaydamak, the Russian populist billionaire, with his tent city in Nitzanim, for people who had fled the north, because of the Katyusha attacks. And the Chief of Staff, Halutz, whom the media would later claim found time to sell his stock portfolio on the first morning of the war.[2] And our divisional commander, a legendary naval commando with a bright future predicted for him, but who had not taken a course to learn about tanks before coming to command an armored division.[3] And the Lubavitcher Hasidim, scampering about the border as the medics moved the bodies into ambulances, dispensing what they supposed to be Jewish truth and logic to the exhausted and disgusted reserve soldiers. And the politicians and their media, each one with his own clever ideas. But it was us, poor fools, suckers, *freierim*, who were there on the border, and whose job was to pay the price in our blood for the complacency and neglect, for the arrogance.

The funeral took place in the graveyard at Hod Hasharon. It was a blazing summer's day. Half of the population of the town seemed to be there, along with Alon's workmates from Teva Pharmaceuticals, and our whole company. His mother and his female cousins wept around the open graveside. There was an awful vividness about it all, in the harshness of the sun. It made you want to close your eyes. But you couldn't. The young regular soldiers of the Armored Corps, in their black berets, lining up and firing the rifle salute over the grave. It was a time of insanity, the war still raging on in the north. Twenty-four hours before, we had been carrying this man's broken body on a stretcher over a watery ditch in a valley below el Khiam ridge. How small death had seemed then. Now, here it was, grown to the proportions that it has in civilian life. Ritual and pain and terrible grief. Mothers, brothers and fathers.

We were numb. We were going through the motions of normality, and I was surprised to see how easy it was to fool people. That one could relate to one's physical self as a sort of puppet, which could be set in motion and would behave in perfect imitation of a regular human being. But behind it, in the part where feelings reside, was nothing but mess. After the funeral, they told those of us who had lost our tanks that we could take the rest of the day off, and that we should head back the following morning. I caught a ride to Jerusalem.

This was unexpected. A chance to breathe for a night, before heading back. The talk on the radio was already about an approaching ceasefire. They were saying it was "crystallizing" but that it was still some way off. But then there were other reports that were still talking about the war widening and Syria being drawn in. The sensible thing would have been to have rested and caught up with sleep. My intention was to hit the bars of west Jerusalem, before heading back north the following day, for the next part of the war.

The city was full of foreign correspondents and a lot of people down from the north. The bars and restaurants were full. Everyone seemed to be having a good time. Hardly any talk of the war, as far as I could make out. In one of my favorite journalists' hangouts, an Arab correspondent with a British accent was good humouredly explaining his support for Hizballah in the war to the young barmaid, who was listening intently. "Well, Mofaz is an animal," I heard him telling her.

Only in Israel, you might say. Only in the Jewish state would it be possible to find that while the nation's young men are killing and dying on the border, it is perfectly acceptable and accepted to hold court in support of the enemy in the hostelries of the capital. With everything treated as a sort of fascinating intellectual discourse which only the impossibly vulgar might think to disturb.

Something about this scene, and the broader sense of unperturbed enjoyment in the packed summer bars filled me with an anger and disgust that I find hard to describe. Something indecent about it. The smug intellectual consensus and the sense of superiority. The foreign journalists happy to take part in the free and open life of west Jerusalem, while cheerfully giving vent to their fantasies regarding those who would like to shut all this down, forever.

And the left wing and fashionable Israelis who don't want to be left out of the international conversation and who therefore accommodate and sometimes parrot this style. And the guns still roaring in the north. And the dead, who had died defending all this, still warm in the ground. His blood cries out from the ground, it says in the Bible.

But who was listening? So I stumbled about like a raging fool for the best part of the night, growing progressively drunker and angrier. Perhaps absurd in self-pity, but anyway heading back to the northern border the following morning.

I stumbled into one of my favorite old haunts at about 3 in the morning. Long past bedtime. Diwan, the same place where I used to come from reserve duty in Mahane Ofer, years before. It is a beautiful old Jerusalem building, lit up in stone and red light. For a while, it became the hangout of international pro-Palestinian volunteers. These were all gone by 2006.

Only a few people still at the bar. I slid into a seat there, and noticed that an acquaintance of mine was seated next to me. This was a young Russian girl, an immigrant from St. Petersburg and a student of photography. I looked at her and she at me, and we said hello and then, for some reason that I do not quite understand, she took my hand. We sat there like that for quite a long time, not looking at each other, and with our hands tightly clasped to one another. All the bloody waste and politicians' lies, the blundering army and the murderous enemy, implacable and meaning to destroy us. And how sad it would be, after living so many years, I thought, to die such a tiny death as the death of a fighting soldier in the last days of a botched and mis-managed war.

Broken families and disgust in it all. Politicians and their fat cigars and their gangster friends. The useless trade union leader of a defense minister. And I was going back the next day, for sure. No real choice in the matter. After all the words I had spent years speaking. Nice that there was still one Russian girl in Jerusalem who felt like holding my hand. After a while, she looked at me again and smiled and at the same time we released each other's hands. I went home shortly afterwards. I had a few hours to sleep. Itzik and I were due to meet the next morning to return to the north.

We set off from Jerusalem next day, which was Saturday. When we arrived back, it was to find that things were changing. The fury and anger after the Marjayoun operation was dissipating and the unit was coming together again. People, one could see, were already a little embarrassed at some of the more extravagant suggestions made in the immediate aftermath of the operation. There was talk of another mission brewing. There was a huge amount of noise coming from further west. This, we would learn later, was the 401 Brigade and the Nahal infantry going through Wadi Saluki, and being cut to pieces, in one of the final follies of the war.

We had no tank, so there wasn't a huge amount to do but wait around and try and make ourselves useful. Itzik and I drove to the border to have a look at what was left of our two vehicles that had taken the missiles, which had since been dragged back to Israel. The company commander's was in the worse state, and looked irreparable. We checked where the missiles had entered. The Kornets that took out the engines of the two tanks, it turned out, pierced at precisely the same point. At the engine grille. But in Alon Smoha's case, the missile had entered, and then continued inwards, flying over the engine, in the area in between it and the outer armor. Then it had penetrated the wall of the driver's compartment, and killed him. In my case, on the other hand, due to a difference in trajectory of no more than a few centimeters at most, the missile had ploughed into the engine, destroying the tank, and leaving me untouched.

We also learned later that a ten-man Hizballah squad had been spotted descending from el Khiam in our direction. Presumably because of the presence of our forces in the area and the carpet of fire laid down in the direction of el Khiam, they had turned back, preventing the firefight I had feared and expected.

There were rival rumors going around of an approaching ceasefire and of an impending new operation. Both, I suppose, were true, and it was simply a case of which would arrive first. For my part, I wanted it to be over, but I knew that there was no way out other than through it, and on to the other side.

On Sunday, in the course of the day, I was asked to replace someone in a crew of a tank being used to extricate wounded soldiers from the zone across the border. This was potentially somewhat dangerous since, as we had already learned, daylight was the time that the anti-tank teams operated. We drove to the border. There was a tense few minutes as we stood by the tank, waiting to hear if we'd be ordered to go in. No one said very much and we avoided each other's eyes. After about ten minutes, we heard that it was a false alarm and we drove back to the rest of the company. War, they told us, is the kingdom of uncertainty.

Finally, on Sunday evening, the contest between the rival rumors was settled. A ceasefire would come in the following morning, at 8 a.m. We received the news without any particular emotion. When you are stuck at the sharpest end of a conflict, as a rank and file soldier, it is difficult to maintain a broad picture of what is going on. But all the same, our overwhelming sense was one of frustration, disgust, and failure. The next morning the Katyusha barrage started at the usual time, and kept on going until 1 minute before 8 a.m. They were falling far off, so I didn't bother getting out of my sleeping bag to greet them. The fact that a ceasefire had come in didn't mean all danger was over. There would be a need to cross the border again to take control of areas before the UN forces returned, and so there was still the issue of mines, and even possible clashes with Hizballah deriving from conflicting orders.

We spent the day waiting. I remember walking into a forest next to where we were stationed outside Kibbutz Kfar Giladi. It was high summer but the scene was one of desolation. The Katyushas had burned everything to cinders, so the ground was all black and gray and the trees reduced to mis-shapen black stumps. It was a scene of silence, made squalid by the clumps of toilet paper here and there left by soldiers from the battalion.

A Norwegian journalist friend called me on my cell phone as I left the forest. We had a strange conversation about a prominent Norwegian writer who had just declared himself opposed to Israel's continued existence. He had said in an article that "For two thousand years, we have rehearsed the syllabus of humanism, but Israel does not listen. It was not the Pharisee that helped the man who lay by the wayside, having fallen prey to robbers. It was a Samaritan; today we would say, a Palestinian." And elsewhere "We do not believe in the notion of God's chosen people. We laugh at this people's fancies and weep over its misdeeds. To act as God's chosen people is not only stupid and arrogant, but a crime against humanity. We call it racism."[4]

This was my first inkling of the very special response of the European left and their Islamist allies to the war. I paced about next to the forest burnt up by Katyushas and my Norwegian friend and I discussed what it meant.

Later in the day, we got the order to cross the border to occupy some village where a lieutenant from our brigade had been killed some days earlier. We were to make it there and wait until further orders. I was put with another crew of men who I didn't know that well. Now that the ceasefire was in operation, the atmosphere had become more normal, and there was general impatience and keenness to be done with the whole thing. We reached the village without incident. It was deserted, just a few stone dwellings in powdery sand. We settled down to wait. We'd been told we could be there for about 48 hours.

In the end, in a perfect postscript to the general run of the war, we received the order after about ten hours, to return across the border. There was some difficult country to navigate in the darkness, but we made it with no problems. The engineering battalion stationed next to us had set up a sound system for a celebration of some kind. So there was trance music thumping out for most of the night. I found a corner of a tent to curl up in. That was the last night of the war. The next day we pulled back to the foot of the Golan Heights.

The division commander, the famous naval commando, came and delivered a little speech to us before we left for home. He would resign a year later, leaving the army, his once glittering career curtailed as a result of the war.[5] Then the brigade commander, whose tank had been hit by the RPG in Marjayoun also spoke. I've little memory of much that they said. At the end, we all sang the national anthem. Then we went to the cars to head south, back to Jerusalem. It was over.

I had often wandered what it would be like to return from a war. This idea had always possessed a certain poetry to me. Dusty citizen-soldiers returning from the front, back to their homes in the cities. In real life, it wasn't quite like that. I returned to my apartment confused and tired, and in the mood for sleeping for a long period. The summer sun was still blazing. People saw me in my reservist's uniform, my skin tanned almost black by the sun, and they avoided my eyes. It was a Thursday, just two weeks after the call up. I went out and got drunk again in Jerusalem, then went back to work the following week.

Thus far the testimony of one soldier of the 2006 Lebanon War.

The war came out of the bright blue sky and left a lot changed. The IDF's assumption in the years preceding it was that Israel was unlikely to face a situation of conventional combat in the foreseeable future. Resources had been poured into air power and missile defense. It had been assumed that what would be needed on the ground in a future war would be small groups of special forces, so there were also investments in this sector. The mass of the regular army and reserves, meanwhile, were required for constabulary duties in the West Bank and (before 2005) Gaza. These duties ate up time and resources.

The combination of these two elements served to create a crippling lack of training and readiness in many frontline units. The operations in the West Bank and Gaza also caused a false sense among many who had experienced them that they were veterans of "combat."

It is important to be precise here. There were of course serious clashes involving considerable loss of life in the West Bank and Gaza in the 2000–2004 period. But these clashes were ultimately of a type and intensity associated with police or counter-insurgency operations. IDF ground forces grew used to operating in areas that were familiar to them, in contexts where the zone of real danger was known and localized. The assumption was that future conflicts would be either of this type, or else high tech clashes led by airpower.[6]

The Iranian Revolutionary Guards Corps, however, through Hizballah and other client groups, was developing a different approach to warfare. Their goal was the creation of a sort of hybrid mode of combat, somewhere between classic irregular guerrilla warfare and conventional operations.

This grew both out of necessity and out of faith. The necessity derived from the fact that by any measure, the armies of the West were more powerful in conventional terms and could not be met head on.

The aspect of faith derived from the belief that Israel and the West did not, in the words of Vietnamese General Giap regarding the US in Vietnam, "possess the psychological and political means to fight a long drawn-out war." Such an approach could not, of course, emerge only from a top-down decision taken by a state agency. It was imaginable precisely because of the Islamist, anti-Western ferment that had swept across the region. The intention was to channel this ideological ferment into a workable strategy.[7]

The realm of perceptions and media warfare was a vital element in this strategy. Cutting Israel off from its natural hinterland of support in the West and isolating it was an obvious aim. For this, the turning of Israel into a monster in the eyes of Western public opinion was an important goal, and would be enthusiastically taken up by the alliance of Islamists and radical leftists discussed in earlier chapters. This too was in evidence during the 2006 war as demonstrations of unprecedented rage against Israel took place across a number of European cities. The demonstrators were mainly European Muslims, with an additional presence of leftists. The Norwegian author and his article was a fine distillation of the spirit that was abroad.

The Lebanon war of 2006 thus offered an example, in miniature, of the form the new Israel-Islamist conflict[8] generated by the meeting of Iranian ambitions with regional Islamist ferment would take.

The deliberate use by Hizballah of undirected Katyusha fire on centers of Israeli population was clearly an extension of the terror campaigns of Hamas in Israeli urban centers a few years earlier. The intention, to recall the words of Nizar the Hamas man in an earlier chapter, is to "raise the price" to a point beyond which the Israeli society is willing to pay. In this way, the muqawama bloc intends to win both tactically and strategically.

But the price mechanism applies not only to civilians. The 2006 war saw Hizballah operating on the assumption that Israel would not attempt a large scale ground operation, because of the losses to soldiers' lives this would entail. And indeed, Israel never did attempt a large-scale ground operation to capture the area south of the Litani River from where the Katyusha missiles were being launched, or at least, not at a time when such a move could have succeeded. Rather, the political leadership vacillated, unsure of quite what it ought to do.

Insofar as Israel in 2006 pursued any coherent strategy at all, it was also attempting to set the price for aggression against it at a rate that Hizballah would be unwilling to pay. So, price-setting and perception was the goal on both sides: for Hizballah, as part of a larger strategy to slowly weaken Israel to a point where it eventually ceases to be a viable society, and for Israel, to convince Hizballah that it was not worth its while to continue this attempt.

It would be wrong to maintain that the war was entirely without gain for Israel. In the first place, Resolution 1701, which ended it, included improved provisions for future arrangements on the border. The Lebanese Armed Forces would henceforth deploy south of the Litani river and control the border area, administered by Hizballah since May 2000. The United Nations forces in the area would be beefed up.

Much, however, depended on the extent of the will of these forces to act to disarm Hizballah in the area south of the Litani. And it rapidly became clear that there was no great determination to achieve this on the part of either force. Instead, arms began to pour in, as the movement sought to rebuild itself and its infrastructures after the damage wrought by Israel in the course of the war.

The border stayed quiet in the period that followed. Hizballah had sustained a blow, and needed time to recover. But few in Israel believed that the quiet was much more than a temporary respite. And even the purchase of this respite should not be allowed to detract from the significant failures at all levels of the Israeli performance.

These began with the very "framing" of the war on the Israeli side. Israel defined its aims in a way that made failure in 2006 a certainty.

The Israeli Cabinet set its aims for the war in a meeting on July 19.

The war's goals included the following three items:

- Freeing the kidnapped soldiers and bringing them back to Israel, with no conditions.

- The cessation of the firing of missiles and rockets against the citizens of Israel and against Israeli targets.
- Complete implementation of Resolution 1559, including the disarming of all the militias as well as the imposition of its sovereignty by the Lebanese government throughout its territory, and also the deployment of the Lebanese army along the border with Israel.[9]

It was never disclosed how the government of Israel thought it was going to achieve item 1 on this list. Short of a commando rescue to bring back the kidnapped soldiers (who, it was later discovered, were already dead at the time of the war), such an outcome was an impossibility. Item 2 could have been achieved, but only by an extensive ground operation begun at an early stage of the war. No such operation was ever ordered. Item 3 could only have been achieved by inducing the Lebanese government or the international community to take action against Hizballah. It is not clear by what mechanism the government of Israel intended to bring this about.

The war exposed the mediocrity and unsuitable nature of significant parts of the political leadership. In particular, the triumvirate of Prime Minister Ehud Olmert, Defense Minister Amir Peretz and Chief of Staff Dan Halutz were revealed to be in the wrong jobs. Olmert and Peretz were entirely lacking in relevant experience. Halutz, the first IDF chief of staff to emerge from Israel's world class air force, nevertheless was woefully ill-equipped to lead a ground war of the type needed.

As a result, in the summer of 2006, an inexperienced and unsuitable leadership took a rusty and poorly prepared army into battle. The uncertainty that we front line soldiers felt, as we waited on the border in the early days of August, was a product of this larger confusion.

The Winograd Committee, which investigated the conduct of the war from Israel's side, was unsparing in its criticism. Some of the evidence revealed of the uncertainty of Israel's political and military leadership during the war is damning. The Chief of Staff was criticized for his failure to adequately prepare for an extensive ground operation in the following terms: "The Chief of Staff did not alert the political echelon to the serious shortcomings in the preparedness and the fitness of the armed forces for an extensive ground operation, if that became necessary. In addition, he did not clarify that the military assessments and analyzes of the arena was that there was a high probability that a military strike against Hezbollah would make such a move necessary."[10]

Winograd also noted confusion in the Cabinet meetings in the final stages of the war, with ministers and generals trying to blame one another as to why a serious move on the ground was being ordered so late. Thus, Chief of Staff Halutz, when berated by Peretz because the army had not presented a plan for an extensive ground incursion, responded that "There was a clear statement that the political echelon does not want a ground operation."[11] Prime Minister Olmert then intervened in the dispute, saying that "The whole way through, the military echelon said: We do not recommend a ground operation."

All this sounds like politicians and generals trying to pass the buck for an operation that they already knew was a failure.

Poor preparation, poor planning, incoherent goals and indifferent execution characterized Israel's war effort in 2006. A "great and grave missed opportunity,"[12] Winograd called it.

All these factors came together in the last operations of the war in a particularly acute way. The story of the final, botched ground operation encapsulates the war. A large-scale move on the ground was approved by the Cabinet on the night of August 7. On August 8, OC Northern Command General Udi Adam was replaced. The operation began on August 9 in the haphazard and piecemeal way that I hope my personal account captures. Then on August 10 it was temporarily abandoned. We are told that on Friday the 11th and Saturday the 12th, the political and military leaderships squabbled among themselves and prevaricated regarding the operation.

With a ceasefire clearly approaching, the push made little military sense. There was no way that in the time remaining, the IDF could properly shut down the Katyusha launchers that were wreaking havoc on northern Israel. On the other hand, perhaps the forward movement of the IDF could gain better terms in the ceasefire. And there was clearly an element on the part of the leadership of a desire to avoid humiliation. The different opinions reached the media, and senior journalists in major papers began demanding their own preferred solutions.

As a result of all this, on Saturday, August 12, the ground operation recommenced. This was the noise we heard as we waited on the border. It was then abruptly called off after a helicopter was downed with the loss of the crew. And that was that.

Fifty-six soldiers died in the last five days of the war, in a series of military acts with no coherent purpose. The description in the earlier part of this chapter is the story of one of them. Multiply it by 56 and you start to get a sense of the Second Lebanon War.

It is hard to connect the two strands. On the one hand, the precise accounting of gain and loss, the meaning of the war for the larger conflict of which it was a part, the lessons to be learned, and so on. The accounts of the politicians and the generals and the journalists squabbling and opining. On the other, the reality of the fighting on the ground. The missiles and bombs and bullets. The filthy threshing ground of the combat zone.

In the months that followed, the war continued to dominate most of my waking hours. Hizballah claimed that it had won a "divine victory," and for a while there was general rejoicing in the pro-Iranian camp. Israel, meanwhile, entered a period of depression and soul-searching, as the country sought an explanation for the unexpected turn of events.

A new war, of a new type, that came like a whirlwind, and the sudden need that it had brought with it for the country to reconsider its assumptions regarding the future. For my own part, I began to dedicate the greater part of my own writing and research work to considering this matter, how best Israel could respond to it, and how the country could avoid ever experiencing a similar systemic failure. I also decided that in order to understand what had happened properly, it was important to travel to Lebanon itself, to see the areas in which the fighting had taken place, and to have a look at Hizballah close up.

This need was half that of a researcher, half something deeper, I suppose. The chance to do this came along a year after the war.

Notes

1. A shortened account of the author's experiences in this operation was published in the *Times* of London, Jonathan Spyer, "Our tank was a death trap," the *Times*, 30 August 2006.
2. Max Boot, "The Second Lebanon War," *Weekly Standard*, 4 September 2006.
3. Amos Harel, "Seven months on, IDF implementing lessons of Lebanon War," *Haaretz*, 7 February 2007.
4. Jostein Gaarder, "God's Chosen People," *Aftenposten*, 5 August 2006.
5. Yossi Yehoshua, "Lebanon War Commander Resigns," *Ynetnews*, 1 June 2007.
6. For further discussion of this issue, see Ofer Shelah and Yoav Limor, *Captives in Lebanon: the Truth about the Second Lebanon War*, Yediot Sfarim, 2007 (Hebrew.)
7. See Ehud Ya'ari, "The Muqawama Doctrine," *Jerusalem Report*, 13 November 2006, for a more detailed appraisal of the thinking behind the strategy adopted against Israel by Iran and its clients. See also Magnus Norell, "A Victory for Islamism? The Second Lebanon War and its Repercussions," Policy Focus no. 98, Washington Institute for Near East Policy, November 2009.
8. This term was first coined by Middle East scholar Martin Kramer.
9. Final Report of the Winograd Committee, 30 January 2008: 219.
10. Ibid.
11. Winograd, 181.
12. Ari Shavit, "Eliyahu's Requiem," *Haaretz*, 7 February 2008.

CHAPTER 8

The Verdict of Deir Mimas

The chance to visit Lebanon arose a year after the 2006 war. It came about as a result of a chance contact with a US journalist closely acquainted with the pro-government Lebanese camp. But what precisely was I looking for?

I wanted to see the war from the other side. To get a sense of who the enemy had really been, what his hometowns looked like. If possible, I hoped to travel down to south Lebanon, and take a trip through the heartland of the 2006 fighting. If possible, I also hoped to get close to the valley where we had been hit. Why exactly it interested me to enter el Khiam and gaze down at the valley, I wasn't entirely sure. Maybe on some level it was a desire to score one over on the people who had tried to kill me last time I had entered the same area, and who had very nearly succeeded.

The decision to travel to Lebanon was slightly foolhardy, from a certain point of view. But I was not the first Israeli journalist to attempt it, and the others had all made it back fine. I traveled from Jerusalem to Amman, and then flew from Amman to Beirut. There was a slightly ominous moment in Amman, when an airport official took exactly five seconds to ascertain that I had entered from Israel. It meant that if I aroused suspicions in Beirut, things would unravel rapidly.

At that time, it had not yet become publicly clear that the security at Rafiq Hariri airport was controlled by Hizballah. So, I was less nervous than maybe I should have been. Hizballah's domination of the airport would become apparent only after the events of May 2008, which were set off by a government attempt to fire the head of airport security. The May events themselves, in turn, were only the latest manifestation of a broader, fundamental problem affecting Lebanon.

Lebanon, in the last half-century, has found itself cast in the unwilling role of an arena for the clash of larger regional forces. The complex and Byzantine topography of its own feudal internal politics has become overlaid and concealed with the bright and simplifying banners of various regional political ideologies. The point to remember about the country is that both the regional political interests and ideologies, and the underlying sectarian landscape must be taken into account in order to understand events. Each feeds off the other. The result in the last 30 years has been much strife.

The conflict between Zionism and the Arabs has been one of the progenitors of Lebanon's woes. Arab nationalism, which sought to subsume the mosaic of Middle Eastern cultural identities into a single, language-based Arab identity, was by its very nature opposed to the essentially pre-nationalist, sectarian nature of Lebanon. A necessary pluralism, of a type bound to antagonize Arab nationalists, is written into the very nature of the country.

Lebanon's eastern neighbor, Syria, considers itself the "beating heart" of Arabism. Syria's use of Arab nationalist terminology has an instrumentalist aspect. The Damascus regime is dominated by a family emerging from a barely-Muslim minority (the Alawi) and therefore with a need to legitimize itself. But the Arab nationalist identity of Syria is sincere enough. It brings with it a certain built-in contempt for the Lebanese, whose pluralist system is regarded as having nothing of value. What this has meant in practice is a Syrian sense that Lebanon constitutes Damascus's backyard, in which interference and involvement is not only acceptable but is in fact natural.

The interference is explained in power political terms — Syria seeks, it says, to prevent Lebanon from falling into the hands of forces committed to Western interests. The result was 15 years of Syrian occupation of Lebanon in the period 1990–2005.

The Israeli-Arab conflict has had no less dire repercussions for Lebanon. As a member of the Arab League, Lebanon was a very minor participant in the war of 1948. However, the country took in a large number of Palestinian refugees following the war. These were consigned to a restricted life as second-class residents, pending their expected return to their homeland. But the country's real entanglement with its southern neighbor began at the end of the 1960s, in the moment following the Six Day War.

There are certain similarities between that moment and the current situation in the Middle East. Following the 1967 defeat, a renewed wave of nationalist enthusiasm swept the Arabic-speaking world. The root of it was the sense of humiliation following the defeat of Arab armies at the hands of Israel in the war. The focus of it was the Palestinian "resistance" of Yasir Arafat and the PLO. Arab intellectuals anointed the Palestinian guerrillas with the mantle ceded by the Arab nationalist regimes after the 1967 defeat. For the Lebanese, the decision proved costly.

In November 1969, PLO leader Yasir Arafat and Lebanese Army Chief of Staff Emil al-Bustani signed an agreement that afforded official Lebanese recognition of the "Palestinian revolution" and agreement to the Palestinians to conduct the "armed struggle" from Lebanese soil.[1]

The remainder of this story is well known. The arrival of the "Palestinian revolution," in the shape of 3,000 PLO fighters, to Lebanon after 1970, the deterioration to civil war, Syrian intervention, Israel's alliance with the Christian Maronites, the Israeli invasion of 1982, and the subsequent long Israeli occupation of part of southern Lebanon. Since we are not writing a history of Lebanon here, there is no need for a detailed treatment of all this. The Lebanese Civil War was a long and brutal affair. And both Israel and Syria have their share of the blame, alongside that of the Lebanese themselves, for its privations.

But what is important to note here is that the Arab nationalist wave that impacted so calamitously on Lebanon spent itself long ago. And as elsewhere, when it receded, it allowed the former contours of the society to resurface. Post civil war Lebanon was under Syrian occupation. But it retained a flourishing civil society, which at a certain point was bound to clash with Damascus. When Damascus was forced to withdraw in 2005, by US pressure and a non-violent civilian uprising, what ought to have then happened was that peace returned to Lebanon. The Israeli occupation of a strip of the southern border area ended in 2000. The Syrian occupation ended in 2005.

But peace did not return. The reason may partly have been because of unresolved issues between the various sectarian communities that make up the Lebanese mosaic. But it was mainly because the country had managed to find itself at the cockpit of the new wave of ideological fervor that was heading across the region, and which sought to fill the vacant spot left by the demise of Arab nationalism. This was and is the wave of radical Islam, and the meeting point between this ideological wave and the regional ambitions of the rising Islamist elite in Iran.

In its time, Arab and Palestinian nationalism tipped the balance of the fragile arrangements holding together Lebanon's various communities. In so doing, it opened the doors to hell — to a civil war, in which more than 100,000 people² (some claim as many as 250,000) were killed. The impact of Islamism and Iran has so far not led to civil war in Lebanon, largely because of the still fresh memories of the last civil conflict, which only ended in 1990, and the consequent unwillingness of the pro-Western element to resist the advance of the pro-Iranian element by force.

But the pro-Iranian, Islamist forces have turned the south of Lebanon once more into the most active frontline of the new conflict. And they brought Beirut to the very edge of war in the early summer of 2008. At that time, renewed strife was avoided only because the central government chose to capitulate to the demands of Hizballah. For a civil war, you need two sides.

Lebanon today suffers from the presence of a movement that has grown beyond the dimensions of the country, and whose actions and ambitions cannot be curtailed by the checks and balances of the Lebanese system.

Hizballah is the chief creation of Iran in the Arab world. The movement gives Iran direct access to the conflict with Israel, and with it the immense legitimating power that pertains to involvement in this conflict. Hizballah has created what is in effect a parallel state in Lebanon that conducts its own foreign policy and possesses its own armed forces. It was this structure that went to war with Israel in 2006, and that defended itself against Lebanese attempts to rein in its power in 2008.

No force in Lebanon, including the national armed forces, can stand in the way of Hizballah. The movement is better armed, trained and equipped than the Lebanese Army. In addition, large proportions of the armed forces are themselves Shia and hence could not be used to fight Hizballah. The army itself in any case is officially supportive of Hizballah's policy of "resistance" to Israel. So Hizballah is an immoveable presence. Yet the structures of the civil society are not prepared entirely to buckle under to it. So two diametrically opposed visions of the country uneasily share the same geographic space. The two sides represent starkly diverse visions of the region, and in this way, the key question that the Arabic-speaking Middle East is asking itself may be seen in sharp focus in Lebanon.

On one hand, are those who desire the path of normal development, good relations with the West, connecting to the globalized economy. This camp retains some of the pathologies of the region, paranoia toward Israel among them. Yet at its best, it also represents a yearning for normalcy, the development of civic institutions and pragmatic ties to the developed world. On the other side, is the local representative of the camp built around the idea of continued defiance of the West, revenge for perceived humiliations, desire for the destruction of Israel, and a religious, supremacist ideology.

As was indicated by the Lebanese elections of June 2009, a large part of the Lebanese population are unwilling passengers in a vehicle being driven by Hizballah. They can vote against the latter, but have no mechanism to ensure that their preferences are not simply ignored.

The process here is a subtle one, and it points to one of the fundamental weaknesses of the muqawama bloc. They have a unique and peerless ability to tap into and make use of symbols of loyalty and identity shared by millions across the region. But in practice, their path seems to bring in its wake mainly ruin and destruction.

The results of the 2006 war frightened all those Lebanese who wanted a return to something resembling normality — Hizballah's claims of "divine victory" notwithstanding. So, in 2009 a sufficient number of Lebanese Christians deserted the Hizballah-led bloc to deny it the electoral victory it had been expecting. But the election results did not change the essential picture. Nor did they have a great affect on the government that eventually emerged. Hizballah's ability to project tacit menace made sure of that.

So, a political culture committed to ideology and war was sharing its house with one committed to commerce, business, economic progress and the good life.

There is something a little resembling H.G. Wells's *The Time Machine* in the Lebanese situation, with the beautiful but helpless Elois at the mercy of the more primitive, but violent Morlochs.[3] Of course, in their time, the Lebanese Christians and Sunnis were very far from being helpless, and very far from being non-violent. But 15 years of civil war have produced a generation with little energy for another go-around. The Lebanese Shia, whose political awakening came only at the tail end of the civil war, and who form the rank and file of Hizballah, are at a very different moment in their history.

Lebanon is unusual in the Arab world because of the weakness of the state, which has allowed the Iran-supported Islamist element to grow to a level of strength only paralleled among that Arab people lacking a state entirely — the Palestinians. But Lebanon is also unusual in that the civil society, opposed to the Islamists, is unusually strong.

The picture is thus neither simple, nor one-dimensional. The Hizballah-led society is not without its own deep social problems, which bely its self-image of Islamic purity. Drugs, corruption, prostitution — all exist in the Hizballah neighborhoods of south Beirut, behind the veil of the propaganda of purity.[4] And the pro-Western Lebanese, whose survival is underwritten by the US, are not quite as helpless as they seemed in the early summer of 2008, though their collective decision to avoid confrontation at all costs means that they are unable to expel the unwanted pro-Iranian guest who has taken up residence among them.

But Hizballah's real enemy is not the civil society of Beirut. The Zionist entity to the south is its main foe. And Israel, despite the best hopes of the Islamists and their allies, is very far from being helpless. Insofar as there is hard power to challenge the designs of Iran and its allies in the Levant, it is the hard power of the Zionists.

There is not, nor will there be, any meeting point between the Israelis and the pro-Western Lebanese. Israelis take little interest in internal developments in Lebanon. Israeli society is turned towards the West and the globalized world. The "Middle East" has always been something of a specialist subject in Israel, with strong connections to and connotations of the country's defense structures. For a while, in the 1990s, this shifted, as peace looked like a possibility. But when the peace process collapsed, the general indifference and suspicion returned.

Regarding Lebanon, such feelings are multiplied because of the failed alliance with the country's Christian Maronite population of the 1980s, and the subsequent transformation of Lebanon, in the minds of many Israelis, into a kind of monster senselessly devouring Israel's young men. Israelis long ago concluded that those Lebanese who might once have shared a sense of commonality with them were now a "broken reed," of little consequence.[5]

Israelis understand that whereas the pro-Western Lebanese have no "hard power" capacity, Israel has no "soft power" to wield anywhere in the region, to use the political science jargon. The prevailing political culture of the Arabic-speaking world, which includes both the Islamists and their opponents, is one in which the existence of an Israeli Jewish conspiracy that wields occult and unseen power across the globe is taken as a given.

So despite Israel's example as one of the few successful, developed countries in the Middle East, the idea that it could be seen as a model or an example by any of the troubled societies that surround it is quite inconceivable. This is so for the societies of countries with which Israel has formal relations of peace — such as Egypt and Jordan — no less than it is for countries with which it remains officially at war, such as Syria. The view of Israel, its desires and its interests in public debate in the Arabic-speaking world, has long ceased to bear anything but a passing resemblance to reality.

But despite the lack of communication between Israelis and pro-Western Lebanese, they are ultimately part of the same camp. By a curious logic, Israel, through its blunt defense of its own interests, plays a subtle, inadvertent role in the complex interaction between pro-Western and pro-Iranian forces in Lebanon. This may have lessons for wider regional processes, as we shall see.

When I arrived in Beirut and stood in the queue for the passport control, each person seemed to be at the booth for a long time, and I was concerned that this meant that everyone was undergoing an in-depth investigation. As I got closer, though, I saw that this was not the case. The pale blue-uniformed airport security men were simply enjoying banter with the passengers, and this was making the process longer. I was struck by the elegance and exuberance and the relaxed manners of the people. When my turn came, the official was jovial and happy to see a foreign journalist. I got through in seconds.

Central Beirut was dark in the evening. There was an immediate sense of heaviness, a kind of oppressive uncertainty that was new to me. The center of the city at that time was still empty in the evenings. My friends and I passed craters left from the bombing of the 2006 war, and went into the protest tent for Rafiq Hariri, full of candles, in the town center. Hariri's killing had precipitated the peaceful uprising of the "Cedar Revolution" in 2005. The issue of the tribunal meant to investigate his death has remained one of the main bones of contention between the pro-Western Lebanese element and the Iranian and Syrian backed forces.

The tribunal, and its failure to bear significant fruit in terms of calling for the arraignment of suspects for the murder, probably represents the limits of the possibility of the pro-Western Lebanese approach. Faced with enemies whose modus operandi is the law of the jungle, the pro-Western Lebanese place their own faith in the law. They have little choice. They are unable, or have decided to be unable, to play any other game. The United States is concerned not to see them go down, so their approach can work, for a time, and to a degree.

In the days that followed, in Beirut, we went from our small apartment in the east of the city. We met with journalists and activists and traveled out of town, the strange contours of the country's dispute revealing themselves to me. At once familiar, and utterly alien. As alien and as familiar as the hills of southern Lebanon had looked just across the border in 2006.

We traveled to the Cedars, the heartland of the Christian Maronites, an area rarely visited by Western journalists. UN troops come up there, though, for rest and recreation. There is skiing in the winter, and little wooden chalet hotels of the type one finds in the Alps. There are cards behind the picturesque reception desks from the commanders of Norwegian army units, thanking the hotels for the rest and recreation afforded their men.

The lingua franca is French, which is spoken by everyone up here, not just by the elite. There are restaurants and clubs where the young people go to dance. The music is a mixture of West and East. One could believe oneself in Europe — were it not for the red symbols on the walls of the Lebanese Forces militia.[6]

The Maronites are an ancient Christian community who made their way to the Lebanese mountains to escape Arab civil wars in the seventh century. They were favored by the French in the nineteenth century, and then delivered a poisoned chalice when France expanded the "petit Liban" of the Christian and Druze areas to take in the Sunni coast and the Shia south in 1920. The Christian share of the population rapidly fell to less than 50 percent.[7] Much of the subsequent history of the country has been of a kind of mini-state system within the tiny boundaries of the country, in which the different communities made and broke alliances with each other.

By 2007, the French speaking mountain area looked like a curious anachronism. For all their ferocity, the people of these areas are deserted by history. The defense they had wished to put up to the advance of Islam and Arabism was not defeated, exactly, but it is far too small and inconsequential to ever make much of an imprint again.

If there was a real challenge to Iran and Syria and Hizballah, it was in the teeming malls of Beirut, and the restaurants and clubs and night-life of the big city. Here was a force that might offer a genuine counter-balance, precisely because it was hooked into the largest center of power in the world, the United States. Here were Starbucks, and shopping chains, and music, and consumption. Almost like Tel Aviv, in a way, in the sense that the conflict seemed hard to imagine.

But of course, when one looked a little deeper, there was a major difference between Tel Aviv and the mall in Achrafiyeh. Tel Aviv may like to see itself as living in a happy bubble, but the bubble is situated behind the iron wall of the Israel Defense Forces.

In Beirut, in 2007, the beautiful people lived their chic and hedonistic lives in close proximity to the dark presence that intended to shut them down. The Elois and the Morlocks. There was little mixing between the sides. Rather, the hedonist, Westernized parts of the city lived next door to Shia south Beirut, which glowered in silent contempt and hostility.

The result was a pervasive paranoia just below the surface, which was in stark contrast to the seemingly light and airy lives being lived. It was coupled with a certain helplessness behind the urbanity and self-confidence. I came across this duality when I began to enquire about ways to reach the south. I had not been prepared for the extent to which southern Lebanon constituted a separate territory, even a year after UN Resolution 1701 supposedly returned it to the full sovereignty of the government in Beirut.

My hosts asked in a charming way whether it was "really necessary" to make the journey. Among the expat crowd, everyone seemed to have their own version of what was required in order to venture to the border area. There were those who maintained that it couldn't be done without checking in with the Hizballah media office in south Beirut. This, however, was inadvisable for two reasons. First, because as colleagues of mine had already informed me, Hizballah were well acquainted with Google. A simple search of my name would reveal several hundred articles of a type unsympathetic to the muqawama.

I also heard from colleagues that Hizballah asked for the address where you were staying in Beirut and a photocopy of your passport if you wanted to register with them. They were experts in subtle and unsubtle intimidation. I was particularly impressed to learn that they even asked for people's hotel room numbers. Just in case you were thinking of feeling safe as you closed the door. There were also some who maintained that Hizballah would insist on giving you a movement escort for the day. The escort would direct you where he wanted you to go and give you a running commentary of the Hizballah version of events.

None of this was what I wanted. There was no question of going near the media offices in the Dahiyeh.

But there were also those who pointed out that entering the area south of the Litani River was forbidden unless you first coordinated it with the Interior Ministry. I wasn't interested in doing that either. I tried to find out what exactly was supposed to happen to people who didn't do any of these things, and who simply set off on the highway out of the city in a southern direction. No one seemed specifically to know, but there was a general sense that it was inadvisable.

What was interesting about all this was the lesson the pervasive atmosphere of paranoia taught regarding who was the real power in Lebanon. The real power, as in when the talking stops, the one who gets to decide. There existed in effect a Hizballah shadow state, with its own institutions, alongside the official state. This shadow state, unlike historical examples of other such entities, did not interfere with the lives of those who bore it no allegiance.

They were free to go to their malls and bars and restaurants and chalet hotels and drink their wine and speak their French and

English, as long as they in turn did not interfere with the actions of the shadow state. If they did, retribution was swift and fierce. As experienced by Lebanon as a whole when the government tried to interfere with Hizballah's control of the airport and its independent communications network in May 2008. The result was a lurch toward civil war as Hizballah swiftly and effortlessly took over West Beirut in a matter of days.

Our Lebanese colleagues assured us that this parallel state itself obeyed certain unspoken rules that were in effect a contract between the Lebanese. Westerners and Israelis, we were told, lacked the ability to understand this. One would be dazzled with myriad examples of names and places.

But the intricacy and elegance of the detail could not obscure certain brute and unavoidable facts. Hizballah had grown to dimensions that meant it was no longer simply another Lebanese militia. Its military capabilities and the alliances of which it was a part were of regional strategic importance. The weak and subtle threads with which the existing Lebanese system sought to bind it would not work. Even if the movement suffered setbacks in elections because large sections of the population did not want to be part of its regional schemes, the election results could not prevent Hizballah from doing what it, or its patrons wanted.

In the end, we found some people willing to take me down to the south. The men in question were Christian veterans of the civil war, who were close to the Lebanese Forces organization. They had taken journalists to the border area before, and were known and trusted by some of my colleagues. Because the whole operation was slightly inadvisable, I was asked not to tell them that I was Israeli.

We set off from Jalal Dib in the morning, in an old Ford. Me in the front seat, a thick-set, good humored man called Kamal driving, and his thin, elegant, slightly devilish-looking colleague, whose name was Antoine, slouched in the back.

We all were about the same age and looked vaguely similar, which was good. I can pass for a Lebanese quite easily. That was important, because we didn't want to attract the attention of the army roadblocks, still less of the other, less visible forces in the south. We traveled down the coastal road, past the cities of Tyre and Sidon, and entered a different world.

The first indication that we were in a separate realm were the posters everywhere. Pictures of martyrs, of the 2006 war and earlier wars, placed by Hizballah and by the rival Amal organization. Faces of very young dead men, gazing down serenely. Strangeness and tension as we drove past the groves of bananas, lemons and oranges outside Sidon. A black car, with tinted windows, driving very fast, overtook us, and Kamal looked at me, smiled and said "don't worry, but that was a Hizballah car. That's the way they drive. Did you see the bearded guys in the front?" I hadn't.

As we neared the border, the traffic began to tail off, except for the white armored vehicles of United Nations Interim Force in Lebanon (UNIFIL) soldiers. The soldiers were Fijians, looking rather bewildered and far from home. Close to their base, as we drove toward the village of Yarine, was an Iranian flag, mounted on a flagpole. Pictures of Nasrallah, Musa Sadr, Khamenei. A different country.

We talked about Resolution 1701 and Hizballah's reconstruction of its infrastructure south of the Litani River. In 2006, the infrastructure had been built mainly in rural areas. Because Resolution 1701 prohibited the organization from holding weaponry south of the Litani, what was now happening was that Hizballah was re-building north of the river and, clandestinely, from within villages in the south.

UNIFIL hardly ever entered the villages, and when it did so, it had to coordinate in advance with the Lebanese Army. The army's rank and file, meanwhile, consisted largely of Shia, who had no desire to clash with Hizballah, and some of whom were probably acting as informers for the organization. Facilities were set up beneath houses, in gardens. Day by day, the infrastructure for the next war was being woven into the fabric of civilian life.

The road into Yarine had recently been repaired, after suffering severe damage from Israeli bombing during the war. There were still some craters remaining. Our intention was to drive along the borderline, stopping in the villages if we saw something interesting. The trip would take us through the towns that had seen the heaviest infantry combat of the war — Ait al-Shaab, Maroun al-Ras and Bint Jbeil. Then we would head further east, into the sector where the "Pillar of Fire" armored division, of which I had been a humble member, had conducted its operations around el Khiam and Marjayoun in 2006.

Large parts of Ait al-Shaab and Maroun al-Ras were still in rubble and uninhabitable. A variety of agencies were engaged in rebuilding. The main effort, of course, was being conducted by Hizballah itself, with Iranian funding. But there were also US aid signs here and there. There was even a metal signpost with a picture of the Emir of Qatar on it beaming outside one construction project.

So we headed east — through the heartland of the 2006 war, through the landscape of destruction. Ait al-Shaab, and then the Maronite villages of Rmeich and Ain-Ebel. These had been used by Hizballah as sites for launching rockets, and had also suffered considerable damage. And then into Bint Jbeil, the worst damaged of all. Posters of Ayatollah Khomeini and Nasrallah, heralding victory. Bullet holes and more pictures of the martyrs. Also, a strange montage depicting a grimacing, grotesque Ehud Olmert and weeping IDF paratroopers.

There was a day of remembrance going on, and the Hizballah youth movement, the Mahdi Scouts, were parading through the town. There were also Hizballah spotters, easily noticeable. Young men in groups of two, wearing black jackets, quietly watching what was going on. It was nerve-wracking as we drove slowly past them, but in the old red Ford, we didn't stand out.

At one point it looked like they had set up a makeshift roadblock. Several young men standing in the road as we approached. But it turned out that they were just milling about as part of the general indifference to the rules that seemed everywhere in south Lebanon. There were cars driving with no headlights, just bare sockets where they had once been. "Those used to belong to the South Lebanese Army," Kamal told me, noticing that I was staring at them. The empty sockets gave the vehicles a strange and evil look.

In the center of Bint Jbeil, there is a restaurant called "al-Tahrir." It was lunchtime, and for a mad moment we considered eating there. But we thought better of it and kept moving. I was in any case impatient to get to the eastern sector. This rubble, these Hizballah men, and the Mahdi Scouts, were not what I had come for. El Khiam and Marjayoun were the places I was interested in seeing. And the valley beneath them. So we kept on moving, only stopping to get out and take a look at the large areas of Bint Jbeil and Maroun al-Ras that were still in ruins.

In Meiss al-Jabal, in the central sector, at the entrance to the village, there was an old T55 tank of the South Lebanese Army (SLA). Hizballah had mounted a cardboard statue of Ayatollah Khomeini on it. When Israel pulled out of southern Lebanon in 2000, a large amount of ordnance and equipment belonging to its erstwhile allies in the SLA was left behind. Some of it has been turned by Hizballah into a monument to their achievement.

Khomeini standing atop a piece of rusting SLA armor sums up the movement's strategic vision rather elegantly. The stern visage of the Iranian leader was everywhere staring down at us as we passed the Fatima Gate, with the Israeli town of Metullah on the other side.

I remembered waiting at Metullah as the darkness came down before we entered Lebanon in 2006. Backed up all the way along the road, with a mad Hassidic sound system blaring away at us. How strange to see it, looking close and distant and strange, from the other side of the gate. With the forbidding visage of the Ayatollah glaring balefully down at us trespassers. He had spotted us, even if his followers had not. I imagined him trying to tell them, furious, constrained by the silence incumbent on statues and representations.

And then, a few minutes later, we were there. The first gray houses of the town of el Khiam, perched on its ridge, with the green valley below and Marjayoun on the other side. This was the place that we had been meant to conquer in August 2006. El Khiam, a Shia town, with its 300 Hizballah gunmen.

The town was very obviously a place built on piety. Nearly all its women were wearing the hijab, and shapeless black dresses. It was known as a particularly militant place too, with overwhelming support for Hizballah.

As we drove through, Kamal suddenly pulled off the main road and began speeding through the narrow side streets. "What are you doing?" I asked him, the thought entering my mind of Hizballah kidnappers and trade offs. El Khiam, having missed me by a whisker in 2006, was going to get me in the end. Radiators and chains in dank rooms in south Lebanon. Days stretching on into years.

Kamal didn't answer me, but kept driving, at high speed, careening down the little winding alley-like streets, kicking up the dust, with the occasional el Khiam resident looking on bemused. Finally, having described a large half-circle, we arrived back at the turning to the main street. Kamal looked from left to right, then muttered, "False alarm. I thought we were being followed," Crisis over.

We resumed our steady progress through the town. As we exited it, with the valley directly below, I asked Kamal to stop the car. We got out. It was a clear, sunny, winter's day. It must have been from a vantage point like this that the Kornet crew that fired on us would have placed itself somewhere around the same area. It would have been impossible to miss. We stood there in silence for a while, and I tried to imagine what our force would have looked like, making our absurd, bobbing progress in the valley that day in August. Menashe, Yuval, Alon, Maoz, Itzik and Amit.

I heard later that the intelligence had been tracing communications in Persian in the area all morning. So, was it Revolutionary Guardsmen, from the other side of the region, who had stood on this ridge with the Kornet launcher in August? Iranians, unintelligible and strange? Or was it local men, Shia, perhaps men from el Khiam itself? Well, I thought to myself, a little smug, I'm here now, so come and get me if you're smart enough to find me. No engine to absorb the blow this time.

After a few moments, Kamal cleared his throat and began to say something. "You know, in the war in 2006, the Israelis did something really crazy here."

No one will believe me when I tell them this, I thought. Kamal was a veteran of the Lebanese Civil War. As such, he apparently knew military mismanagement when he saw it. "What did they do?" I asked him.

"They sent a whole column of tanks down this valley, in the daylight. It was toward the end of the war. Just crazy. And they'd attacked Marjayoun, which is a Christian town, and friendly. But here in el Khiam, which is Hizballah, they didn't enter."

"So what happened to them?"

"Of course they were all blown away by Hizballah, firing from up here. What a mess."

We waited there a little while longer. The day was bright and clear. I remembered the tadpoles and the flies in the irrigation ditch in which we'd hidden after the destruction was complete. With the body of our comrade beside us, and the useless communications equipment. Grim and silent.

After a while, Antoine said, "It's getting late. We should head to Marjayoun if we're going there." So we trudged back to the car.

Nor was the war finished in that place. Not in any part of south Lebanon, that we traversed in the course of the day. With Kamal driving, and me making notes frantically in the front seat, and Antoine slouched coolly and elegantly in the back, watching from left to right. We drove through Lebanese Army roadblocks, past Hizballah spotters, past the white armored vehicles of Fijian soldiers, underneath the grim visages of the Ayatollahs looking down at us. With Metullah just the other side of the Fatima Gate. And the war was not over.

Finally, we pulled into Marjayoun, the last stop. I had been here before and remembered the houses as I had seen them in the early morning light. There was a monument to the SSNP RPG-29 crew that our brigade commander's tank killed on the night of 9 August. More faces of young men. We ate in a restaurant in the town, owned by a Christian family. The young man managing the place, had a screen saver on his computer reading "Nasrallah — go to hell" which made us laugh. But we didn't stay too long. It was late afternoon by now and we wanted to get back to Beirut before darkness fell.

Before we began the drive back in the direction of Nabatiyeh,

Kamal suggested that we stop outside of the village of Deir Mimas. The village was a few miles from Marjayoun. He wanted me to see a 600-year-old monastery that had been destroyed in the 2006 war.

The monastery was set a little apart from the village. It was established to commemorate a famous child saint from the vicinity who was executed by the Emperor Aurelian, in the third century, for refusing to renounce Christianity. Before the 2006 war, a single Polish priest had lived there. During the fighting, Hizballah had used the area as a site for launching Katyusha rockets. As a result, the Israeli artillery had fired back and destroyed the old structure.

We walked down to the remains of the monastery. It was a scene of silent desolation. Torn Christian holy books in French and Arabic strewn about. The structure itself smashed to bits. In the graveyard there were broken tombstones. The books were slowly detaching themselves as the paper rotted, and loose pages blew about. I picked up a little booklet about the life of Saint Mimas, in French and Arabic, as a souvenir. Kamal told me that the adjoining Shia village of Kafr Kila had been nearly untouched in the war. Deir Mimas and its environs was the preferred site for Hizballah to launch their unguided rockets in the direction of Israel. As a result, 119 houses in the village had been destroyed, and the ancient site around which the village had grown lay ravaged.

There was silence around as we walked the remains of the monastery. The sun was setting and in the distance we could still see the Beaufort Castle, the great Crusader fortress that offers strategic control of south Lebanon. In the 1982 war, the Golani commando company had fought a desperate battle with Fatah forces to take the castle. Later, it had become a routine stopping point for Israeli troops in the time of the Security Zone. Now there was a massive Hizballah flag flying above it, and the light fading behind it. And a simmering tension, unmistakable, giving off its low hum all around.

These hills, that have seen many conquerors passing, from Alexander the Great, by way of Rome and the Crusaders, the Arabs, the Turks, French, British, Americans, Israelis, Syrians, now in the hands of the Shia clients of Iran.

Deir Mimas and the sorry state of its monastery seemed to me to confirm the underlying dynamic of events in Lebanon. The Greek Orthodox village was hardly noted for its pro-Israeli sentiments. Maronite border villages such as Rmeich and Ain Ebel were famous for the high proportion of fighters, whom they had produced, on the Christian side in the civil war. Orthodox Deir Mimas, on the other hand, was the home village of Souha Bichara, who was jailed after trying to assassinate Antoine Lahad, commander of the Israel-allied SLA. She is a heroine of the small Lebanese far left and its allies.

The village's illustrious tradition of resistance against the Zionists, however, had been of little use to it in protecting it and its ancient sites from use by Hizballah as a launch site, and from Israeli retribution.

Here was the helplessness of the non-Hizballah Lebanese at its most obvious. Whatever the sentiments of the villagers of this or that location, the important point was that they had no ability to say no to the parallel armed forces of the parallel state maintained by Hizballah in the south of Lebanon, and in a different way throughout the country. And being non-Shia, and hence not supporters or members of the organization, they, their lives and property were of secondary interest to it.

But it wasn't only a single Orthodox village that was in that situation. As would subsequently become clear, it was all of Lebanon that was in the predicament that Deir Mimas faced in the summer of 2006. And the intricate and elegant civil society of the country, of which its people were so proud, was no less vulnerable than the beautiful, broken monastery outside the village.

After Deir Mimas, we began the drive back to Beirut, passing through Nabatiyeh. We were back in the city by early evening. We went out and had a sort of celebration. More impossibly elegant people in the bars and restaurants of Gemayze, in the east of the city. Something about the way they built the houses, to catch the light, which seemed so perfectly to reflect the landscape. Even in the city.

I looked at them all on the final night of our stay and thought of the next war, the war that may well be coming — between Israel and Iran and its local allies in this country. The next war, and the last one, in which I had participated. We had circled el Khiam in the night-time in August, and blasted it with tank shells. The civilians of the town had for the most part been temporary refugees in Beirut at that time. As Jerusalem too had filled up with Israelis from the north. Next time it would be worse.

So it was a tragedy, and there were probably more tragedies ahead. Usually one can live with that very easily. Anyone who has been involved in war and come out of it sane knows all about compartmentalization. About finding a sparse, gray, bare room in your head in which you can reside when hard and tough moments are around.

The really vulnerable time is when you start to consider the sadness of all this from a different place. One that lets you admit to the possibility of forgiveness and friendship. One that lets you realize that at the true level, all people are equally close, or equally strangers to one another, outside of the bonds and duties imposed by history and identity. This was how it was on the final night I spent in Beirut.

The day I left it was raining, and it took a long time to get to the airport because there were traffic jams caused by fighting the night before, between supporters of Hizballah and followers of Saad Hariri. The clashes related to attempts by the Hizballah supporters to take down posters put up by the Hariri men on the fault line between a Sunni and a Shia neighborhood. I smoked in the airport waiting room, as I sat waiting for the plane to Amman. I was back in Jerusalem by the evening.

A few months later, the events of May 2008 determined decisively who had the final word in Lebanon. The May fighting was sparked by a government attempt to move against Hizballah's control of the Rafiq Hariri airport, which Hizballah turned into a trial of strength and won hands down. May and June stripped a lot of the ambiguity from the situation. From this point, it was clear that there was no internal force either willing or able to issue a hard power challenge to Hizballah.

The strategy that the pro-government Lebanese have chosen is not an absurd one. It may well be the only option available, since another civil war seems, apparently, unimaginable to them. They have chosen to rely on the notion that international legality has meaning and purchase, and to appeal to its authority in the face of the encroachments of Iran and Syria, and the activities of their proxies on Lebanese soil. The close links possessed by the Hariris to the West, via the key regional state of Saudi Arabia, and the current US desire to preserve Lebanese sovereignty, mean that this strategy has not yet decisively failed, though the choice of pacifism does mean that the situation of those Lebanese who do not support Hizballah is precarious in the extreme.

The Lebanese experience offers a number of somber lessons regarding the elements arrayed against the alliance of Islamist Iran with other Islamist groups across the region.

The first lesson is that no weight can realistically be placed on those forces most resembling Western liberals and democrats in the Middle East. For the moment at least, such currents can at most be protected and nurtured by the West in the Arabic-speaking world. But they have neither the energy nor the will nor the ability to themselves form a bulwark against the wave of Islamism and its allies. This may change in the future, but it remains so in the present.

So the forces arrayed against one another in the Arabic speaking world are on the one side the Islamists — who want to transform the region into a series of states modeled on Iran, the current regime in Sudan, the Hamas enclave in Gaza, and Hizballah's mini-state in southern Lebanon — and on the other side, the existing dispensation, that consists largely of corrupt and ineffective politicians, officers, and monarchs. They have demonstrated — in Egypt, in Saudi Arabia, in Jordan, among the Palestinians — a tenacious talent in one area only. Namely, that of staying in power. For the moment, it is this order or the Islamists. There is no third way.

From Israel's point of view, the election results in Lebanon in June 2009, also showed the role that Israel may play in the larger drama in the region. It will be a thankless one.

In the past, it has been Israel, and the desire for its destruction, that has served as the focus for the waves of ideologized anger that have swept the Arab world. They have derived their charisma from their opposition to the Jewish state, and from their contention that they have, finally, discovered the means whereby the string of infuriating and bewildering defeats at the hands of this hated entity can finally be reversed.

This was the claim of the Arab nationalism of the Egyptian officers' regime of Gamal Abdel Nasir in Egypt. Nasir's regime had a developmental model too, but the idea of successful military struggle against Israel was at its center. The Nasir regime as a model for "resistance" and development never recovered from the defeat of June 1967. The "guerrilla" resistance of Fatah and the PLO was the next to receive the anointed crown of "resistance" in the eyes of the Arabic-speaking world. But their version proved no more successful in the end.

The Islamist movements across the region, and their Iranian patron, are currently bidding for the same crown. In Lebanon, 2006, for a moment they succeeded in persuading many across the region that the key to strategic victory had been found.

The reality was somewhat more complex. The destruction wrought by the war was very great. The civil society of Lebanon had no real desire to see it repeated. They were too afraid to offer real resistance to Hizballah in May 2008. When they got the chance to vote in the elections a year later, however, a sufficient number of Christians deserted the Hizballah-led bloc to deny it the victory it expected. Hizballah held its power in the coalition negotiations that followed. But its charisma had suffered a setback, in a chain reaction begun by the war of 2006 and the May events of 2008. It kept its control. But there was a little less legitimizing fabric around its iron fist.

The ruined landscape of the south of the country that I traveled through was hardly an advertisement for the muqawama bloc. Towns in part still uninhabitable a year after the fighting ended. A new military infrastructure that turned the civilian population into human shields.

Hizballah's electoral setbacks, of course, had no bearing on the shadow state they had established, which was not available for replacement through the polls. But the electoral decision at least had the virtue of clarifying the situation. The Lebanese majority were not attracted to the muqawama idea. But they were hostage to it, since they had decided to give up the possibility of challenging it head on.

Hizballah's hard power remained intact. No other political force in the country could challenge it. But the price that its postures of defiance before Israel demanded made more and more non-Shia Lebanese choose against it when they had a chance.

Hizballah's Islamism, like its predecessor ideologies, could offer a politics of military theater. Of ritualized rejection of perceived humiliation. But the result was ruined landscapes and hostage populations. The predecessor ideologies had also started in euphoria, and ended up holding power by force and coercion, long after the promises had proved empty.

After the 2009 elections, Hizballah was already looking just a little more similar to the hollow parade of Arab military power of the past. The elections were an early sign that the fate of the latest wave of political violence might in the end prove not too different to its predecessors.

Only an early sign, to be sure. But it showed the role played by Israel as the exposer of Arab illusion, the element that time and again has turned a cruel and modern light on the intoxicated picture show.

For the moment Hizballah's guns and its willingness to use them would keep its state within a state safe from any internal interference. Decline, as its threats prove repeatedly self-destructive and its claims of integrity and purity prove more and more tenuous is its likely eventual fate. Not that this will mean the default victory of the other Lebanon. After all, if the example of the rest of the Arab world is anything to go by, Arab military power remains of great use against its own subject populations, even after it has ceased to offer any threat to its external enemies. Which further underlines the chief lesson of all this.

The main lesson from the events in Lebanon is a relatively simple one. It is one that all major forces in the Middle East understand very well, though they rarely admit it in polite company: the region remains under the dominion of the sword. Force, and nothing else, has the final word. The new ways of interaction between states and nations that many in the West believe have replaced this ancient master do not exist here. Rights-based systems, free societies, group self-determination, the pursuit of knowledge and advancement, all will continue to exist for as long as and insofar as they can be defended. This is doubly so in the case of entities created or dominated by regional minorities.

Regimes, ideologies, justifications might change. But this hierarchy remained and remains unshifting. The fate of the non-Hizballah Lebanese is a reminder of what happens to people who fail to pay it tribute in this unforgiving landscape; the verdict of Deir Mimas. Precious sites broken and ravaged. Pages detaching from beloved texts. It is a message that Israel itself has long internalized.

Notes

1. Helena Cobban, *The Palestine Liberation Organization: People, Power and Politics*, Cambridge: Cambridge University Press, 1984: 7.
2. Lebanon Civil War 1975–90. http://www.globalsecurity.org/military/world/war/lebanon.htm Acessed: 17.5.10
3. H.G. Wells, *The Time Machine*, 1898.
4. See, for example, Hanin Ghaddar, "Dahiyeh back to Lebanon," *Now Lebanon*, 25 September 2008. http://www.nowlebanon.com/News ArchiveDetails.aspx?ID=60328 Accessed: 17.5.10. The article describes the spread of crime, particularly drug abuse and prostitution, in the Hizballah-controlled Dahiyeh area of south Beirut following the May events of 2008. See also "Hezbollah's Constitution" by the same author.
5. This phrase was used by then Israeli foreign minister Moshe Sharett to describe the Maronites of Lebanon in 1955. Sharett was reacting to a plan formulated by then Prime Minister David Ben-Gurion and IDF Chief of Staff Moshe Dayan for an Israeli alliance with the Maronites. See Ze'ev Schiff and Ehud Ya'ari, *Israel's Lebanon War*, London, Unwin Paperbacks, 1984: 14.
6. The Lebanese Forces was an alliance of Christian militias during the Lebanese Civil War. Today it is one of the leading political formations among Lebanese Christians.
7. William Harris, "Reflections on Lebanon," in ed. Barry Rubin, *Lebanon: Liberation, Conflict and Crisis*, New York, Palgrave Macmillan, 2009: 16.

CHAPTER 9

The Transforming Fire

The conflict between Israel and the Arabs passed through a period of dormancy. From the mid-1970s onwards, it appeared to be edging toward permanent solution. A number of factors combined to ensure that this did not happen.

Firstly, a genuinely partitionist politics had not emerged in the secular Palestinian national movement itself. Palestinian nationalism, when required to take the final, irreversible step toward accepting the partition of the area of former Mandate Palestine, found itself unable to do so.

This should not have come as a surprise. Observation of the central articles of faith of mainstream Palestinian nationalism would reveal that the idea of the "return," that is, the reversal of the 1948 partition is central to it. Palestinian nationalism is not and has never been the movement for the creation of a small Palestinian state — for the recognition of partition. So the failure and collapse of the "peace process" in the summer of 2000 was predictable — and predicted.

What was less foreseeable came next. The collapse of the peace process led to the emergence for the first time in a generation of a real rival for the control of the Palestinian cause. This is of far more than local importance, because the Palestinian cause remains the great legitimating project in the Arabic-speaking world, and to a lesser extent in the Muslim world as a whole. It is a cause to which leaders pay lip service, and about which broad publics care passionately. Bernard Lewis referred to it as the "licensed grievance" in an Arab world dominated by socio-economic dysfunctionality and controlled by dictatorships.[1]

The presence of Israel is intimately connected with the sense of humiliation and anger that remains dominant in Arab political culture. As the historian Jacob Talmon expressed it "For decades the Arabs have been obsessed by memories of past glories and prophecies of future greatness, mocked by the injury and shame of having an alien and despised race injected into the nerve center of their promised pan-Arab empire, between its Asian and African halves, just at a time when the colonial powers had started their great retreat from their colonial possessions in Asia and Africa."[2]

The new contender for control of the cause was the Islamist Hamas movement. The "resistance" strategy adopted by this movement was directly inspired by the example of Hizballah in Lebanon in the 1990s. Hizballah was presented as having discovered the key that could finally reverse the string of defeats at the hands of the Jewish state.

This idea of prolonged popular war underlay the Second Intifada of 2000–2004. The notion was that Israel was a weak, disunited, and artificial society, predicated on a falsehood and therefore lacking the resources of social fortitude available to its enemies. On the tactical level, this was supposed to mean that it could be forced to retreat by inflicting losses on it. On the strategic level, in some more vague way, endless war was meant to wear Israel down, eventually bringing about its wasting away, decline and collapse.

The contrasting size of the two camps — tiny Israel, opposed by the vast Arab and Muslim world, has long contributed to the profound strategic optimism at the root of Israel's enemies' perceptions.

Both Hamas and Hizballah, each in their different ways, are part of a larger political and social phenomenon currently under way in the Middle East. This might be called the "Islamic revival," or the growing centrality of politicized Islam across the region.

Radical Islam, defiance of the West, and of course hatred of Israel, each possess tremendous legitimacy in the eyes of the populations of the Arabic-speaking countries. The existing regimes of the Arab world, while adept at holding power, have little to offer in opposition to the legitimacy enjoyed by the forces of Islam and defiance, the forces of "muqawama" — resistance. The belief that these forces represent a chance to regain dignity, and to defeat Israel, is central to their appeal.

But, is this not merely a pipe dream? After all, Israel has one of the largest and most powerful armies in the region, as well as a probable nuclear capacity. Are not the plans of the forces of muqawama, and their supporters throughout the region, merely the frustrated hopes of subjugated populations? Certainly, Israel successfully resisted and turned back the assault of the period 2000–2004. Israel did not accept the rules of attrition. Rather, its conventional superiority was brought to bear against the Islamist and nationalist militias that had declared war against it. And their campaign was broken.

In order to understand why this was not the final word on the matter, it is necessary to broaden the focus, to take in the geo-strategic picture of the region. The danger facing Israel today is not only or primarily from local Islamist militias. If it was, it would be of no great consequence. The challenge, rather, derives from the meeting of three related processes: the spread and popularity of political Islam, which has put fresh wind in the sails of the belief that Israel is a temporary imposition that can be defeated and destroyed; the development by supporters of political Islam of a long war strategy intended to bring about this defeat in the decades and years ahead; and the emergence of a state sponsor for this long war, and for the ambition to destroy Israel.

It is state sponsorship that turns the ambition of the muqawama from a boastful delusion into a serious strategy. The key state sponsor is Iran. Iran is in the process of an attempt at a "second revolution." Within the regime, a group of radical Shia Islamists are on the road to power. This group, centered on the Revolutionary Guards Corps and on a number of conservative political associations, emerged closer to complete domination of the Iranian system following the suppression of the unrest that took place after the allegedly rigged elections of June 2009.

It is in the process of turning the Iranian semi-representative clerical regime into something quite different: namely, a security state, ruling with little concern for the consent of the public. Such regimes are commonplace in the Arab world, though much more alien to the Persian tradition.

The goal of this emergent regime is not eschatological or otherworldly. It is interested in its own power and its expansion. Its ideological stances are not hollow and cynical. They are undoubtedly sincere. But they are also an instrumental force in building the regional power and hegemony that the rulers of Iran seek. The nuclear ambitions of the Iranian regime are an integral part of this larger project. A nuclear capacity would allow Iran freedom of maneuver to expand its power and reach across the region, with little prospect of serious interference.

The new regime in Iran wishes to present itself as the rising force in the region, representing all those elements in favor of resistance and the perceived authentic cultural patterns of the Middle East, as opposed to the supposedly declining power of the US and its hireling allies.

This is a somewhat strained intellectual construct, given that the Shia Persians are no more "insiders" in the Arabic speaking Middle East than are any other neighboring foreign power. However, given the undoubted widespread support for leaders and movements who can defy the West and Israel in the region, and support the Palestinians, the regime in Iran's desire to take ownership of this cause is quite rational and pragmatic. They know that this is the only form of "soft power" that matters in the Arabic-speaking world.

The widespread popular appeal of anti-Western and anti-Israel stances is borne out by all reliable polls. In 2008, 86 percent of respondents in Egypt, Jordan, Lebanon, Morocco, Saudi Arabia and the United Arab Emirates named the Palestinian cause as among the three most important issues. Ninety-five percent of respondents said Israel was the "biggest threat" to their countries.[3]

The most popular regional leaders named by those polled were Hassan Nasrallah of Hizballah, President Mahmoud Ahmedinejad of Iran and President Bashar Assad of Syria, in that order. So defiance pays off in terms of building regional popularity.[4]

The meeting of Islamic revivalist movements with a rising, ambitious new regional elite in Iran is transforming the geopolitics of the region. A central result of this is to re-ignite the old Israeli-Arab conflict in new form, and to return the existential aspect to this conflict.

Why do the forces of the muqawama think they can win? We saw, with the Hamas men Nizar from Ramallah and Salah in Mahaneh Ofer, that their self-confidence derives from a deeply rooted conviction in the temporary, ephemeral and flimsy nature of Israel. This was the sentiment enshrined in the speech given by Hassan Nasrallah in Bint Jbeil in 2000, in which he described Israel as weaker than a "spider's web." It is the core assumption of the muqawama bloc, from which all its subsequent positions derive. The idea of Israel's concealed, inner feebleness makes possible the belief — held very strongly among supporters of the muqawama and its doctrine — that they are on the road to victory.

This item of faith was inherited from Arab nationalism. It appears impervious to refutation based on evidence. Neither Israel's deep historical roots, nor its present day vitality have yet dented the confidence of the muqawama bloc.

Perhaps this is because the needs satisfied by the muqawama ideology are situated at a deeper level than that of rational debate. This outlook may be an attempt to cover a sense of shame and humiliation with a furious declaration that the enemy's apparent success and victory is momentary and illusory. Such a claim is made feasible by the deeply held regional view of the Jews as a traditionally helpless and subaltern people — who have upset the rules of nature by departing from this situation. But again, the need addressed by this belief system does not mean its adherents are insincere in their faith.

The muqawama bloc of Iran and its allies has developed a doctrine and strategy for the long war against Israel. This doctrine takes into account the areas in which Israel is undoubtedly stronger than its enemies, and also its points of vulnerability. Israel's economic and conventional military superiority is unchallengeable. The muqawama bloc, however, considers that Israel suffers from a series of fundamental weaknesses.

How does Israel's supposed societal weakness make itself manifest, in the view of its enemies? Israel's small size and small population are of primary importance. The Jewish state is seen as inordinately sensitive to casualties and therefore subject to being pressured through attrition. The muqawama bloc thus believes that Israeli tactical goals can be frustrated by the imposition of a casualty rate beyond the country's capacity to absorb.

So, militarily, the strategy is one of slow attrition: focusing war on the imposition of casualties, both civilian and military, as a means for breaking Israel's will, rather than reaching a decision on the battlefield, which is currently beyond the capabilities of the muqawama bloc.

On this basis, the development of ballistic missiles for indiscriminate use is a key element. The latest information suggests efforts to build a hybrid military strategy utilizing the methods of terrorism, but bringing them into a military framework, for example, through the employment of small groups of fighters intended to be inserted into civilian areas at a time of conflict, where they will wreak havoc.

Earlier, we referred to this as the practice of military theater, rather than conventional war as it has traditionally been understood. This does not imply a lack of seriousness in the strategy. Rather, it means that these are practices designed to destroy the enemy's will and political ability to continue, rather than his physical ability to do so. In such a war, the political struggle takes place alongside the military one.

The uses of international forums, of the media, of the transnational communities made possible by modern technology are all integral parts of the strategy. Israel's diplomatic position is seen as exposed and vulnerable. Iran and its allies have a natural home in the bloc of Muslim states. Israel, however, has perhaps a more precarious set of alliances. Its friendship with the United States is firm and deep rooted. With Europe and to a greater extent with other emerging world powers such as India and China, relations are healthy, but based purely on mutual self interest, rather than deep rooted cultural and historical affinity.

Iran and its allies intend, therefore, to heat up the conflict to a point where Israel's friends will no longer see it as worthwhile to maintain their alliances with it. The automatic majority in the UN General Assembly for any motion condemning Israel, and the corresponding anti-Israel majority on a number of vital UN committees — most notably, the UN Human Rights Council — facilitate the focusing of disproportionate attention on Israel's supposed misdeeds vis à vis the Palestinians.

The investigations following Operation Cast Lead in 2009 are a blueprint for the kind of political/judicial warfare with which Israel's enemies hope to make it impossible for the Jewish state to respond effectively to their attacks. The use of civilians as human shields, widely noted in Gaza, is an example of the cold blooded tactics by which the muqawama is fighting its war. We love death as you love life, it tells its enemies. The death the muqawama has in mind is that of many of its own civilians, as well as those of its enemy.

Iran and its allies are therefore developing a strategy for a prolonged war, to be fought simultaneously on a variety of fronts — military, paramilitary, political and diplomatic. The positive side of this strategy, from the point of view of the muqawama bloc, is that it does not have to end in victory in order to bear fruit. Rather, by the very process of maintaining the two currently active fronts in the conflict between Israel and its enemies, and magnifying world attention on Israel, the bloc intends to purchase for itself the regional legitimacy which Teheran desires.

However, the utilitarian aspect of the strategy should not blind observers to the seriousness of the muqawama bloc's intentions. Its war aim is the termination of the Jewish state.

This war is one of broken borders. It is not primarily about territory, rather, it is about ideas and symbols. For this reason, the struggle between Israel and the Islamist forces of the muqawama cannot be settled by compromise. Israel can offer compromise on one basis only — that of renewed partition in return for the definitive end to the conflict. The prospect of an end to the dispute based on partition is unimaginable to this enemy.

The preceding chapters traced the emergence of the new conflict over the last decade, and the experiences of one front-line participant in it. Terror war against civilians, and the desperate fight of the IDF to close the way to the bombers into Jerusalem in 2000–2004. The growing role of religion in the conflict, and the broadening of the circle of participants in it, as Muslims from Western countries began to play an active role as supporters and sometimes combatants. The rise within the Iranian power structure of a new, radical, generational group. The vital role of Iran as the impresario that pays the bills, and trains the fighters. The Lebanon war of 2006 as the first full scale war between Israel and an Islamist force.

This renewed conflict, like the old one, is ultimately a debate about the Jews, and about Israeli society. The medieval Islamic scholar Ibn Khaldoun developed the concept of "asabiya," usually translated as "social cohesion." According to Ibn Khaldoun, it is in the nature of civilizations to follow a kind of life cycle. He depicts nomadic and peripheral groups, possessing a clear, simple sense of identity and group solidarity as likely to threaten and eventually conquer older, settled civilizations grown decadent, lazy, and fractious. But, Ibn Khaldoun says, it is in the nature of things that the conquerors, over time, will themselves become accustomed to ease and luxury. The pristine, simple beliefs that sustained them will fade. Laxity, disunity, and indiscipline will set in.

At this point, the one-time conquerors will become vulnerable to the advance of a new set of "barbarians" from the periphery. A younger, more hungry, seemingly more primitive society will make its bid for domination, will defeat and destroy the grown-lax, effete kingdom and the cycle will begin anew.[5]

It is the contention of Israel's enemies that the Jewish state has reached this point of development. Nizar, in Ramallah, scoffed at the shrinking ambitions of the Zionists, as he characterized them. First, he said, the Jews wanted to build an empire from the Nile to the Euphrates. Then they wanted to absorb all the land between the Jordan River and the sea. And now, he said, all they hope for is to be left alone in order to continue to dominate the small area of pre-1967 Israel. But this too, Nizar thinks, is only a passing moment. The inexorable process, he considers, is of the premature aging and encroaching senility of his enemies. The muqawama bloc as a whole makes great use of this kind of rhetoric. Its representatives claim to have discovered the hidden truth regarding Israel, and to be exploiting it.

I wanted here to consider this claim seriously and carefully, and to set out to look at the society of which I am a part in light of it. It was my own experience of the 2006 Lebanon War that was the spur for this. The war of 2006 was a harbinger of further wars to come. The centrality of the home front, the attempt to use the possibility of attrition as a deterrent. The openly stated strategy of, over time, rendering Israel's continued existence an impossibility.

On the border in 2006, my comrades and I glimpsed for a moment what it would look like if things did not hold together. In that botched war, the full extent of the muqawama bloc's strategy toward Israel was revealed. And Israel, under a leadership indeed defined by decadence and laxity and loss of vision, did not rise to the challenge.

The balance between the sides, and the Israeli advantage, which was the result of the efforts of earlier generations, meant that no great disaster took place. Rather, even with an incompetent leadership and an under-prepared army, Israel succeeded in extracting a very high price from Hizballah for its aggression. But the Jewish state for a moment was confused, shocked, flailing.

So, I set out to examine the extravagant claims of the enemy regarding the likely future direction of events. I was aware throughout of two separate possibilities for error — the first was an easy, contemptuous dismissal of these claims, the second was to be duped by the psychological pressure of the muqawama bloc into affording its assertions a seriousness which they did not deserve. Of course, I cannot assert that I have achieved the correct balance. But I have sought to soberly measure this enemy's depictions against events, awarding him neither the awe which he sees as his due, nor the arrogant dismissal which breeds complacency.

What did I discover in this exploration? If one delves into Israel — into the society, its assumptions, the ideas that govern it, its deep and secret motivations, one discovers a complex picture very different from the fantasies of the country's enemies. The bottom line from the conversations I held and the searches I made, causing me to quiz close friends, comrades and acquaintances as to their deepest motivations, is that Israeli society is itself in a process of transformation. This process is in part a result of the new reality imposed upon it by the threat of the muqawama bloc. However, this is not the only factor driving it.

Israeli politics have been transformed by the failed peace process of the 1990s, and the subsequent emergence of the new hostile coalition. The old, passionate debates between advocates and opponents of the idea of "land for peace" have largely been replaced by a general consensus accepting of partition, accompanied by doubt that there is a partner for peace among the Palestinians. The doubt is justified. Insofar as a genuinely partitionist politics exists among the Palestinians; it is small and kept relevant largely by Western aid and patronage.

At a deeper level, Israeli society is becoming more traditional, more sentimentally religious and less European than was formerly the case. A new, localized version of sovereign Jewish identity is emerging, which is neither Sephardi nor Ashkenazi, and neither secular nor fully observant in the ways in which these terms have in the past been applied to analysis of Israel.

This process of societal change is reflected in a number of areas of national life — notably in the shift of elites in the military, where officers and soldiers of national religious origin are acquiring increasing prominence. Other formerly peripheral groups — Jews of north African origin, Druze Israelis, Russian and Ethiopian immigrants — are also taking an increasingly prominent role in the IDF.

The societal fatigue and collapse predicted by the muqawama bloc is not taking place. Israeli society and culture is youthful, full of vitality, and hungry for life. The Israeli economy, under conditions of conflict, is one of the most robust in the Western world. A less naïve, less ideological, more realistic Israel — simultaneously more religious and more disenchanted, more traditional and more pluralist, is in the process of being born. It is this entity upon which the muqawama bloc has declared war to the end.

The war between Israel and Islamism is likely to continue in the coming years, and to end in the defeat and decline of one of the combatant sides. From Israel's point of view, the strategic goal is to maintain the country as a majority-Jewish state. The muqawama's goal is to destroy Jewish sovereignty. Since peaceful reconciliation is impossible, Israel needs to last out the muqawama, delivering heavy blows where necessary to inflict demoralizing defeats and deter the enemy from attempting aggression.

Israel is exponentially stronger than its enemies in a central regard — its conventional military capacity. Indeed, the entire doctrine of the muqawama bloc might be called a (hoped for) recipe for how to achieve success in an existential struggle in spite of chronic conventional inferiority. The focus on levels higher than the conventional (the pursuit of weapons of mass destruction), and lower (the use of terror and paramilitary methods) along with the concentration on political warfare and delegitimization take place because of an obvious absence of a conventional military option.

It is in Israel's interest, therefore, to focus precisely on conventional military operations. Rather than allowing itself to get bogged down in wars of attrition that play to the enemy's advantage, Israel will seek to deliver set-piece, conventional lessons to the various components of the muqawama bloc. These lessons will be intended to serve to remind the enemy of the true state of the relative strength between the two sides.

Such operations should be of short duration, with clear objectives, uncompromisingly pursued. Israel has no interest in, and no ability to positively affect, the image its enemies have of it, or their more general views on the nature of the world. But what it can do, through ferocious responses to aggression against it, is to strip its enemies of any halo of achievement, and inform the publics behind them of the high cost of pursuing a policy of war against the Jewish state.

In the 2008 movie "Under the Bombs," which deals with the 2006 Lebanon war, a Christian Lebanese taxi driver called Tony says with reference to the Hizballah action that precipitated the war "It's stupid to poke a wasps' nest."[6] Thoughts of this kind are precisely the ones that Israel hopes to plant in the minds of its enemies. This can be done only through uncompromisingly effective military responses to aggression. Examples of actions of this kind are the raid on the Syrian plutonium reactor in September 2007, and Operation Cast Lead in Gaza, in 2008/2009.

The tactical goal of such responses is to achieve a de facto balance of terror between the Jewish state and its would-be destroyers. The strategic implication of success in this regard may go beyond this. As I discussed earlier, previous waves of anti-Western radicalism in the Middle East have singled out Israel as the central local representative of the enemy. They have ridden along for a while on the charisma derived from anti-Israel radicalism. But defeat at the hands of Israel served to strip them of much of their appeal, and to initiate their period of decline. This pattern was followed by secular Arab nationalism in the 1950s and until the 1967 war, and by the Palestinian guerrilla movements in the 1970s and until their destruction as a military factor in Lebanon in 1982.

Israel knows that it has no soft power in the region to affect the way it is viewed. The overwhelming Arab view of Israel is in line with the fictional Lebanese taxi driver's comparison of the country to an insects' nest.

Nevertheless, in the past, the use of Israeli hard power has over time also produced soft power results. By stripping anti-Western movements of part of their charisma, it has hastened their decline. Israel's strategic goal is survival. It is uncompromising with its enemies. Their discomfiture has, in the past, been beneficial not only to Israel itself, but also to its allies and backers, and to pro-Western Arab states. The same will be true in the event of Israel's proving victorious in the long war against the muqawama bloc.

The precise form that Israel's conventional actions will take, will depend partly on the actions of its enemies. It is not hard to envisage extreme scenarios in which very drastic action is taken against Hizballah in Lebanon, and perhaps also against Hamas in Gaza. Such an eventuality might occur, for example, if Israel were to carry out a raid on Iran's nuclear program, and this were to be met by Hizballah missile attacks.

However, because of the nature of the current conflict, an old-fashioned reliance on conventional superiority will not be sufficient. The diplomatic and political levels and Israeli internal society are all fronts in this war. The blows Israel will strike against the muqawama bloc and against its main backer in Teheran will be of a conventional military nature. But the tasks of maintaining a society supportive of the struggle and an international stage at least willing to tolerate the measures Israel deems necessary for its defense are no less vital.

In all these areas, the challenges are immense. Nevertheless, eventual success is likely. Iran and its allies suffer from the fundamental problem that they cannot produce societies in which people actually want to live. Rather, they create immensely repressive internal arrangements, coupled with an endless repeat of acts of military theater, which then bring down retribution and suffering on the populations they control. The anger and sense of humiliation that they are focusing on is real. But once it becomes clear that they are not in fact able to bring the victory, they are likely to decline.

Two years after the 2006 war, I traveled back to the depot of our unit at the foot of the Golan Heights. I remembered the chaos of that first night of the call-up. Confusion and roaring engines and lights shining on piles of rifles. In the fall of 2008, the depot could not have been more peaceful and pastoral. The wind blowing the fallen twigs and leaves. Far from the burned forests near Metullah in 2006, black and ash beneath the summer sun. Far from the military funerals that took place in the blinding light of that July and that August. Routine and silence had returned. The tanks like great iron statues, silent and waiting.

But the quiet and the peaceful, even tranquil atmosphere that prevails at army depots on autumn weekday mornings was an illusion.

The factors that set us rolling toward south Lebanon in the summer of 2006 have not disappeared, and the conflict set in motion a decade ago is still continuing, and has almost certainly not yet reached its height.

When we returned to the front line a few days before the ceasefire in August 2006, it was not with any faith in our own commanders or in the national leadership above them. All of us reservists knew that to a degree we had chosen the short straw, and were part of an unprepared force, dispatched to its task in an inept way by an irresponsible and short-sighted leadership.

We were not children, and we were being asked to acknowledge this fact, in all its starkness, and nevertheless to return to the front and to continue the war. It seemed unfair. One lives, after all, just once. All the same, there was nothing between the hand of destruction and the northern towns and villages of Israel except the army of which we were a part. We returned. To be anywhere else at that moment would have been unimaginable. But we also made a common vow that, if and when we came through the rest of the war unscathed, we would do our utmost to prevent anything like the mess and confusion of 2006 from happening again. Each in his own field. This has been my attempt to honor this pledge.

Jerusalem, 2009

Notes

1. "Islam and the West: a conversation with Bernard Lewis," *Pew Forum on Religion and Public Life*, 27 April 2006.
2. Jacob Talmon, *Israel Among the Nations*, London: Weidenfeld and Nicolson, 1970: 169–70.
3. Professor Shibley Telhami, Principal Investigator, 2008 Annual Arab Public opinion poll — Survey of the Anwar Sadat Chair for Peace and Development at the University of Maryland, 2008.
4. Ibid. It is worth noting that respondents were asked to name the leader they most admired outside of their own country.
5. Ibn Khaldoun (1332–1406) is regarded as one of the fathers of the modern disciplines of sociology, historiography and cultural studies. His theory of asabiyah is outlined in his most well-known work, the

"Muqadimah," which is the first volume of a larger historical work. He is widely seen as one of the greatest historians and social theorists of any age.

6. "Under the Bombs (Fr. Sous Les Bombes)," dir: Philippe Aractingi, Lebanon, 2007.